LINCOLN AND THE NEGRO

Abraham Lincoln portrait by David Bustill Bowser, contemporary Negro artist
Courtesy of The Lincoln National Life Foundation

LINCOLN
AND THE NEGRO

BENJAMIN QUARLES

A DA CAPO PAPERBACK

Library of Congress Cataloging in Publication Data

Quarles, Benjamin.
    Lincoln and the Negro / Benjamin Quarles.
        p.   cm. — (A Da Capo paperback)
    Reprint. Originally published: New York: Oxford University
Press, 1962.
    Includes bibliographical references and index.
    ISBN 0-306-80447-6
    1. Lincoln, Abraham, 1809-1865 — Relations with Afro-
Americans. 2. Lincoln, Abraham, 1809-1865 — Views on slavery.
3. Afro-Americans — History — To 1863. 4. Slavery — United
States. I. Title.
E457.2.Q3   1991   91-18201
973.7'092 — dc20   CIP

To Vera: In Memoriam

Published by Da Capo Press, Inc.
A Subsidiary of Plenum Publishing Corporation
233 Spring Street, New York, N.Y. 10013

Foreword

To SAY that Abraham Lincoln is the most studied about and written about of all Americans is to say two things about him: he was at the helm when a great and terrible crisis gripped his country, and he has become the best-loved American in our history.

The Civil War holds an enduring interest for Americans, in part because it enlarged the boundaries of human freedom. The war was a testing ground for the American experiment in a government by the people; the war was a rendezvous with the created-equal doctrine of the Declaration of Independence. These paramount issues were crystal clear to Lincoln's searching mind. Indeed, his grasp of the meaning of equality, coming as it did at a high moment in America's destiny, gave to Lincoln's career its most abiding quality.

To say, therefore, that Lincoln lives in history is to say that he met head-on the greatest challenge to his country as the land of the free—the challenge of the Negro. To Lincoln the status of the black man was the touchstone of American democracy; the fate of the Negro was interwoven with America's role as "the last, best hope of earth." Lincoln believed that the Civil War itself was brought on by the Negro question. As he told a delegation of five Negroes who came to the White House on August 14, 1862, "Without the institution of Slavery, and the colored race as a basis, the war could not have an existence." But whether or not the Negro was central to the Civil War, he was of the greatest significance in Lincoln's life as a national figure.

The man who was elected President in 1860 brought to his task a grasp of the political and constitutional aspects of slavery unsurpassed by any public person of his day. This deep learning did not come from first-hand knowledge of slavery or the Negro, yet Lincoln's early years were not barren of contacts with either. Any gaps in his acquaintance with the Negro vanished during the White House years. To the desk of the chief magistrate came any number of problems growing out of the collapse of slavery and the condition of the freed slave. Calling at the executive mansion to help solve these problems, or to bear him gifts, came Negro delegations and visitors.

The Lincoln that the Negroes met and heard about was to them a figure to admire. They viewed him as a humanitarian, one whose love for his fellows embraced all sorts and conditions of men. Doubtless the Negro's attitude toward Lincoln was tinged by wish-fulfillment, seeing him as they wanted him to be. On plans for freeing the slave and extending to Negroes the right to vote, Lincoln actually seemed to drag his feet or, at best, to lead from behind.

Yet the Negroes of his day saw him as a man growing in knowledge and wisdom, and to them he was "emancipator, benefactor, friend and leader," in the words of a group assembled at the Fifteenth Street Presbyterian Church in Washington two days after his death. To the mass of Negroes, Lincoln had passed from history to legend even before Booth's bullet. The flesh-and-blood Lincoln paled before this legendary figure—a figure who came alive in the hopes and aspirations of colored Americans. "My mother used to talk much of Abraham Lincoln," wrote school principal Joseph L. Wiley: "Though she had never seen him, she talked as if she had."

His Negro admirers are not to be blamed if they did not see Lincoln in the round—few people did, in his day or afterward. It is not so much that Negroes saw only one aspect of Lincoln's character as it was that, as a rule, only one aspect of Lincoln's complex and many-sided character ever seemed to present itself to an observer. To those who held communion with him, Lincoln, like nature, spoke a various language.

The Negro mirrors America, and his concept of the folklore Lincoln was a part of the general pattern. For Abraham Lincoln was destined for the number one spot in America's gallery of heroes. "We all know Lincoln by heart," said Frederick Douglass, a Negro contemporary. And, in a sense that Douglass would not have ruled out, that is how the American rank and file came to know Lincoln—by heart rather than by mind. He became a symbol, and hence a product of something more than memory alone.

If the people's evaluation of Lincoln tended to be uncritical, it was not unimportant. Americans are the sum of the influences brought to bear upon them, and one of these influences has been the pervasive spirit of this towering figure who "came out of the wilderness, down in Illinois." In him, Americans realize themselves. He lives because he was a man the people loved. No other group symbolizes this deep affection as do colored Americans. They have not bothered to claim any superior devotion to his memory, yet it is a matter of historical record that they loved him first and have loved him longest.

In fine, Lincoln became Lincoln because of the Negro, and it was the latter who first reflected the image of the Lincoln that was to live. Hence, this book.

I am indebted to the following library staffs: the Illinois State Archives and the Illinois Historical Society, both at Springfield; the Chicago Historical Society and the Newberry Library, in Chicago; the Kentucky Historical Society at Frankfort; the Boston Public Library, the Boston Athenaeum, and the Massachusetts Historical Society, in Boston; the New York Public Library and its Schomburg Collection branch, and the New-York Historical Society; the Library of Congress, Manuscripts Division, the National Archives of the United States, and Howard University, in Washington; and the Enoch Pratt Free Library, the Maryland Historical Society, Johns Hopkins University, and Morgan State College, in Baltimore.

For answers to requests, made by mail or in person, for information, I owe thanks to Clyde C. Walton, James T. Hickey, and Mrs. Marion D. Pratt, of Springfield, Lincoln authorities all; Mrs. Edith S. Reiter, formerly Curator of the Campus Martius Museum at Marietta, Ohio; John Chavis, Curator of the Education Division of the Detroit Historical Museum; Stephen T. Riley, Director of the Massachusetts Historical Society; David McKibbin, Secretary of the Art Commission of the City of Boston; Mrs. Dorothy B. Porter, librarian of the Moorland Foundation at Howard University; Pauli Murray, author of *Proud Shoes,* and Victor Searcher, author of *Lincoln's Journey to Greatness.*

I am especially grateful to Sheldon Meyer, Trade Editor of the Oxford University Press, for his helpfulness at every stage of the work. I wish to express my thanks to President Martin D. Jenkins and the Trustees of Morgan State College for a sabbatical year. And to my wife, Ruth Brett Quarles, I owe a number of assists in getting this manuscript out.

B. Q.

Baltimore, Maryland
December 1961

Contents

List of Illustrations

1

CHARLOTTE SCOTT'S MITE

ONCE AGAIN it was Good Friday, April 14, the first Good Friday to fall on that date since the assassination of Abraham Lincoln eleven years earlier. What better date to unveil a monument to the martyred President? What better place than the nation's capital city, scene of his final, greatest years? And what better group to have raised the money for a bronze statue than those whom he had helped free?

The unveiling of the emancipation monument was recognized as something out of the ordinary. It was, wrote the Washington correspondent of the *Baltimore Sun*, "the event of the day." In its observance, Congress had passed a joint resolution setting aside that particular April 14 of 1876 as a general holiday so that "all persons desiring to do so should be given the opportunity of attending" the exercises. President Ulysses S. Grant, congressmen, and Supreme Court justices had accepted invitations to attend; members of foreign legations were also expected as guests; and the most prominent Negro of his times had been scheduled for the oration.

If the exercises at the unveiling of "Freedom's Memorial" were to be made newsworthy by the presence of high-ranking government officials, the origin of the monument was to be found in the sacrificing spirit of an obscure "washerwoman."

THE ORIGINAL and foundation subscription for the Lincoln-Negro monument came from Charlotte Scott. Born a slave on a plantation near Lynchburg, Virginia, she had been given by her owner to his daughter, Mrs. William P. Rucker. When the Civil War broke out, William Rucker's sympathies for the Union cause led to his spending seventeen months in a Confederate prison, after which the family fled to Marietta, Ohio, taking Charlotte along. Freed in 1862, she stayed on with the Ruckers, living in their home. She was well thought of, according to Rucker, for her industry and her honesty.

Although over sixty when freed, she was still hale and active and had no trouble getting work washing clothes. She had just managed to scrape up her first small savings when the dread news of Lincoln's assassination reached Marietta.

On that mournful Saturday in April 1865, the deeply distressed Charlotte said to Mrs. Rucker, "The colored people have lost their best friend on earth. Mr. Lincoln was our best friend, and I will give five dollars of my wages toward erecting a monument to his memory." The sympathetic Ruckers suggested that the money be placed in the hands of C.D. Battelle, a local clergyman. Taking this suggestion, Charlotte went to see Battelle and asked him to act as agent for the colored people, receiving their contributions and holding them for the time being.

Battelle bestirred himself at once: "I received her offering, and gave notice through the press that I would receive other donations, and cheerfully do what I could to promote so noble an object." The project quickly caught the fancy of Brigadier General T.C.H. Smith, in command of the military post at St. Louis, who hit upon the idea of turning it over to an organization that could best reach prospective Negro contributors, the Western Sanitary Commission whose headquarters was in the city. Late in June the Reverend C.D. Battelle sent Charlotte's mite to James E. Yeatman, president of the commission. In Yeatman's mail the same day came a letter from Rucker emphasizing that every dollar toward the monument should come from former slaves.

Now that the Western Sanitary Commission had become the active agent in collecting funds, the project got off the ground. In

Negro circles the commission was well known. It had been founded in September 1861 to minister to the sick and wounded of the Western armies, but it had taken on the task of helping the needy former slaves along the Mississippi, who by the fall of 1863 had numbered some 50,000, from Columbus, Kentucky, to Natchez.

Upon receiving the letters about the Charlotte Scott proposal, Yeatman lost no time in sending notices to newspapers and to officers commanding Negro troops, informing them about the monument and inviting contributions. The black wearers of the blue quickly responded, subscribing some $12,000 in two months. The largest gift, $4770, came from the Sixth U.S. Colored Heavy Infantry ("those that Forrest's men did not murder at Fort Pillow," wryly added paymaster W.C. Lupton, in a covering letter to Yeatman). Another regiment in the District of Natchez authorized Lupton to deduct one dollar for each of its nearly 1700 men. At Rodney, Mississippi, where the Seventieth U.S. Colored Troops donated $2949.50, Colonel W.C. Earles felt it necessary to caution the officers "to check the noble generosity of my men rather than stimulate it." Before the winter snows fell on Lincoln's grave, the soldiers and freedmen along the Mississippi had sent a total of $16,242.00.

Once the money was collected, the task of the Western Sanitary Commission shifted to the erection of the monument. While a tribute to the generosity of its black donors, the sum raised was not nearly enough for a statue of large design. But the commission was in for a piece of luck. One of its five members, the clergyman-college president William G. Eliot, happened to be in Florence in 1869, where he visited the studio of Thomas Ball. Boston-born, although making his home in Italy, Ball was well known as a result of several excellent works, among them the equestrian statue of George Washington in the Boston Public Garden.

While at Ball's studio Eliot's attention was caught by a half life-size model of Abraham Lincoln and a liberated slave, a piece Ball had executed shortly after receiving the news of the President's death. Having difficulty in finding a good model for a slave,

Ball had sat for himself and with the aid of mirrors had made "one of my best nude figures." (At least, wrote Ball, he could not have had a better model "for the money.")

The visiting Dr. Eliot observed the marble statuette very closely, storing up the details in his mind. Upon his return to America he told his fellow commissioners about the striking piece. Soon came a letter to Ball's studio asking him to furnish the Western Sanitary Commission with photographs of the emancipation duo and his terms for a nine- or ten-foot bronze. After examining the pictures Ball sent, the commision offered him the job, expressing the hope that he would accept such a small amount as $17,000 in light of the fact that it had been raised by former slaves. The commissioners had one other stipulation: in place of Ball's slave model of himself, they asked him to substitute the features of an actual Negro. To these terms Ball agreed. Thereupon Dr. Eliot sent him several photographs of the man who was to be the model for the slave, Archer Alexander.

If his past experiences give to a model's face the values the artist is seeking, Archer was a good choice. He was a man with a past, colorful if humble. A slave in Missouri when the war broke out, he had in February 1863 brought information to Union troops about a bridge over which they were scheduled to pass, but whose timbers had been sawed by Confederate sympathizers. Before his highly suspicious anti-Union master could punish him, Archer fled to St. Louis and took employment with Dr. Eliot.

Eliot let it be known publicly that he was willing to pay as high as $600 "ransom money" to Archer's master, but the offer was ignored. One afternoon, as Archer was working around the Eliot yard, he was seized by three of his master's henchmen and taken to the city jail—"the last fugitive slave taken in Missouri under the old laws of slavery." Before his master could rush him to Kentucky, Eliot managed to secure his release from jail and put him on a steamer to Alton, Illinois. Archer subsequently returned to St. Louis, where he became an organ-blower at Dr. Eliot's

Church of the Messiah. He took a lasting pride in the memory of his son, Tom, who had been killed in battle.

It was, then, the face and figure of an ex-bondman that filled Ball's eye as he modeled his slave. Ball had some experience in working from photographs, having done so in executing a marble bust of Liszt. When the emancipation piece was finished, Ball sent it to Munich to be cast at the Royal Foundry. The statue then came to the United States, where Congress permitted it to pass the customs free of duty and also appropriated $3000 for a pedestal.

The bronze work was elevated into its position in Lincoln Park on April 13, being covered with American flags until the unveiling scheduled for the following day. The committee of five Negroes appointed by the Western Sanitary Commission to make arrangements for the exercises had done its job. All was in readiness for a day to remember.

IT WAS ELEVEN in the morning. The sun would not show itself, but the showers had held up although, as a reporter from an out-of-town newspaper put it, "the sky continued of that uncertain cast that made umbrellas the most satisfactory companions." Optimistic now that the rain had stopped, the celebrators went ahead with their plans.

Gathering at their places along a half-dozen blocks on K Street were some twenty Negro organizations—companies of the National Guard, benevolent and charitable societies like the Good Samaritans and the Sons of Purity, and workers' groups like the Labor League. All bore banners, and most were gaily attired, the Knights of St. Augustine sporting black hats with yellow plumes and blue, sword-ensheathed baldrics. Interspersed between these groups were marching bands and the carriages bearing the orator of the day and his party. Heading the line of march was a yellow-sashed chief marshal, with a squad of mounted police a few paces behind.

The assembled line was soon ready to move. Passing through the streets, where flags were flying half-mast from the house tops, the marchers came to the Executive Mansion. They passed in review, after which they made their mile-long way up East Capitol Street to Lincoln Park. Here the grounds were "packed with human beings," fully half of them white, hiding the park's chain fence and posing a threat to its handful of slow-growing trees.

In front of the covered statue was a stand for the speakers and a railed platform for the dignitaries. At half-past one President Grant and his party of two—Ulysses S. Grant, Jr., and Secretary of the Interior Zachariah Chandler—got out of their carriage and were conducted to reserved chairs. Revolving around, finding seats on the platform, were some sixty figures of lesser importance.

Shortly before two o'clock the Marine Band struck up "Hail to the Chief," and the exercises were on. A bishop said a prayer. Then J. Henri Burch of Louisiana read Lincoln's message to Congress approving and signing the act freeing the slaves in the District of Columbia, which, as coincidence would have it, had taken place fourteen years ago to the day. The audience, taking advantage of its first opportunity to cheer, greeted the reading by Burch with "as much enthusiasm as if it had just been written." James E. Yeatman, representing the Western Sanitary Commission, then gave a sketch of the origin of the project, ending up by presenting the monument to John Mercer Langston, the presiding officer.

An Oberlin graduate, dean of the Howard University law department, and destined to be the only Negro ever to represent Virginia in the Congress, the slender, bearded, steady-eyed Langston was at home on the public platform. He responded to Yeatman by expressing the thanks of the Negro for the commission's work. Then, just as everyone was waiting for him to unveil the statue, Langston turned to President Grant and asked him to pull the cord. It was a very happy inspiration.

Whatever his shortcomings as a presidential leader, Grant could muster an impressive dignity. Rising and stationing himself in front of the flag-draped bronze, he paused for a moment to let the silence sink in. Then he gave a tug to the silken cord, the covering fell away, and the figures were finally exposed to view. The resultant din was deafening, compounded of spontaneous cries of admiration—a claque could have done no better—noisy handclapping, the booming of cannon, and the brassy strains of the Marine Band.

The statue that drew such applause was a twelve-foot bronze. It represented Lincoln standing beside a column bearing the face of George Washington, and upon which rested the Emancipation Proclamation, one corner of which Lincoln was fingering. Lincoln's face was turned toward a half-kneeling Negro, although his eyes seemed to be peering into the future, rather than focusing upon any object. Lincoln's left hand was poised over the Negro, as if in protection or benediction. His wrist shackles broken, the muscular former slave was in the act of rising, with one knee off the ground, like a sprinter getting set. His upward-looking face bore no pronounced expression. At the base of the piece was the single word EMANCIPATION in raised twelve-inch letters. The statue rested upon a ten-foot granite pedestal bearing two metal plaques, one telling of Charlotte Scott and the other quoting the final phrases of the Emancipation Proclamation.

When the applause had spent itself, the program proceeded with a poem, "Today, O martyred chief, beneath the sun," by Cornelia Ray, which was read for her in her absence. Miss Ray's stanzas abounded in such passages as:

> While Freedom may her holy spectre claim,
> The world shall echo with "Our Lincoln's name."

But if the young New Yorker's eighty-line eulogy did not add notably to the Lincoln literature, it gave the audience time to settle back for the second and final high light of the overcast afternoon: the oration by Frederick Douglass.

To see that striking head again and to hear that rich baritone voice lifted in oratory would in itself attract an audience. Here was a man whose life read like a saga. After his escape from a Maryland slave master, he had become a polished speaker and a forceful writer, devoting his skills to reformist movements such as the abolition of slavery and equal rights for women. Like his career, his appearance was arresting. With a wealth of white hair and beard, a healthy glow to his skin, and a bit of a bulge around the middle, he gave one the initial impression of a Santa Claus in brownface. But a second look brought a different reaction: his piercing eyes, his formal bearing and no-nonsense air reminded one of an Old Testament patriarch.

As Langston, the presiding officer, completed his introduction of the "orator of the occasion," Douglass arose, manuscript in hand. He had brought to the writing of his address some firsthand knowledge of Lincoln, as he had had two White House audiences with the President. He owned a cane of Lincoln's, which Mrs. Lincoln had sent him and which he viewed as "an object of sacred trust."

In his lengthy address, however, Douglass let himself be swayed by no sentimental memories. After the opening congratulations to the assembled "friends and fellow citizens," he devoted his attention almost exclusively to one question: Was President Lincoln devoted to the welfare of the Negro, or were his actions on behalf of the colored man forced by the pressures of the times?

There was but one answer, said the unsparing Douglass, as he described Lincoln's slowness in coming around to the point of view held by those who had no patience with slavery. Lincoln "was preeminently the white man's President."

But, went on the orator of the day, this was far from the whole story. The Negro's faith was often taxed to the limit while the President "tarried in the mountain," but it never failed. And Lincoln finally proved himself worthy of this faith: "Though he loved Caesar less than Rome, though the Union was more to him than our freedom or our future, under his wise and beneficent rule we saw ourselves gradually lifted from the depths of slavery to the heights of liberty and manhood." In the person of Abraham Lincoln the hour and the man of "our redemption" had met.

It was on this latter, emancipating Lincoln that Douglass brought his oration to a close. The cheers of the audience indicated that this was the Lincoln they preferred to remember. The closing minutes of the program took on a fitting note of devotion, with the band playing Rossini's "Sicilian Vespers" Overture and Dr. J.P. Newman pronouncing the benediction. "The occasion," editorialized the *Washington Chronicle*, "could not fail to impress everyone with feelings of the most profound respect for a people in whom the sentiment of gratitude is so strongly ingrained as it is in those whose voluntary contributions paid for the magnificent memorial which commemorates the crowning act of Lincoln's life."

Dear, dear Charlotte Scott. In his address Douglass had not spoken her name. But who more than she gave meaning to his words: "When now it is said that the colored man has no appreciation of benefits or benefactors, we may calmly point to the monument we have this day erected to the memory of Abraham Lincoln"—who, more than this former slave, who lived to be over a hundred, dying in 1892 at her birthplace four miles from Lynchburg?

LORADO TAFT, art critic and himself a sculptor, had a high opinion of the Lincoln monument, describing it as one of the most inspired works produced by an American: "a great theme expressed with emotion by an artist of intelligence and sympathy, who felt what he was doing." Also impressed by the emancipation duo was Moses Kimball of Boston, businessman and long-time member of the state legislature, who commissioned Ball to do a replica. Kimball gave this copy to his native city, which held dedication exercises at Faneuil Hall on May 30, 1879. Attended by the governor of the state and opened with a prayer by Phillips Brooks, the exercises featured an oration by Mayor Frederick O. Prince and an occasional poem by John Greenleaf Whittier, who was "the slave's poet" of a bygone day but was still quick to point a moral:

> Amidst thy sacred effigies
>   Of old renown give place,
> O city, Freedom-loved! to his
>   Whose hand unchained a race.
>
> Stand in thy place and testify
>   To coming ages long,
> That truth is stronger than a lie
>   And righteousness than wrong.

The Kimball gift was erected in Park Square, where it was to stand, then as now, on a little plot of land completely engulfed by traffic.

The widest public knowledge of the Ball statue came in 1940 when the Post Office issued a three-cent-stamp reproduction of it, running off an initial order of forty million. The step was taken upon the urging of Negroes, who wanted the government to do something in observance of the seventy-fifth anniversary of the amendment abolishing slavery. Printed in deep violet, the stamp was first placed on sale at the New York World's Fair branch post office, on the occasion of the diamond jubilee celebration of the Thirteenth Amendment.

Despite the apparent popularity of the Ball monument, not all Negroes cared for it. Frederick Douglass found that it left him cold: "It showed the Negro on his knee when a more manly attitude would have been indicative of freedom." A subsequent critic, Freeman Henry Morris Murray, had a more inclusive bill of indictment against the piece in Lincoln Park.

Ball, said the dissenting Murray, had really not modeled his piece as an emancipation group, but as Lincoln and the kneeling slave. Hence the face of the sculptured Negro bears none of the elevated emotion of one who is and ought to be free; it was, rather, like that of a man who has just escaped the hangman's noose by a last-minute commutation of sentence. The statue reminded Murray of a conventional portrait of Jesus and the Magdalen, with the deified Lincoln saying, "Go, and sin no more." All in all, said Murray, the monument could have been improved, perhaps, by removing the ex-slave completely.

If many Negroes were destined to become lukewarm about the monument, this attitude was never transferred to Lincoln. In Negro circles his fame remained untarnished. In large measure this was due to former slaves, to whom Lincoln was a folk hero, legendary and semireligious. Typical of this mood was seventy-nine-year-old Bob Maynard, of Weleetka, Oklahoma: "I think Abe Lincoln was next to the Lord. He done all he could for the slaves; he set 'em free. 'Fore the election he travelled all over the South, and he come to our house and slept in Old Mistress' bed. Didn't nobody know who he was."

By no means was this worship of the Civil War President confined to the unlettered Negro. The cult of "Lincolnolatry" took firm root among the colored leaders, led by Booker T. Washington. Lincoln's was "almost the first name I learned," wrote this Negro who lunched with Theodore Roosevelt in the White House, and on whom Harvard University conferred an honorary degree. "I confess," said Washington, "that the more I learn of Lincoln's life the more I am disposed to look at him much as my mother and those early freedmen did..." To Kelly Miller, another listened-to spokesman for the colored man, Lincoln was "a genius of the first order," one who dwelt upon the "radiant summit." An executive director of the New York Urban League, James H. Hubert, found in Lincoln a familiar American theme, but one with especial appeal to minority groups. To Hubert, himself from a family of above-average achievement, the life of Lincoln said, "You may climb from the bottom to the top." And on one February 12, Mordecai Johnson, best known of the Negro clergyman-educators, gave a radio address entitled "The World-Significant Soul of Abraham Lincoln."

Most of these twentieth-century Negro leaders had succeeded in convincing themselves that Lincoln had been slow in striking at slavery because he had preferred to follow his own timetable, and not because he did not care about the slave. Now and then a Negro voice might cry out, "He was not our man," but such a minority report was not even discussed and died because no one would second the motion. Negroes of high degree, as well as of low, seemed to agree with the Lincoln sentiment expressed by their greatest poet, Paul Laurence Dunbar:

> Earth learned of thee what Heav'n already knew,
> And wrote thee down among her treasured few!

As CONCERNS SLAVERY and the Negro, what was the background of this man who was destined to give to Negroes a sense of belonging, a sense that America was really their country? What was the actual "Negro story" of this man to whom the colored people turned during the war and in the years immediately after as reform spent itself and the war's bright promises faded? What of this man whose bearded, kindly-eyed face looked down from the blackboard rails of a thousand colored schoolhouses and from the walls of a hundred thousand cabins?

2

LINCOLN: THE SHAPING YEARS

FIVE WEEKS after he had been elected to the presidency, Abraham Lincoln was asked a question: Had he been a speaker at a meeting held by free Negroes who were presenting a silver pitcher to Governor Salmon P. Chase of Ohio? Although flooded with mail, the President-elect did not wish to ignore this query, for it came from Henry J. Raymond, editor and co-founder of the influential *New York Times* and one of the original organizers of the Republican party. Moreover, Raymond's letter carried a note of urgency: "If you can find time to say a word about the silver pitcher speech it will be serviceable in my comments on these matters."

From his Springfield, Illinois, home town Lincoln sent an immediate answer. Terming the story "a forgery out and out," he said that he had never seen a pitcher presented by anybody to anybody. What's more, wrote he, "I never was in a meeting of negroes in my life..."

But the Lincoln who was preparing to depart for the White House was by no means unfamiliar with the colored man. Some two weeks before the Raymond letter, Lincoln was relaxing with some old acquaintances who were lounging on the sofa and in the half-dozen armchairs of the governor's room at the Illinois State House, which had been turned over to the President-elect. Snatching a few minutes from his correspondence, Lincoln was reminiscing over the past and speculating about the future. As he paused for a moment, someone remarked that it was too bad that when he reached Washington, the first question facing him would be that of slavery. Lincoln's response was a typical mixture of the serious and the comic. According to Henry Villard of the *New York Herald*, Lincoln "told the story of the Kentucky justice of the peace whose first case was a criminal prosecution for the abuse of slaves. Unable to find any precedents, he exclaimed at last angrily: 'I will be damned if I don't feel almost sorry for being elected when the niggers is the first thing I have to attend to.'"

The Lincoln of November 1860 hardly needed anyone to tell him of the insistence of the slavery theme. The role of the colored American, slave and free, was no new topic to him. Lincoln's early environment, his years as a practicing lawyer, and his political ambitions for the Senate and the presidency had all combined to give him an unusually broad grasp of the Negro question.

LINCOLN'S EXPOSURE to slavery dated from his earliest days. Born in 1809, he spent the first seven years of his life in a slave state, Kentucky, and in a county, Hardin, that in 1811 listed 1007 slaves, an average of two slaves a family. Hardin County was second to none in America for the bitterness over the slavery issue, and the three successive homes of the Lincolns, all within a fifteen-mile radius, were in the eye of the storm over the pros and cons of Negro bondage. Lincoln's parents, Nancy Hanks and Thomas, held no slaves, and the Baptist churches they attended were opposed to slavery. The emancipating Baptist churches of the frontier, like the ones the Lincolns joined, were the leaders in 1808 in the formation of the Kentucky Abolition Society.

By the end of 1816 Thomas Lincoln was ready to move elsewhere with his wife and their two children. Discouraged by his trouble over land titles on three separate occasions, not liking slavery, and perhaps resentful of being looked down upon by those who held slaves, the elder Lincoln had had enough of Kentucky. He decided to make his way to near-by Indiana, which was on the point of being admitted as a free state.

It was in November or December 1816, while the Lincolns were en route to their new home, that young Abraham's first recorded experience with a Negro took place. At Hardinsburg the Lincolns stopped for some minutes in front of the home of Colonel David D. Murray. Here, at the doorstep, the Murray servant, Minerva, "gave young Abraham milk . . ." Continuing their ninety-one-mile trip, the Lincolns crossed the state line and made their way to Little Pigeon Creek in southern Indiana.

The fourteen years Abraham Lincoln spent in Indiana brought him in personal contact with very few Negroes. Originally a part of the Northwest Territory, from which slavery was barred, Indiana even in the latest years of its territorial period had only a sprinkling of Negroes—630 in 1810, as against 23,890 whites. Living on a heavily timbered backwoods farm with fewer than a dozen families whom they could call neighbors, the Lincolns led a restricted social life, highlighted by the camp meeting and the husking bee. And of the limited number of people they knew or met, probably none was a Negro, since there were only five in the entire county in 1820.

But this scarcity of colored inhabitants did not mean that the Negro question was unimportant in the Indiana of Lincoln's boyhood. Indeed, the fewness of the Negroes was due in part to a continuous agitation to keep them out. At virtually every session of the legislature, whether of the territory or later of the state, bills prohibiting Negro immigration were presented. From the time of the Missouri Compromise in 1820, stipulating where slavery might and might not go, the whole question of human bondage, emancipation, and the free Negro was widely discussed in the Indiana region where Lincoln grew up.

The most notable experience of Lincoln's Indiana years was a trip to New Orleans. During the closing weeks of 1828 the nineteen-year-old Lincoln was one of a two-man crew that took a cargo of farm products along the Ohio and down the Mississippi. Shortly before reaching New Orleans the young Lincoln had an experience that he never forgot. One night while tied up below Baton Rouge, the flatboat was boarded by seven Negroes bent on plunder. Lincoln and his companion, although hurt in the scuffle, managed to drive off their assailants. But not caring to risk a return engagement, the two young men hoisted anchor and pulled away from the wharf.

Young Lincoln was to make a second flatboat trip to New Orleans some twenty-eight months later, altogether spending some five weeks in this thickly slave-populated metropolis. According to one of the best-known Lincoln stories, it was at a slave auction in New Orleans that Lincoln made an eternal vow. A beautiful mulatto girl was up for sale, and the manner in which she was handled and inspected by the prospective buyers left Lincoln flushed with anger. "If I ever get a chance to hit that thing I'll hit it hard," he muttered as he walked away.

New Orleans was famous for its "fancy girls" for fancy purchasers, but the Lincoln-mulatto girl story will not stand up, as it was told by a man who did not accompany Lincoln on either of his trips. While in New Orleans, however, Lincoln could have scarcely missed seeing one or more of the public sales of slaves. Mistress of the domestic slave trade, New Orleans was an auctioneer's paradise, her main traveled streets studded with slave showrooms, show windows, and depots. In most of the city's some two hundred slave-auction marts the traffic took on a somewhat dehumanized aspect, with Negroes being put on the block simultaneously with such other salables as horses, carts, furniture, and casks of wine.

After his return from the second New Orleans trip Lincoln struck out on his own. By then his family had moved to Illinois, having left the Little Pigeon Creek home in March 1830, a few weeks after Lincoln reached his twenty-first birthday. Leaving his father's roof, Lincoln took residence at New Salem, a village on the Sangamon River, twenty miles below Springfield. During the six years at New Salem, Lincoln had a varied experience—store clerk, captain of a volunteer company in the Black Hawk War, store merchant, postmaster, and county land surveyor. Capping these

hibited, but that all contracts for service then in existence were binding. The constitution of thirty years later ordered that laws be enacted keeping Negroes out of the state. The legislature, however, needed little prodding. Between the time of the admission of Illinois to statehood and the outbreak of the Civil War, thirteen measures relating to Negroes were placed on the books. A person was prohibited from harboring runaway slaves, for example, or from granting a license for a marriage between a Negro and a white. State law would not permit a Negro to sue for liberty, to serve as a witness in court, to vote, or to serve in the militia.

The numerous enactments concerning Negroes meant that many court cases would inevitably result, testing the constitutionality of a law or its specific application. Such cases called for legal services; a practicing attorney in Illinois might expect to be called upon sooner or later to handle a suit involving the Negro, slave or free.

Lincoln was admitted to the bar on March 1, 1837, and some six weeks later he moved from New Salem to Springfield, which had just been chosen as the new capital city. Here Lincoln was to practice law nearly a quarter of a century. While still in the early years of his legal career, Lincoln became a party to a much-to-be-cited case concerning the legal aspects of slavery. This case, *Bailey v. Cromwell*, argued in the State Supreme Court in the summer of 1841, centered upon a Negro young woman named Nance.

Nance had been purchased by David Bailey, who had been assured that she still had seven years to put in as an indentured servant, and who had been promised legal proof of Nance's servitude. Bailey had not paid cash for Nance but had given a promissory note for $400. When the note fell due, Bailey refused to honor it, contending that Nance had left him after six months, and that the seller had never produced the title papers to her. Representing Bailey in the circuit court and now, upon appeal, in the higher court was Abraham Lincoln.

The young attorney presented an impressive argument to the judges assembled in the courtroom of the Capitol building. He pointed out that, during the years when Nance was alleged by the plaintiff to be an indentured servant, she had actually held a wage-paying job. She had made purchases and had established credit at the local stores; presumably she had an income. Moreover, argued her attorney, the burden of proof did not rest with the party asserting freedom, and no evidence had been produced that Nance was not free. She was free by the Ordinance of 1787 and the state constitution, both of which forbade slavery. Hence, concluded Lincoln, the promissory note issued by Bailey was void because it involved an act that was against the law—the sale of a human being.

The three judges pondered Lincoln's words. Six months earlier, in *Kinney v. Cook*, they had declared free a Negro who had been claimed as a slave, but for whom no supporting evidence had been produced. But although they had rendered this decision in December 1840, they had not yet delivered the written opinion. They listened, therefore, as Lincoln spoke, for it was obvious from the numerous authorities he quoted that he had made a painstaking examination of the case. Deciding in his favor, the court pointed out, as he had, that Illinois law presumed that every person was free regardless of color, and that the sale of a free person was illegal. Nance retained her freedom, and, thanks to Lincoln, the courts had been supplied with a mass of data supporting the principle of freedom. Certainly this was one of the most far-reaching of the nearly 250 cases in which Lincoln was to appear before the state's highest tribunal.

In another instance involving a Negro's freedom, Lincoln went into his pocket when his legal representations brought no results. Here the person in jeopardy was John Shelby. Early in 1857 young Shelby had hired himself out as a deckhand and cabin waiter on a Mississippi River steamer. On reaching New Orleans, Shelby made the mistake of going ashore without first obtaining a written pass from the boat's captain. Shelby apparently did not know that in New Orleans a Negro caught on the streets after curfew would be jailed unless he could produce one of three things: "free papers," a permit from his master, or a pass signed by a ship captain.

It was Shelby's fate to be stopped by the police and asked for his papers. Within minutes the young Negro was on his way to the jail to be locked up for the night. At the hearing the next morning he was unable to pay the fine levied against him, and so was brought back to his cell. With his steamboat gone up the river, the penniless Shelby faced the dismal prospect of being sold into slavery to pay the cost of his mounting jail dues.

Lincoln learned of Shelby's misfortune through Benjamin F. Jonas, a New Orleans lawyer. His reasons for bothering Lincoln were twofold, wrote Jonas: he remembered Lincoln as a long-time acquaintance of his father, and young Shelby had told him that Lincoln would be concerned about his plight. Lincoln did regard Abraham Jonas as a "valued friend," and he did know young Shelby and his mother, Polly Mack. He decided to see what he could do for the luckless Negro in faraway New Orleans.

With William H. Herndon, his law partner, Lincoln went to see the Governor of Illinois. But after a second visit the two attorneys were told that the Governor's office was powerless to do anything for Shelby. Thereupon Lincoln and Herndon made inquiry as to how much it would cost to pay Shelby's fine and jail dues. The partners raised the necessary $69.30 and sent a check in that amount to New Orleans. This step, wrote Herndon, "restored the prisoner to his overjoyed mother."

If the Nance trial and the John Shelby incident seemed to place Lincoln on the side of human freedom, such cannot be said of the Matson slave case. Quite the contrary. For here was an instance in which Lincoln's services were engaged by a Kentucky slaveowner who was seeking to recapture a family of runaways.

Robert Matson owned land in Coles County, Illinois, on which he employed slaves brought in from his Bourbon County, Kentucky, plantation. Matson took care not to keep his slaves in Illinois all year round: to have done so would have exposed him to heavy fines for harboring Negroes who had no certificates of freedom. Hence, Matson brought his slaves into Coles County in the spring and returned them to Kentucky after the fall harvest. But in the latter part of 1845 Matson had sent Jane, a favored mulatto, and her four children, one of whom had blue eyes and long red hair, to Coles County and had permitted her to stay there continuously for nearly two years. This sojourn in Illinois was particularly gratifying to Jane, since she could be with her husband, overseer Anthony Bryant. But one day Jane ran afoul of Matson's influential white housekeeper, who threatened to have her and her children returned to Kentucky and sold.

Under cover of night the alarmed Bryant quietly loaded his wife and children in a four-horse wagon and made his way to Oakland. Tavern owner Gideon M. Ashmore had promised asylum to the fugitives, and he proved to be as good as his word. With Hiram Rutherford, a young physician, Ashmore rounded up a corps of volunteers to prevent any effort to retake the runaways. Matson, not to be denied, engaged a lawyer. Quickly a writ was issued for the Bryants, and soon they were on their way to the county seat, Charleston, where they were put in jail as absconding slaves.

The justice of the peace who was to try the case knew perfectly well the excitement the incident had aroused. He knew that a Matson henchman was waiting with a covered wagon, in case the verdict was favorable, to hustle Jane and the children off to Kentucky. He knew, too, that ten armed men were standing outside his door, determined that the slaves would not be turned over to Matson. The nervous justice of the peace hit upon a ruling designed to avert any violence at his doorstep: He decreed that his court lacked jurisdiction on a question of freedom. But, added he, since the Negroes had no letters of freedom, as required by state law, they must be turned over to the sheriff.

With the Bryants back in jail, their two champions applied for a writ inquiring into the legality of their imprisonment. In turn, Matson brought suit against Ashmore and Rutherford, claiming damages of $2500 for seizing his slaves. Thereupon Rutherford set out for Charleston, bent on retaining a lawyer. By this time the case of the Matson slaves had become the chief topic of conversation throughout Coles County.

Lincoln rode into the county seat with the judges who were to hear the case, and it was at this stage of the proceedings that his services were engaged. Matson's lawyer persuaded Lincoln to join him as co-counsel. The trial was held in a packed courtroom, with sympathy running strongly for the Bryants, who had been behind bars for nearly seven weeks. The two-man bench listened to Matson and one of his retainers. The latter testified that his employer had not intended for the slaves to be permanently domiciled in Illinois.

Soon after Lincoln arose, it was obvious that the crux of his argument was to be an elaboration of the point of view expressed by the Matson henchman. Lincoln held that the key point in the case was Matson's intention: if he had brought the slaves into Illinois with no thought of establishing their residence in the state, he did not confer freedom upon them. Jane and her children were seasonal workers, contended Lincoln, and nothing more.

The judges apparently were not convinced by the temporary-domicile argument; at any rate they ruled that the Bryants were to go free. It was a popular verdict. Ashmore was able to raise money to send the former slaves to New Orleans where, under the auspices of the American Colonization Society, they took passage for Liberia.

It is not easy to say just why Lincoln consented to represent Robert Matson. Possibly he may have felt that even the devil was entitled to an advocate, that every litigant, no matter how unlovable, should have his day in court. It might be noted, too, that the Matson case took place in 1847, and that Lincoln's strong anti-slavery views seem to have been a product of the 'fifties. And even if his role in the Matson case were questionable, Lincoln could hardly be judged by one fall from grace.

Lincoln's "Negro business" as a member of the bar was not limited to questions involving slavery or freedom. Negroes sought his services in general cases, to represent them in husband-wife quarrels or to handle their legal business. An all-round lawyer whose cases ran the gamut of litigation, Lincoln was not choosy as to his clients. He had an especial attraction for those of small means.

"You must think I am a high-priced man," wrote he to a Quincy resident to whom he was returning a portion of the $25 fee sent to him in the mails. In one instance Lincoln and Herndon charged a Negro client a modest $5 for defending him against a suit brought by another Negro; Lincoln and Herndon's Fee Book of 1847 listed the case as "Negro vs. Robert Smith (Negro Bob)."

Typical of Lincoln's colored clients was Mary Shelby, for whom he filed a bill of divorce in the Sangamon Circuit Court in March 1841. Until two years previously, stated the Lincoln-drafted petition, his client and her husband (facetiously described in the court record as "a gentleman of colour") had lived together, "though not in the highest state of connubial felicity." But since then they had gone their separate ways. Moreover, so ran the charge, Mary's husband was a habitual drunkard and had contributed nothing to her support. Hence Lincoln asked the judge to decree that the marriage bonds between the Shelbys be dissolved.

Lincoln's most prosperous colored client, and certainly the Negro who came the closest to being a personal friend of his, was William de Fleurville, "Billy the Barber." Born in Haiti at the turn of the century, Billy had been sent to Baltimore, where he had picked up the barbering trade. While on his way to Springfield in the fall of 1831, he had stopped at New Salem, penniless and forlorn. Lincoln took him to the local tavern and explained his plight to the guests. Billy got several customers on the spot and left for Springfield the next morning with a much lighter heart.

Billy's barbershop, the first in Springfield, was a gathering place for the single men of the community, an ideal center for swapping tall stories. Lincoln's law books might be found lying about in Billy's shop; it was "his second home" before his marriage in 1842. And, of course, nobody in Springfield could shave him except Billy. When in the fall of 1860 Lincoln decided to grow a beard, he followed Billy's advice about trimming it and thinning it out.

A man with a funnybone, Lincoln may have liked Billy for his bubbling humor. Billy had not been in Springfield a year before he put an ad in the *Sangamon Journal* begging leave to inform the public that he was in the business "of scraping chins and cropping fore-tops." Some lines of doggerel followed, beginning:

> I scrapes the chin with hand so light,
> That to be shav'd is mere delight.

Two years later, in the same newspaper, Billy issued a "proclamation" in which pride in the birth of his first-born was shrewdly interwoven with a plea to slow-paying customers:

It will bring joy to the hearts of my faithful subjects to know that a princess has been added to my illustrious family, which in consequence of the abrogation of the salique law, is heir to these realms. On such an occasion, fraught with matters of such moment to my people, I must announce to them that the expenses incident to the proper support of her royal highness, renders it necessary that the funds due my treasury should be forthwith deposited in its vaults.

Given under my hand this 1st day of January, 1834.

William, IV.

Billy seemed to be popular among the townspeople generally. He played clarinet in the military band of the Springfield Artillery when it made its first appearance in full uniform in August 1835. Some years later the Springfield daily carried a "human interest" story on him, informing its readers that he loved gumbo and fricasseed chicken and "wouldn't object to a crapeau," besides being "one of the politest men." Billy was looked upon as one of the leading spokesmen for Springfield's Negroes. In 1855 a law was enacted stating that in townships with Negroes the school taxes paid by them should be used for colored children. Billy headed the movement to get such a school started in his home town, one of his first steps being to place a newspaper advertisement for a schoolmaster who could teach spelling, reading, writing, arithmetic, geography, and grammar. Billy's civic interests were broad; Catholic himself, he contributed generously to the charities of various religious groups.

Lincoln's main legal business with Billy was the handling of his

27

real estate. "I am in a little trouble here," wrote Lincoln from Bloomington in September 1852, as he sought the assistance of a fellow attorney in obtaining a decree for the conveyance of four lots that the well-to-do barber had acquired. Two of these lots Billy had purchased; the other two came from a steady customer whom Billy had contracted to shave for life. But Billy's deed to his holdings had not been properly recorded. "Billy will blame me," added Lincoln, "if I don't get the thing fixed up this time."

The Bloomington lots continued to be troublesome, however. A year later, still seeking a clear title, Lincoln represented Billy in the case of *William Floville v. James Allen*. Eventually the deed was obtained, and Lincoln then took on the job of paying the taxes from year to year. In 1860, a political campaign year, the taxes slipped Lincoln's mind for a time. But no damage was done; he had a Bloomington lawyer associate, Major W. Packard, pay the fees and mail him the receipt.

In February 1861, when President-elect Lincoln left Springfield for Washington, one of his most sorrowful farewells was at the old barbershop on Fifth Street, where Billy waited on him for the last time. Lincoln did not forget his colored fellow townsman. On two occasions while at the White House, he sent verbal regards and best wishes to his former barber-client, using as messengers his friend and physician, Anson G. Henry, and Governor Richard Yates.

His INTEREST in national politics accounts in great measure for Lincoln's profound study of the Negro question. Ambitious of political honors, Lincoln came to realize the overriding importance of the slave issue as he moved into the national arena, first as a one-term member of the House, then as a candidate for the Senate, and finally as an aspirant to the presidency itself.

It was as a member of the Thirtieth Congress that Lincoln had the opportunity of sensing the dominance of the slavery question. After four terms in the Illinois legislature, Lincoln ran for Congress in 1846, winning out against Peter Cartwright, the fiery, circuit-riding church elder. Early in December 1847 the thirty-four-year-old Lincoln arrived in Washington to take his seat as a Whig from the seventh congressional district of Illinois.

Although Lincoln's career in Congress was to be brief, he was called upon to take sides on the dozens of slavery bills that found their way into the hoppers. To a great degree such measures dealt with slavery in the territories and with the slave trade and slavery in the District of Columbia.

In a record not always marked by consistency, Lincoln voted for measures prohibiting slavery in the territories. In February 1848 he voted against tabling a resolution forbidding slavery in territory to be acquired from Mexico, a measure quite similar to the Wilmot Proviso. Later in the first session Lincoln voted to uphold a bill applying the Ordinance of 1787 to the Oregon Territory. In the early days of the second session he voted for a resolution instructing the Committee on Territories to incorporate an antislavery proviso in a bill establishing territorial governments for California and New Mexico.

Proposals for abolishing the District slave trade and for regulating slavery therein were nothing new when Lincoln came to Congress. More often than not during his one term, he supported measures opposing the slave trade. Within the first month after he had taken his seat, he voted against tabling two petitions that sought the stopping of the Washington slave traffic. Likewise in his early weeks he voted against tabling a motion to inquire into the expediency of either repealing the laws that sustained the District slave trade or moving the nation's capital elsewhere. Introduced by Joshua R. Giddings, staunch abolitionist from Ohio, this measure grew out of an incident at a local boardinghouse where a Negro waiter had been seized by three slave traders. During his last week in Congress, Lincoln presented a petition against the District slave trade signed by his constituents in Morgan County.

But Lincoln sometimes seemed to blow hot and cold. On two occasions he voted against resolutions directing committees to report bills abolishing the District slave trade. He also went on record against a resolution ordering a report on a bill abolishing slavery in the District. Possibly Lincoln's pattern of voting was not clear-cut because most of the measures had some feature that he disliked. He had his own ideas on slavery in the District, and these he presented in mid-January 1849.

As read to the House, Lincoln's proposed enactment would have granted freedom after January 1, 1850, to children born of slave mothers in the District, and would have compensated masters who consented to free their slaves. The municipal authorities of Washington and Georgetown would be required to arrest and deliver fugitives promptly, lest the District become a mecca for footloose slaves. Before becoming law these proposals would first be placed before the white voters. Lincoln claimed that this plan had the support of some fifteen of Washington's leading citizens. But he never formally introduced it for action, knowing that it would not be reported out of committee, especially since, as he later explained, "I was abandoned by my former backers."

Although he had submitted a plan of his own for promoting freedom in the nation's capital, Lincoln took no part in the heated discussions and bitter debates over slavery. When Washingtonians were aroused over the recapture of eighty slaves who had escaped from a steamer docked at Georgetown, Lincoln was among those who voted to shut off the angry exchanges that took place on the floor of the House. On slavery issues Congressman Lincoln voted when he had to. He introduced a petition or advanced a point of view when he felt that he had to; otherwise he held his peace. But his ever receptive mind had taken in a lot.

Lincoln left Washington when his term expired. He had not stood for re-election and would perhaps have been defeated anyhow—the fate of the Whig candidate in his district. For the five years following his return to Springfield, Lincoln was in political eclipse. But this "sleeping lion" period was marked by a heightened social awareness.

"IF SLAVERY is not wrong, nothing is wrong. I can not remember when I did not so think, and feel," wrote Lincoln in the spring of

1854. Actually, Lincoln's antislavery views were slow in coming to the fore. They were unmistakable by the summer of 1855, when he wrote to Joshua F. Speed about a boat trip they had taken fourteen years previously, during which a dozen slaves were aboard, shackled with irons in two groups. "That sight was a continual torment to me," wrote Lincoln in August 1855. Yet in September 1841, while the trip was still fresh in his mind, he spoke of the slaves in a letter to Mary Speed, but he expressed no dislike of slavery. Indeed, wrote he at the time, the slaves he saw in chains on the *Lebanon*, despite their bleak prospects, "were the most cheerful and apparently happy creatures on board." One of them "played the fiddle almost continually; and the others danced, sung, cracked jokes, and played various games with cards from day to day."

As early as October 1845 Lincoln, in a letter to abolitionist Williamson Durley, said that nothing should be done to prevent slavery from dying a natural death. But he did not at that time condemn the practice. Lincoln's hatred of slavery was no sudden conversion, the consequence of a single experience or event. It was, rather, a slow growth, as difficult to pinpoint as the merging of one season into another. Although he did not denounce slavery in forthright language until the mid-fifties, his dislike for it may well have been fermenting in his mind for ten or fifteen years.

Lincoln's hatred of human bondage had many possible roots. One of these was grounded in his own observations of slavery. On invitation from Joshua F. Speed, he had in the summer of 1841 visited Farmington, the Speed family plantation near Louisville. Here he could see slavery in operation; it is possible that a slave was assigned to him for his personal needs. However, in his thank-you letter to Mary Speed, mentioned above, he did not mention slavery at Farmington.

Six years later Lincoln again came to Kentucky to visit, this time in Lexington. He was then en route to Washington to take his seat in Congress. Lexington was his wife's home town, where she had been born and raised. Daughter of a prominent political figure,

Mary Todd had grown up in a household and in a region where slavery was almost second nature.

Early in November 1847 the four Lincolns—parents and baby boys—arrived at the Todd home in Lexington. For three weeks Lincoln had a second opportunity to observe slavery in Kentucky. He would come to know the Todd household slaves, particularly Mammy Sally, the best loved and most influential of "our colored contingent," as they were called by one of the Todds. The vacationing Lincoln, strolling around, could not have missed the slave pens, less than three blocks away, which almost surrounded the home of Mary's aged grandmother. Quite possibly he saw slaves put on the block; he liked to visit the courthouse, and the enclosure in front of that building was a favored spot for slave auctions.

While in Washington as a House member, Lincoln was exposed to slavery in another setting. Its two thousand or so bondmen were much in evidence. The buying and selling of blacks was a flourishing business. From the windows of the Capitol, Lincoln could see what he later described as "a sort of negro-livery stable, where droves of negroes were collected, temporarily kept, and finally taken to Southern markets, precisely like droves of horses."

Possibly something of what he saw of the slave traffic in Washington may have taken deep root in Lincoln's mind. Possibly, too, a second, shorter trip to Lexington some months after his term in Congress may have added its bit to his growing impression of slavery as a combination of the whipping post, the crowded pen, and the auction block.

LINCOLN'S INTENSIVE STUDY of slavery began in 1854 with the passage of the Kansas-Nebraska Act, repealing the Missouri Compromise. Passed in 1820, the Missouri Compromise had prohibited slavery in the Kansas-Nebraska Territory; and as long as this measure remained on the books, many Northerners felt that slavery would eventually die out. Its repeal in the spring of 1854, an invitation to the extension of slavery, was bitterly condemned in the North. It had the effect of a blow on the head, wrote Horace

White, a journalist friend of Lincoln, "which causes a man to see stars in the daytime."

With a depth of feeling new for him, Lincoln, too, was stirred. Prior to the Kansas-Nebraska Act his political ambitions were self-centered, lacking any burning convictions. As a member of the House he had been a good party man, following the Whig line and expecting favors for his faithful support. But the opening of new territory to slavery marked his great awakening. "I was losing interest in politics," wrote he, "when the repeal of the Missouri Compromise aroused me again."

Destined so significantly to shape Lincoln's subsequent career, this measure plunged him into an intensive study of the politics of slavery. He did not start from scratch. As postmaster of New Salem, while just entering manhood, he had read in detail the newspapers that passed through his hands, and slavery and the free Negro were public questions that these mass-circulating sheets could not ignore. Building on such early foundations, the newly aroused Lincoln began to read fully from the *Chicago Tribune*, the *Anti-Slavery Standard*, and the *New York Tribune*, balancing these with such proslavery dailies as the *Richmond Enquirer* and the *Charleston Mercury*. He subscribed to all of these jointly with his law partner.

Billy Herndon, a great admirer of abolitionist leaders like William Lloyd Garrison and Charles Sumner, kept scrapbooks of newspaper clippings that condemned slavery. These he constantly pressed on his senior partner. Although Lincoln considered Billy's views "too rampant," he did not hesitate to familiarize himself with the extensive information his office mate had compiled.

Lincoln made his exhaustive study of slavery with one purpose in mind—to equip himself to return to politics. It was inevitable, therefore, that he would join the Republicans, a party that came into existence against the repeal of the Missouri Compromise. By the fall of 1856 Lincoln had moved into the forefront of the new party, receiving 110 votes for the vice-presidential nomination at its first convention, held in Philadelphia in June. The party went down to defeat that year, but it showed surprising strength outside the South.

In 1858 the Illinois Republicans chose Lincoln as their candidate for the United States Senate. In running for this office, Lincoln challenged his Democrat opponent to a series of joint debates. Stephen A. Douglas, the incumbent, thought it best not to refuse, even though he might have far less to gain than the relatively unknown Lincoln. Possibly, too, Douglas concluded that he might as well debate Lincoln openly as to have him keep showing up at the tail end of the well-planned Douglas rallies and inviting the audiences to remain and hear him.

Seven debates were arranged, each in a different county. These meetings were colorful affairs, with torchlight processions, companies of artillery and light guards, costumed young women on horseback, all enlivened by brass bands, cannon, and fireworks, with flags and banners everywhere. But the holiday atmosphere in which the debates were staged could not dim their basic seriousness. The exchange between the two candidates pivoted around their differing views on slavery—its extension and its morality.

Douglas eloquently supported the doctrine of popular sovereignty—the principle whereby a territory or a state could determine its own way of life. Hence, said the Little Giant, if a community wanted to have slaves, that was its business. Lincoln challenged popular sovereignty, maintaining that it tended to spread and to perpetuate slavery. And slavery, asserted Lincoln with increasing conviction every time he faced Douglas, was wrong.

Lincoln lost his bid for the Senate seat, and Douglas was reelected. But in the great debates Lincoln gained much. He had stood toe to toe with an opponent of national reputation, giving blows as hard as those he took. As a result his name emerged from the shadows and became known in Republican circles throughout the North. He had taken on the stature of a "dark horse" for his party's nomination as its standard-bearer. But this was not all. He had done much to fix upon the coming presidential campaign the overriding issue of slavery, with all of its explosiveness.

THE VIEWS expressed by Lincoln in the great debates furnish an excellent prewar mirror of his mind. But they do not stand in isolation from his other speeches and writings during the late fifties. Important as the debates were, they furnish only a part of the Lincoln output. Ever since the repeal of the Missouri Compromise Lincoln saw to it that no one suffered from an information gap as to his attitude on slavery: he shared his thinking with all who sought it—personal correspondents, newspaper editors, civic organizations, and political groups. A summary of these views is essential to an understanding of the Lincoln who was to move into the national spotlight in 1860.

Lincoln opposed slavery, and for many reasons. One was its effect on the white worker. Lincoln held that slavery was contrary to the best interests of the wage earners in the North, who were forced to compete with unpaid laborers. "The mass of white men," said he in a Cincinnati speech in September 1859, "are really injured by the effect of slave labor in the vicinity of the fields of their own labor."

Lincoln charged that slavery endangered democracy. The relation of the master to the slave was a denial of the great principle that governments derive their powers from the consent of the governed. Lincoln held that no man was good enough to govern another man without that man's consent. "As I would not be a slave," wrote Lincoln, "so I would not be a master. This expresses my idea of democracy."

Lincoln opposed slavery on moral grounds, as an evil. It was a contradiction of a basic law of God—that of freedom. We live in an ethical world, one that holds us accountable. Hence, said Lincoln, a man who did not wish to be a slave should not proceed to enslave anyone else—"Those who deny freedom to others, deserve it not for themselves; and, under a just God, can not long retain it." Because in the Lincoln-Douglas debates, the Little Giant refused to consider slavery in terms of right and wrong, Lincoln said of him: "He is blowing out the moral lights around us, when he contends that whoever wants slaves has a right to hold them."

Lincoln was opposed to slavery because it was contrary to the ideals of the Declaration of Independence. No man in public life ever surpassed Lincoln in his devotion to this great document; it was, said he, "an immortal emblem of humanity." He held that the "all men are created equal" phrase in the Declaration included the colored man. Obviously slavery was at variance with the fundamental American principle which, said Lincoln, until recently "was held sacred by all, and thought to include all." To Lincoln there was no reason in the world "why the negro is not entitled to all the natural rights enumerated in the Declaration of Independence, the right to life, liberty and the pursuit of happiness. I hold that he is as much entitled to these as the white man."

However, it must be noted that while Lincoln supported Negro freedom, he was no advocate of Negro equality. "I have no purpose," wrote he in 1858, "to introduce political and social equality between the white and black races." Lincoln did not believe that the Negro was on a par with the white man in mental endowment, and he supported the Illinois law forbidding intermarriage. He was not an advocate of Negro voting, or Negro office holding, or of Negroes serving on juries. Lincoln believed in equality of opportunity for all Americans, but he did not fully sense that a denial of any basic right was, in effect, a denial of equal opportunity for advancement.

Lincoln was not anti-Negro, however, despite the strong racial prejudices so prevalent where he lived. In the campaign for the Senate in 1858, the jibes of his opponent forced him to declare himself in opposition to Negro equality. But Lincoln regarded the issue of racial equality as something of a bugbear, a mysterious specter with uncanny power to affright.

A man without bigotry of any kind, Lincoln believed that there was no necessity for a conflict between whites and blacks. In America there was room enough for all to be free, for all to earn a decent living. As mentioned previously, Lincoln did regard the Negro as inferior. But this did not mean that he was to be deprived of his American heritage. Like Thomas Jefferson, whom he so greatly admired, Lincoln held that a man's rights were not contingent upon his abilities.

Lincoln's views on slavery were dominated by the idea that had brought him back into politics—the conviction that slavery should be restricted to the states in which it existed, and kept out of the territories. This cardinal belief is well summed up in his own words: "toleration by *necessity* where it exists, with unyielding hostility to the spread of it."

Lincoln would put up with slavery in the states because he believed that Congress had no legal right to do anything about it. Slavery in the states was constitutional. So, too, as Lincoln saw it, was a fugitive-slave law. Again and again Lincoln asserted the right of Congress to enact a law enabling masters to recover their bondmen; such a law, however, should protect a free man from being sold into slavery. Obedience to law was second nature to Lincoln; because he felt that the fugitive-slave laws passed by Congress were legal, he did not, as an attorney, take cases in behalf of runaways, although his partner, Herndon, welcomed such suits.

Lincoln's belief in the legality of slavery in the states was accompanied by a somewhat paradoxical belief that slavery would fade away in time. In 1854 Lincoln expressed the opinion that the autocrat of all the Russians would resign his crown sooner than American masters would free their slaves. But somehow Lincoln reconciled this opinion with the hope that slavery would one day spend itself and go off and die. He predicted that a house divided could not stand, and yet he expected that slavery would wear away of itself.

These comforting beliefs about the peaceful passing of slavery received a mortal blow in the Dred Scott decision. Handed down by the Supreme Court in 1857, this ruling permitted slavery in the territories. Lincoln was dismayed. To him the Dred Scott decision meant that slavery was again on the march and would possibly be forced upon the free states themselves.

In common with most Republicans, Lincoln believed that the plantation owners and their supporters in Congress and on the federal bench made up a slavocracy which was plotting to rule or ruin. Lincoln and his party felt that a new President was needed, one who would appoint new justices to the Supreme Court, which would then reverse the decision permitting slavery in the territories.

Just as the Kansas-Nebraska Act fixed his purpose, so did the Dred Scott decision strengthen the determination of the Lincoln who with the coming of 1860 had set his sights upon the highest office in the land.

Two watershed events:
K-N Act
Dred Scott

3

"AMONG US, YET NOT OF US"

THE LINCOLN who moved into the national picture in 1860 did not have a rounded knowledge of the colored people. Lincoln knew little of Negro life, of the Negro's hopes, and of his efforts to move into the mainstream of American life. Lincoln was well schooled, as has been noted, in the historical record of slavery in America, but prior to the Civil War he never had a heart-to-heart talk with a runaway slave. A prominent Negro would not have escaped his attention; he had heard of Frederick Douglass. Indeed, Lincoln's political opponents had taken pains to identify him with the famed Negro orator; in June 1856 the *Illinois State Register* reported of Lincoln that "his niggerism has as dark a hue as that of Garrison or Fred Douglass." And in his series of debates for the United States senatorship in 1858, his opponent repeatedly identified Lincoln with the Negro leader, mentioning the latter's name three times in the very first debate at Ottawa, Illinois. But although a widely known Negro might come into Lincoln's ken, he knew little of John Doe, colored.

A great lover of humor, Lincoln was, of course, quite familiar with the folk Negro of mirthful anecdote. Like most whites, Lincoln believed that the Negro as such was funny. He enjoyed Negro dialect stories and had his own repertoire. Wrote fellow congressman Moses Hampton on March 30, 1849, to Lincoln: "Do you remember the story of the old Virginian strapping his razor on a

[handwritten marginalia: L, linked to D.]

certain member of a young negro's body which you told and con-
nected with my mission to Brazil?"

Lincoln liked minstrel shows with their black-faced performers
singing, strutting, and telling jokes. His friend, attorney Henry C.
Whitney, accompanied Lincoln to one of these shows and noted
"the spontaneity of Lincoln's enthusiasm and the heartiness of
his applause." Lincoln was fond of Negro ditties and often asked
another lawyer friend and associate, banjo-playing Ward Hill
Lamon, to sing "The Blue-tailed Fly":

> When I was young I used to wait
> At massa's table 'n hand de plate,
> An' pass de bottle when he was dry,
> An' brush away de blue-tailed fly.

Sally Brown was another Negro in song whom Lincoln remembered, quoting, in an address at the Springfield Scott Club in
August 1852, one of the stanzas about her:

> Sally is a bright Mullatter,
>   Oh, Sally Brown
> Pretty gal, but can't get at her,
>   Oh, Sally Brown.

The Lincoln of 1860 knew the Negro of dialect story, minstrel
stage, and sea chantey. The last five years of his life would give
him a much fuller picture of the Negro. A sketch of the general
nature and outlook of the Negro community on the eve of the
Civil War will shed light on the critical issues that faced Lincoln
and the country during the fateful sixties.

In 1861 George T. Downing, a successful New York caterer,
expressed a guarded optimism about the Negro's lot in the North.
Contrasting the outlook then with that of twenty years ago, he
noted "the most hopeful changes." Less than a quarter of a century
ago,

> a colored man had to take the gutter side of the pave, and dared
> not show his face in a concert, lecture or library-room; schools,

colleges and literary associations closed their doors against him; he had to pace the deck all night amidst howling storms while going up and down the rough tempestuous sound; the teachers teaching his children "no hope in this country," instructing them to be good menials.

Things were different now, continued Downing:

Colleges and schools are alike open to all on equal terms, as are also the lecture, the concert and the library room; railroads and steamboats free to him; see him in legislative halls, in person or by petition; see him participating at the bar, in the workshop, in the studio, occupying professorships, and then say, if you can, there is no hope for the future.

Downing's optimism was shared by Thomas Hamilton, also of New York City, and publisher of a literary monthly, the *Anglo-African Magazine*. "We maintain," wrote Hamilton editorially, "that no one thing is beyond the aim of the colored man in this country." Indeed, Hamilton's chief fear was that the colored people aimed too low: "A society for the demolition of boiled turkeys would be wonderfully popular with us." What was the ideal of Negro young men, "they who should be scaling the Rocky Mountains, or felling the timber of the Utah region"? Apparently their ideal was "a Morphy cap, one well-fitted suit of clothes, patent-leather boots of the latest fashion, an ingot or two of gold in the form of a chain hanging over their breast, a long nine and a sherry cobbler at the St. Charles." On rolled Hamilton's unsparing pen: "And the young women—ladies I presume I must call them to avoid offense—they who are to be the mothers of the Gracchi— What is their ideal? Our fear is that it reaches no higher than the polka and the redowa, and agreeable flirting at a picnic."

Downing's rosy picture and Hamilton's exhortation were meant as spurs. Neither was blind to the many difficulties that environed their fellow blacks. Indeed in 1860 Downing himself had been summoned to court for refusing to state the value of his holdings, his reason being that the government did not regard him as a person and that property could not own property. Like other leaders of their race, Downing and Hamilton well knew that for the Negro in the North "freedom" generally meant insecurity rather than equality.

In every walk of life there were evidences of discrimination. Public conveyances discriminated against Negro riders. In New York City as late as 1855 there were special horsecars bearing a sign that ran along their entire length, "Colored People Allowed in This Car." In 1854 the Reverend James W.C. Pennington, a Doctor of Divinity from Heidelberg, after urging his congregation to stand up for their rights, boarded a Sixth Avenue car not reserved for colored, and was badly roughed up.

Shrines of learning offered no serious challenge to the color line; no welcome mat beckoned the black-skinned student into the halls of ivy. "In one Northern college," reported Unitarian clergyman James Freeman Clarke, "a Negro was told he might be admitted by testifying under oath that he was of French and Indian extraction and had no African blood in his veins." In view of the thumbs-down attitude of the colleges, Negroes were particularly vexed over the remark attributed to John C. Calhoun, "that if he could find a Negro who knew Greek syntax, he would believe that the Negro was a human being and should be treated as a man." Alexander Crummell, holder of a bachelor's degree from Queens College, Cambridge, raised a question: Where could a syntax-aspirant Negro go for his training? "It is manifest that Mr. Calhoun expected the Greek syntax to grow in Negro brains, by spontaneous generation."

On the labor front, Negroes in the North were employed as a rule in not more than a dozen of the three hundred occupations that the census listed as engaged in by whites. Acute in many cities was the competition for the menial jobs that once had been Negro monopolies. Recent immigrants were quite willing to become maids, cooks, waiters, porters, and dock hands. This crowding out of the Negroes was recorded by one of their newspaper editors: "Formerly blacks were almost the exclusive coachmen in wealthy families; this is so no longer; white men are now employed and, for aught we see, they fill their servile state with the obsequiousness as profound as that of the blacks."

Many of the Negro's difficulties stemmed from a denial of the ballot. Even though numerically small in proportion to the white population, Negroes were disfranchised in many Northern states. To vote in New York a Negro had to own real estate worth at least $250.00. Such restrictions aroused strong protest. Toward the ballot many Negroes shared the sentiment of Sojourner Truth, that tall, pure black, Negro reformer who had furnished her own name: Sojourner, she said, because the Lord had commanded her to travel throughout the land; Truth, because she was divinely commissioned to reveal His purposes. A fighter for political equality, Sojourner Truth's greatest dread was to enter the Kingdom of Heaven disfranchised.

The plight of the Negro in 1860 as it appeared to him was reviewed by Dr. J. McCune Smith. A New Yorker well known in reformist circles for his labors in the Liberty party and the Radical Abolitionist party, Smith had received his medical education in Scotland. A successful practitioner and an author of medical monographs, Smith somehow found time for civic interests. Among Negroes he was listened to, and his views generally struck a common chord.

> What stone has been left unturned to degrade us? [ran his summing up]. What hand has refused to fan the flame of popular prejudice against us? What American artist has not caricatured us? What press has not ridiculed and condemned us? Few, few, very few, and that we have borne up with it all—that we have tried to be wise, although pronounced by all to be fools—that we have tried to be upright, when all around us have esteemed us to be knaves—that we have striven to be gentlemen, although all around us have been teaching us its impossibility—that we have remained here, when all our neighbors have advised us to leave, proves that we possess qualities of head and heart, such as cannot but be commended by impartial men.

The many discriminations against the Negro were not without an improving quality: Negroes worked zealously to better their lot. The opinion expressed by Smith, for example, was distributed in a pamphlet issued by the New York City and County Suffrage Committee of Colored Citizens, of which he was chairman. With more than twenty branch clubs in New York City alone, this committee was organized on a statewide basis. In upstate New York the key figure was Stephen Myers of Albany, newspaper editor, underground railroad agent, and lobbyist in the halls of the state legislature.

The Negro's efforts for self-improvement were notable in education. As taxpayers they waged a persistent struggle to get their children admitted to the public schools. A few Negroes were able to afford private instruction; James Forten, owner of a sail loft in Philadelphia, hired tutors for his eight sons and daughters. Other Negroes, acting in concert, set up and financed their own schools so that qualified applicants would be prepared to enter Northern colleges when the color bars were lowered. In Washington, D.C., forty of the fifty-two colored private day schools established between 1807 and 1861 were founded and conducted by Negroes themselves.

Another expression of the Negro's impulse toward self-improvement was the prevalence of literary societies, founded for "the stimulation of reading and the spreading of useful knowledge by providing libraries and reading rooms." The pre-Civil War existence of no fewer than forty-five such societies has been traced in the North. Their names are suggestive. Baltimore boasted the Young Men's Mental Improvement Society for the Discussion of Moral and Philosophical Questions of All Kinds, and the Negroes of Pennsylvania's second largest city prided themselves on their Young Men's Literary and Moral Reform Society of Pittsburgh and Vicinity. Rochester had its Ladies Literary and Dorcas Society, and the 120 Negro families inhabiting the sparsely populated frontier Greenville settlement in Randolph County, Indiana, reported themselves as having "a very good Literary Debating Society."

The earnestness shown by these Negroes impressed many

thoughtful whites. In the main these interested whites were reformers. Of their many enthusiasms—woman's rights, universal
peace, land reform, no capital punishment, and the temperance
agitation, to name but a few—the abolition of slavery was paramount. Into their ranks these abolitionists invited Negroes. Frown-
ing on the principle of segregation and holding that "complexional
anti-slavery societies, as such, are absurdities," the organized anti-
slavery movement opposed the formation of Negro abolitionist
societies.

Negroes were gratified at this joining of hands. "It is better,"
one of them had said, "to be the part of a whole than to be the
whole of a part." To work hand-in-glove with white reformers gave
them an opportunity to prove that Negroes were concerned with
the problems of all peoples. "We are men," proclaimed the motto
of the Negro weekly, the *Ram's Horn*, "and therefore interested in
whatever concerns men."

The abolitionists, white and black, attacked slavery not because
it denied freedom to men of a particular color, but because they
regarded it as by far the worst of all the wrongs in America. To
clergyman Henry Highland Garnet slavery was "the highly con-
centrated essence of all conceivable wickedness." To Frederick
Douglass it was "a Hell-born monster." J.W.C. Pennington, who,
like Garnet and Douglass, had known slavery at first hand, nodded
in accord: "The being of slavery lives and moves in the chattel
principle, the bill of sale principle; the cart-whip, starvation, and
nakedness are its inevitable consequences, warring with the dis-
positions of men."

In directing their efforts toward freeing the slaves on the Southern plantations, the abolitionists reflected the social ferments and
the humanitarian impulses which characterized America in the
'forties and 'fifties. Conscience-driven men and women, spurred
by the teachings of Christianity and by the ideals implicit in the
Declaration of Independence, could not hold their peace. To the
abolitionist, slavery was the major malady—a foreign substance in
the body politic, requiring surgery. To the reformers it seemed ob-

vious that a sound and healthy democracy could not exist in "the land of the free and the home of the slave."

Prior to 1840 the driving spirit behind the organized abolitionist movement was Theodore D. Weld. Despite a stern and forbidding countenance—a friend likened it to the Inquisitor General's—Weld had great personal charm. His deep religious convictions gave to his oratory a compelling ring. At Lane Seminary in Cincinnati and at Oberlin, the students who heard him lecture fell under his spell and became ardent reformers. Weld trained antislavery agents for work in the field, edited antislavery publications, acted as a research assistant for the handful of abolitionists in Congress, and compiled a notable best-selling handbook, *Slavery As It Is, the Testimony of a Thousand Witnesses*, which was second only to *Uncle Tom's Cabin* in its antislavery influence.

Weld retired from active agitation in 1844, his mighty voice burnt out from a decade of extraordinary exertion. But before his retirement the American Anti-Slavery Society had come under the influence of another force to be reckoned with—William Lloyd Garrison of Boston.

Garrison's abolitionist career had an early beginning. On January 1, 1831, when only twenty-five, he launched the *Liberator*, setting the type with his own hands. This notable addition to the literature of social protest never paid expenses, "but its message became known from coast to coast and across the Atlantic." A year after the *Liberator* appeared, Garrison organized the New England Anti-Slavery Society. Thirteen months later, in December 1833, he was one of the founders of the American Anti-Slavery Society, drafting the uncompromising Declaration of Sentiments, which became the society's platform. Almost as unpopular in his home town as elsewhere, Garrison was seized by a Boston mob one October afternoon in 1835 and dragged through the streets with a rope around his waist.

Garrison's rough handling was witnessed by Wendell Phillips, who had left his law office to investigate the commotion. As the hooting and jeering mob left Wilson's Lane with their prey,

Phillips walked thoughtfully back to his office. Abolition had made a convert. In Phillips the reform movement acquired a powerful supporter. He was a true patrician: by birth, with five generations of distinguished ancestors; by education, having graduated from Boston Latin School, Harvard College, and Harvard Law School; and by appearance, reminding one of "a young Apollo." Deserting the law, Phillips brought to the reform movement oratorical abilities unparalleled in America and soon became "abolition's golden trumpet."

Phillips and Garrison became intimate friends. Their antecedents were not similar—Garrison had come from a broken family and had no formal schooling—but their beliefs were identical. They were root-and-branch abolitionists, and their goal was immediate, uncompensated emancipation. Compromise was not in their make-up: between two evils, said they, choose neither. Freedom-shriekers with a high impatience quotient, they stood ready to break a lance with friend or foe.

The Garrisonian abolitionists drew much of their support from their Negro members. In the early years of the *Liberator* the majority of the subscribers were Negroes, and the first substantial cash contribution to the paper was made by James Forten. When in 1832 Garrison was pondering a visit to England and needed $200 passage, Nathaniel Paul, a Baptist minister of Albany, came to his rescue. Three Negroes sat on the twelve-man executive committee of the American Anti-Slavery Society in its first year.

During the 'fifties Negro lecturers were the greatest "drawing cards" among the Garrisonians. After joining their ranks in 1841, Frederick Douglass became their prize exhibit. Preceding Douglass in the movement was Charles Lenox Remond—spare, thin-faced, and dark skinned—the first Negro to take the field as a professional antislavery lecturer. William Wells Brown was also effective on the abolitionist platform, delivering over a thousand lectures for the Massachusetts Anti-Slavery Society. An escaped slave with an unusually adventurous background, Brown became a prolific writer.

He was the first American Negro to try his hand at the novel, the drama, and travel literature.

Two other steadfast Negro Garrisonians were Robert Purvis and William C. Nell. The son of an Englishman and a free colored woman of Charleston, Purvis resided at Byberry, Pennsylvania, in comfortable circumstances. His magnificent orchards and approved breed of livestock made him the heaviest taxpayer in the township. A man of high principles, Purvis was one of the signers in 1833 of the national society's Declaration of Sentiments. Unlike Purvis, who was educated at Edinburgh, Nell was self-taught. Although he was not particularly effective as a speaker, he brought to the cause a knowledge of abolitionist journalism acquired as publisher of the *North Star* and in the offices of the *Liberator*. Nell's *Colored Patriots of the American Revolution*, published in 1855, was the first serious attempt by an American Negro to write history.

The agitation of the abolitionists seemed to be making some headway in the 'fifties. The chief factor enabling them to spread their influence was the dispute over runaway slaves. On September 18, 1850, President Millard Fillmore signed the Fugitive Slave Law. It turned out to be one of the most vulnerable measures ever passed by Congress; the storm of protest it aroused never subsided.

By denying the testimony of the alleged runaway and by assuming that he was guilty rather than innocent, the measure immediately became a powerful propaganda weapon for the reformers. The abolitionist press referred to it as "the Man-Stealing Law" and "the Bloodhound Bill." The legal claims of the master notwithstanding, the free men of the North, as Frederick Douglass pointed out, "can never be brought to look with the same feelings upon a man escaping from his claimants, as upon a horse running away from its owner." Thundered Samuel Ringgold Ward, a Congregational clergyman so richly pigmented that, according to Phillips, when he closed his eyes, you could not see him: "We the people will never be human *bipeds* to howl upon the trace of the fugitive slave."

The unpopularity of the Fugitive Slave Law thus dated from the hour of its passage. Highly dramatized by the abolitionists was the plight of thousands of Negroes. The law was ex post facto, reaching back to runaways who had been living unmolested for years. A few of them breathed fire. Proclaimed Jermain Wesley Loguen, the short, stockily built pastor of the African Methodist Episcopal Church at Syracuse: "I am a fugitive slave from Tennessee. My master is Manaseth Loguen—the letter of the law gives him a title to my person—and let him come and take it. I'll not run, nor will I give him a penny for my freedom." Ward warned that "if anyone came to take him he had better perform two acts for the benefit of himself and his family. He should first make his will and then make his peace with his Maker."

Many runaways, however, made preparations to reach the Canadian border. Within fifteen days after Fillmore signed the bill, over three hundred Negroes left Pittsburgh, "armed with pistols and bowie knives, determined to die rather than be captured." In Columbia, Pennsylvania, home of William Whipper and other prosperous Negro lumber merchants, and one of the principal avenues of escape for fugitives, the Negro population fell from 943 to 487. Of the 115 members of the Colored Baptist Church in Rochester, New York, only two remained. The Reverend Hiram Wilson of St. Catherine's, whose business it was to receive runaways, reported that 3000 took refuge in Canada from September 1 to December 1 in 1850. During the ten years following the passage of the bill, from 15,000 to 20,000 Negroes crossed into Canada.

Many of the latter, however, came directly from the South via the underground railroad. Aiding fugitives "to get Canada under their feet" had become to abolitionists a high moral duty. Hundreds of runaways were assisted by such devoted workers as Harriet Tubman, an escaped slave who carried her rescues to the cotton field and the cabin door, and the great-hearted David Ruggles of New York City, who sheltered innumerable fugitives under his own roof. William Still, who received hundreds of them in Philadelphia, was another outstanding operator among the not less than

140 Northern Negroes who manned underground railroad stations.

But the Fugitive Slave Law did far more than arouse a natural human sympathy for runaway Elizas pursued by bloodhounds. The abolitionists also called attention to the basic principles involved: freedom of transit, trial by jury, protection from ex post facto legislation, and the presumption of innocence rather than of guilt. By arousing a deep concern for the preservation of civil liberties in America, the abolitionists broadened their appeal. More and more the public listened.

As the 'fifties wore on, the abolitionists did not doubt that their cause would prevail. "We have turned Whigs and Democrats into Republicans and we can turn Republicans into Abolitionists," wrote one. In the meantime, pending the arrival of that glorious day, the slaveowner could know no peace of mind. So Frederick Douglass assured his fellow abolitionists at a convention held by the national society:

> The slave power might silence the voice of Wendell Phillips, or the pen of William Lloyd Garrison. They might blot out our anti-slavery organization in order to give peace to the slaveholder. They might cut out my tongue, and all our tongues. They might gather all the Anti-Slavery literature, "Uncle Tom's Cabin" included, set a match to it, send its flames toward the sky and scatter its ashes to the four winds of heaven, and yet the slaveholder will be ill at ease; for deep down in his own dark conscience would come an accusing voice: "Thou art verily guilty concerning thy brother."

THAT THE 383,637 SLAVEOWNERS in 1860 felt a sense of guilt was not a provable assertion. Indeed, these men believed that "slavery is the natural and moral condition of the Negro," as Alexander Stephens phrased it. Another eminent spokesman for the South, John C. Calhoun, concluded after an exhaustive inquiry that slavery was "a positive good." Slavery was a benefit to the Negro, said Jefferson Davis, because "the negro was a child race, and slavery was its training school." The slaves on Briarfield, Davis's plantation on an island in the Mississippi below Vicksburg, were treated with great consideration and always referred to their master as a "very fine gentleman," but Davis was wedded to the Southern belief that slavery, as he saw it, was "but a form of civil government for those who by their nature are not fit to govern themselves."

To white Southerners race and color were not mere descriptions of superficialities; on the contrary, race determined mental and moral traits. Whites in the South believed that Negroes comprised an inferior breed. The New Orleans *Bee* summed up a sectional philosophy in a sentence: "As for the complaint that we do not recognize negro equality, we answer that we cannot recognize what does not exist."

Another belief widely held in the South was that no crop could be produced under a free-labor system, that the Negro would work only as a slave. It followed, then, that the Negro existed for the special object of raising cotton, tobacco, sugar, and rice, in the status of "chattels personal, to all intents, constructions and purposes whatsoever," in slave-code language.

Slavery was not only an economic way of life, it was also a system of racial adjustment. Southerners who personally deplored slavery agreed with the majority that the Negro needed controlling and that slavery alone could furnish adequate safeguards. Even those who were devoid of the feeling expressed by one Southerner, "A man feels good when he owns twenty or fifty negroes, and can say to one go, and he goes and to another come, and he comes," nonetheless feared the revolutionary change that would attend the disruption of a time-hallowed institution like slavery. Some masters who favored emancipation felt that to free their slaves would be to dodge a responsibility. These benevolent slaveholders could not appreciate such abolitionist parodies as colored man Simpson's "Slave-Holder's Hymn—To be sung at Evening Prayers (Short Metre)":

> A charge to keep I have
>   A negro to maintain,
> Help me, O Lord, whilst here I live
>   To keep him bound in chain.

What was the actual lot of the slave? Many white Southerners depicted the slave as happy and slave life as one long interchange of coon and possum hunts, barbecues, fish frys, and Saturday night breakdowns where bucks and gals enjoyed "de pleasures ob de dance." The last week of the year was vacation, and on December 25 the slaves came to the big house and shouted, "Crismus gif," and lingered meantime for the "sweetened dram."

This idyllic picture drew a derisive snort in some quarters. Southern publications, wrote *L'Union*, a French-language weekly issued by New Orleans Negroes, pretended to present the truth about slavery, but their writers were not slaves to the truth. To the editors of *L'Union*, as to abolitionists, the slaves were thought to toil "from day-break to back-break," subject to the beck and call of sadistic Simon Legrees, hellbent on maximum crop production whatever the cost in human values.

The actual picture is a combination of light and shade, with the latter predominant. The lots of the slaves varied, since there were different kinds of slaves. In the towns there were many slaves who were virtually free, their masters permitting them to bargain for their own employment. Out of their earnings they turned over to their masters a weekly sum, averaging three dollars. The remainder they put aside as savings to buy their freedom.

The plantations had two types of slave—the domestics and the field hands. But whether he lived in the big house or along slave row, the bondman bore his lot, because over the years there had developed an "etiquette" of slavery, a code of social manners and usages which enabled him to know just what was the expected thing to do. This etiquette was a complex system of slave behavior and response, involving his manner of greeting, saluting, and conversing with whites and his conduct whenever he was in their presence.

IN THE OPINION of Southern whites, if there was one thing that might make the slave dissatisfied, it was the presence in his midst of the free Negro. The quarter of a million Negroes in the South had become free in various ways. Some had purchased their own freedom; some had been manumitted by kind and grateful masters; and some had become free as a result of meritorious military service in the Revolutionary War and the War of 1812. These free Negroes were a constant source of disquiet to the slaveholding population. "Wherever the free Negro is found he becomes for the most part a pest and a nuisance," wrote a Southern editor; "he gets drunk, debauches our slaves, or preaches insubordination to them."

To keep the non-slave Negro in his place, the states below the Potomac had erected a variety of controls. To begin with, color indicated condition, and if one had a dark skin, it was up to him to prove he was not a bondman. Unless he could produce his "free papers," a Negro without a master was presumed to be "an absconding slave." In Mississippi free Negroes were required to secure special licenses from county boards of police, in the absence of which they would be sold into slavery. In South Carolina the free Negro must wear a diamond-shaped copper badge; caught without it, he must pay $20 or go to jail. In Savannah the law required that a free Negro have a guardian—a combination protector, go-between, and overseer.

In the courts the free Negro, like the slave, was held incompetent to testify for or against white persons, except in Delaware and Louisiana. In the latter state the Civil Code affirmed that while "the circumstance of the witness being a free colored person is not sufficient cause to consider the witness as incompetent," it may "diminish the extent of his credibility." In South Carolina the free Negro could be sold into slavery in default of payment of jail fees or court fines. In Petersburg, Virginia, from 300 to 500 Negroes a year were sold for failing to pay their taxes. The precarious position of the black man without a master was incisively described by Chief Justice Joseph H. Lumpkin of the Georgia Supreme Court: "The free Negro resides among us, and yet is a stranger. A native even, and yet not a citizen. Though not a slave, yet he is not free. Though not in a condition of chattelhood, yet he is constantly exposed to it."

Since the very existence of free Negroes was an implied censure of slavery, the planter class made a concerted effort to keep their numbers down. Laws existed whereby masters were permitted to free their slaves only upon legal guarantee of transporting them out of the state. In many towns and counties the immigration of free Negroes was prohibited. Freedom of travel was restricted; a free Negro who left Charleston was not permitted to return.

In the South the effort to reduce the number of free Negroes reached its highest point in the late 1850's with the sharpening of sectional hostility. Southern state legislatures adopted measures prohibiting manumissions, inviting free Negroes to enslave themselves, and removing free Negroes from the state. Typical of the antimanumission measures was a Georgia law of 1859 that prohibited emancipations by will of the deceased master. In Alabama the *Huntsville Southern Advocate*, labeling the free Negro "a loathsome pest," urged the legislature to check the "morbid growth of free-niggerdom." Taking heed, the General Assembly in the session of 1859-60 declared void all wills that emancipated slaves. Maryland in 1860 prevented masters from freeing slaves.

Some states invited the free Negro to renounce his liberty and select a master. In Louisiana the legislature provided in 1859 for the voluntary enslavement of Negroes. Virginia's law granted permission for free Negroes to make application before a county court to become slaves. Any debts or liabilities of the petitioner would be assumed by his new master. In Maryland free Negroes above eighteen years of age might get court permission to renounce freedom. If they were females with offspring under five years old, the latter would also become slaves. Alabama passed, in the 1859-60 legislative session, a "Re-enslavement Act." In South Carolina in 1860 there was "much sentiment" for forcing the state's 9914 free Negroes to accept the status of slaves.

Typical of the measures to remove free Negroes from the state was the action of the Arkansas legislature in 1859. If the seven or eight hundred free Negroes (there were 608 in 1850) did not leave the state by January 1860, it became the duty of the sheriffs to seize them and hire them out to the highest bidder for one year; the net proceeds of their labor would enable them to buy a railroad ticket and get out. Arkansas' free Negroes made inquiries about where they might go, issuing "An Appeal to Christians Throughout the World." Composed by Francis Ellen Watkins Harper, abolitionist lecturer and literary light, the appeal dramatized the plight of the free Negro wherever he might be found: "We turn to the free North, but even here oppression tracks us. Indiana shuts her doors to us. Illinois denies us admission to her prairie homes. Oregon refuses us an abiding-place for the soles of our weary feet."

ALTHOUGH THE 'FIFTIES had been for the Negro a decade of unfulfillments, the election of Abraham Lincoln to the presidency brought some consolation. To Negroes, Lincoln was not the ideal candidate, nor was the Republican party the ideal party. Indeed, in the early stages of the campaign, Negro leaders were extremely cool toward the party ticket. Voicing this initial disrelish for the Lincoln nomination, twenty-eight-year-old H. Ford Douglas denounced his fellow Illinoisan for "his pro-slavery character and principles," citing Lincoln's advocacy of an effective fugitive slave law. Moreover, during the months when the colored people of Ohio were "agitating the question of suffrage in that State," Lincoln, in a speech at Columbus, had made it clear that he opposed the political equality of the races. Also, charged Douglas, when he went to see Lincoln in 1858 and asked him to sign a petition to repeal the Illinois law forbidding Negroes to testify against whites, Lincoln turned him down.

But if Negroes were unenthusiastic about Lincoln in the election of 1860, they were even less happy about his opponents in the four-cornered race that developed. The Northern Democrats nominated Stephen A. Douglas on a platform affirming that the status of slavery in the territories should be determined by decisions of the Supreme Court. The Southern Democrats, desiring more positive assurances for slavery and a candidate from their own section, proceeded to nominate John C. Breckinridge of Kentucky on a platform affirming the duty of the national government to protect slavery in the territories. A new party, the Constitutional Union party, nominated conservative candidates and simply swept the explosive slavery issue under the rug, winning the derisive dubbing of "Respectable Old Gentleman's Party."

To Negroes the Republican-Lincoln ticket was the least objectionable of the four. Moreover, although the Republicans made no play for the small Negro-abolitionist vote, it came to them through the tactics of their opponents. Lincoln's political foes charged him with having furnished John Brown with two rifles, with favoring racial equality and with being a "nigger worshiper." In one of their campaign songs the Democrats portrayed Lincoln and the Negro as one and inseparable:

> Then, Union men, let's work away—
>   We've got the Blackies tight, sir:
> Old Abe will fall on 'lection day,
>   No matter how they fight, sir.

Lincoln's running mate, swarthy Hannibal Hamlin, got the tar-brush treatment. "If the Black Republicans," said influential R. Barnwell Rhett, at Charleston, South Carolina, in early July, "succeed in electing Lincoln and Hamlin, then we shall have to look to ourselves. Hamlin is what we call a mulatto. He has black blood in him. They put a renegade Southron on one side for President, and they put a man of colored blood on the other side of the ticket for Vice-President."

Such racial attacks made the Republicans more palatable to Negroes. Frederick Douglass informed the readers of his monthly that, while he had resolved to vote for the Radical Abolitionist party candidates, he hoped for the triumph of the Republicans. "I love everything the South hates," said H. Ford Douglas at Boston's Tremont Temple in the closing days of the campaign, "and since they have evidenced their dislike of Mr. Lincoln, I am bound to love you Republicans with all your faults." In a few spots, notably in Pittsburgh, Negroes managed to work up enough enthusiasm to form marching clubs—Wide-Awakes—with their glazed hats and oilcloth capes.

In general, Lincoln's victory seems to have been received with pleasure by Negroes. To the colored inhabitants of Maryville, California, who did not get the news until six days after the election, it brought "great rejoicing." In Philadelphia the Library Club, made up of the city's black intelligentsia, held a December debate at St. Thomas Episcopal Church: "Will the election of Abraham Lincoln be advantageous to colored people?" The answer seemed to be a yes, with reservations. In Baltimore in the days right after the election, the Negroes were said to have adopted as their rallying cry "Go in, Mr. Lincoln," and one bold person of color was alleged to have boarded a white streetcar, asserting that as Lincoln had been elected, he could ride like any man. To the President-elect came a letter from Sue H. Burbridge of his native state informing him that the Negroes of Logan County had "commenced their work of poisoning and Incendiaryism," having taken up the notion "that as soon as you were elected they would all be free."

If such stories seem overdrawn, Lincoln's election to the presidency undoubtedly heartened Negroes and their friends. They felt that although slavery would be safe under the new administration, the Republican victory was a blow to the political power of the slaveowners. Moreover, reasoned slavery's foes, Lincoln's triumph demonstrated the possibility of an abolitionist's eventually being elected President. Lincoln's emergence would thus set in motion a law of increasing returns. "A pawn on the political chessboard, his value is in his position; with fair effort, we may soon change him for knight, bishop, or queen, and sweep the board," said Wendell Phillips, to the applause of a Boston audience, on the day after the election results were known.

But such gloating was short-lived. For Negroes and reformers the postelection weeks quickly turned out to be a Walpurgis Night during which "the South had moved North." The four months' interval between Lincoln's election and his inauguration was for the Negro and his abolitionist supporters the most trying period in their stormy experience. In the Yankee world during that tense and jittery secession winter, the spirit of compromise and conciliation mounted with every fresh dispatch from the aroused Southern states. Shaken by the action of South Carolina in dissolving, on December 20, its union with "the other States of North America," many Northerners felt that something had to be done to convince the South that her established customs were in no danger.

One way of reassuring the slave states was by throttling the abolitionists and breaking up their meetings. Such gatherings were by nature disorderly. Because they incited combativeness on the part of those who disagreed with them, abolitionists were case-hardened to tumult. Indeed, reformers like the erratic genius Stephen S. Foster "measured the success of anti-slavery meetings by the number of windows and benches broken and the quantity of eggs thrown." But in the four months following Lincoln's election a record number of abolitionist meetings came to abrupt and violent adjournment.

Boston set the pace. Four weeks after the elections the abolitionists and Negroes met at Tremont Temple to discuss the question "How shall American slavery be abolished?" The meeting had hardly been called to order when hired hoodlums invaded the hall and rushed to the platform, determined to take control of the proceedings. Battle was joined, but not for long; in rough-and-tumble pugilism the abolitionists were good amateurs, but this time they were pitted against professionals. The rowdies threw or pushed from the platform the abolitionist speakers and themselves chose a chairman, organized a meeting, adopted a set of resolutions, and passed them by acclamation. Their sword wrested from them, the abolitionists brandished the pen. Wrote the *Anti-Slavery Standard*, "The claim of these 'heroes of the kerb-stone' to be gentlemen rested solely upon their coats being whole at the elbows and their shirts not noticeably dirty."

At the Music Hall, six days after the Tremont Temple meeting, Frederick Douglass was roughed up by "a handful of very coarse samples of human nature." Fearing "mobocratic proceedings," the pastor of the Joy Street Church, J. Sella Martin, gave up his plans for a first anniversary celebration in honor of the three Negroes who died with John Brown at Harpers Ferry. Clergyman Martin had correctly judged the Boston temper, for when at the annual meeting of the Massachusetts Anti-Slavery Society, Ralph Waldo Emerson started to protest against any further concessions to the South, he was interrupted by hisses, groans, and cries of "Dry up" and "Put him out." A man of such culture and refinement that he regarded laughter as ill-bred, and one who (according to James Russell Lowell) "dwelt in that ampler and diviner air to which most of us, if ever, rise only in spurts," Emerson was obviously out of his element. It was the first time the world-famous philosopher had ever faced a mob, and after several attempts to begin he finally took his seat unheard.

In New York State, as in Boston, mob violence held sway at abolitionist gatherings. At Association Hall in Albany the mayor personally escorted to the platform the great triumvirate among the women reformers—Susan B. Anthony, Elizabeth Cady Stanton, and Lucretia Mott. These pioneer workers for women's rights were abolitionists also. Their antislavery zeal stemmed in part from the staunch support that Negro leaders had given to the woman's rights movement at its organizational meeting at the Wesleyan Methodist Church, Seneca Falls, New York, in the summer of 1848, and thereafter. Appearing at this meeting in Albany was for these three women's-righters, therefore, simply one such attendance out of hundreds. But this meeting was different in one respect; an air of high tension pervaded the hall. Plainclothes policemen were stationed throughout the hall while Frederick Douglass and philanthropist Gerrit Smith delivered addresses. Stiffly on the platform sat the mayor, clutching a loaded gun. No overt violence took place, but the strain told on the mayor, and he requested the reformers to cancel their scheduled second meeting.

In other New York cities the abolitionists were less fortunate. An attempted meeting at Syracuse could best be described in a single word: bedlam. "The friends of freedom," ran an angry report to the abolitionist press, "were prevented from meeting by grogshop soakers, bruisers, and 'Vinegar Hill' roughs, all stirred up with strychnine whiskey." At an abolitionist meeting in Auburn someone threw red pepper upon the hot stove, and suffocating fumes filled the hall. One of the speakers thereupon advised the chairman, "As we are so near hell, I would suggest that the meeting be closed with prayer, if there is a clergyman present who will offer one." In Rochester an abolitionist meeting was graced by the presence of the sheriff, the mayor, several aldermen, and the chief of police. The stately bearing of these worthies made little difference. The "wild and boisterous excitement" abated only when the chief of police adjourned the meeting. After this occurrence the abolitionists were unable to rent a public hall in Rochester, and the only church where an abolition lecture could be delivered was the Zion Methodist Episcopal Church, seating 150.

Baltimore avoided any demonstrations against Negro gatherings by simply prohibiting such gatherings. The city Board of Police would not permit the African Methodist Episcopal Conference to hold its annual meeting there, declaring such a meeting unlawful under an old statute prohibiting nonresident Negroes from coming into Maryland.

Concerning these widespread infringements on freedom of assembly, the pulpit spoke in subdued tones. "Clergymen of every degree and religious denomination," wrote a contemporary, "exhorted their flocks to be firm in faith, patient in hope, careful in conduct and trustful in God." Liberal newspapers that before the election had shouted, "Who's afraid?" were now cooing in peace-dove accents. As for those sheets that were opposed to abolitionism, they had less space for discussing freedom than for publishing letters proposing an "American Anti-Abolition Society," whose platform aimed "to disabuse the mind of the false theories of the Abolitionists, and to expose and counteract the dangerous tendencies and inevitable consequences of their doctrines." Such an organization would provide "The Remedy for Negro Mania," declared the *New York Express*.

A further attempt to conciliate the South was the repeal of the "personal-liberty laws." Passed during the 'forties and 'fifties, these state statutes had been designed to offer protection to runaways. Such laws were made possible by a Supreme Court decision, *Prigg v. Pennsylvania*, delivered in 1842, which permitted states to forbid their officers to assist claimants to slaves. With such a go-ahead signal, Northern legislatures had proceeded to deny the use of state jails for the holding of fugitives, had forbidden state judges to assist owners, had extended the right of trial by jury to Negroes claimed as slaves, and had gone as far as to require state attorneys to act as legal advisers for Negroes thus accused.

Such measures were hateful to the South, and if she were to be won over, they would have to go. To this end, a meeting of Republican governors was held in New York in December 1860. These chief executives agreed to recommend to their state legislatures that the personal-liberty laws be repealed or drastically modified. In response, Rhode Island, Massachusetts, and Vermont adopted such recommendations.

The abrogation of these protective measures created consternation in Negro circles. Those who had come North via the underground railroad now felt as unsafe as in the early days of the Fugitive Slave Law of 1850. Even Harriet Tubman, that "whip-scarred woman of earth," whom John Brown had introduced to Wendell Phillips as "General Tubman, one of the best and bravest persons on the continent," was persuaded to hurry off to Canada.

Perhaps in no other city were Negroes more apprehensive than in Chicago. During the first week of April 1861 the Negro community was panic-stricken by the rumor that a group of federal marshals were about to swoop down on the black population. Former runaways were admonished to hasten to Canada. "Don't let the grass grow under your feet ... Strike for the North Star," urged a friendly newspaper.

Sunday, April 7, was made memorable by an exodus such as no

city in the United States had ever witnessed. At one Baptist Church alone, 115 Negroes had gathered. One of them, a sick woman for whom return-to-slavery writs had been made out, arrived by dray on a mattress. Many brought food for others less fortunate, "very much like white folks under the same circumstances," wrote the *Chicago Tribune* reporter, adding that "at Delft Haven it might have been nearly the same, very like indeed," for the Pilgrims. After praying and singing together, the group went to the Michigan Southern Depot, where an immense crowd had assembled to bid them Godspeed. Don't forget us, ran the refrain of those on the platform, when you reach "the other side of Jordan."

Perhaps some of these involuntary emigrants reflected that they were leaving a city whose first permanent settler had been a French-speaking Negro. (Indeed, the Pottawatomie Indians who traded with Jean Baptiste Pointe de Saible in the 1790's had a saying, "The first white man to settle at Chicagou was a Negro.") As the train sped from the metropolis, some of the departing black passengers may have observed that the receding signposts, "Chicago, Ill.," not only located the city in space but also described its state of mind.

While municipalities and states were acting to appease the South, similar efforts on the national level were every whit as intensive. John H. Rapier, a young, light-skinned, rolling-stone journalist, expressed impatience over the "rose-water policy" of the North. William Wells Brown found the spirit of compromise so strong toward the close of 1860 "as to cause serious apprehension on the part of the friends of freedom for the future of American liberty." With a certain class of politician, editorialized a New York weekly, the greatest question of the day seemed to be "how to make a new compromise."

President James Buchanan, in a message to Congress at its opening session on December 3, 1860, recommended an "amendment recognizing the right of property slaves," and "the duty of protecting this right in all the common Territories throughout their Territorial existence." Both branches of Congress appointed committees "to receive, consider and report upon plans for pacification."

Of the many compromise schemes, the one coming from Senator John J. Crittenden of Kentucky received the most attention. The main proposals of the Crittenden compromise were that slavery be prohibited in the territory north of the old Missouri Compromise line but that it be protected below that line; that Congress should not interfere with slavery in the states or in the District of Columbia, and that the interstate transportation of slaves should also be outside the scope of Congressional action. These measures were to be written into the Constitution and were not to be subject to future amendment.

These proposals were acclaimed in business circles. Merchant and manufacturing groups in the large Eastern cities sent numerous resolutions to Congress "earnestly requesting your honorable body" to take favorable action.

No such resolutions came from Negro groups. On the contrary, Boston Negroes petitioned the state legislature to send a communication opposing the compromise, and also drew up "An Appeal to White Citizens." Negroes were especially wrathful about the resolutions that Crittenden had bracketed with his proposed unamendable amendments. These resolutions would pledge Congress to recommend to the Northern states that they repeal the personal-liberty laws—termed, in the language of the resolution, "those laws which in their operation, impede, hinder or delay, the free course and due execution of laws for the recovery of fugitive slaves."

The Crittenden compromise, like other similar plans, came to nothing. The responsibility for the failure of such proposals rests in part with the President-elect. It was his belief that the object of all of the proposed compromises was "to put us again on the high-road to a slave empire." Lincoln would give no word of encouragement to the Crittenden plan because it opened the prospect of extending American slavery into Cuba and elsewhere below the Rio Grande.

Conciliators in Congress made one last attempt to do something before the new President took office. They succeeded in pushing through a thirteenth amendment that would forbid Congress to interfere with "the domestic institutions" of any state, including state laws relating to "persons held to service or labor." Never ratified, this measure, if not too little, was certainly too late. It was passed only two days before Lincoln was inaugurated, and by then seven Southern states had left the Union.

It need only be added that the heated and futile discussions of the compromise measures intensified sentiment against the colored man. He was held to be the source of all discord. "The *everlasting Negro* is the rock upon which the Ship of State must split," ran a widely reprinted, angry editorial in a Providence, Rhode Island, daily. "Will the people stand for this much longer? Will they make the Negro their god . . . ?"

Even in the Far West, where the impulses of equality and democracy were supposedly strong, the Negro noted a sea change. "In California public sentiment is more intense against the colored man than at any previous period," wrote an observer in 1860. This was in sharp contrast with race relations in 1850, when "the black men and white men could be seen working in the same mine, traveling together, eating at the same board, drinking at the same bar, and staking on the same card." And now, only ten years later, the California legislature was looking with apparent favor on the enactment of "black laws."

Such was the inflamed mood of America as Abraham Lincoln arrived in Washington to take the reins of a nation already in travail, sundered physically as it had long been rent in spirit.

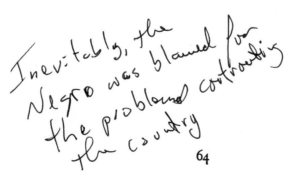

Inevitably, the Negro was blamed for the problems controuting the country

4

HALF SLAVE, HALF FREE

OF THE MILLIONS who awaited Abraham Lincoln's words upon his taking office on March 4, 1861, no group exceeded the Negro in hopeful anxiety. And after the incoming President had delivered his inaugural address, and its contents had become quickly and widely circulated, no group exceeded the Negro in disappointment. As the weekly, the *Anglo-African*, expressed it, "We gather no comfort from the inauguration of Abraham Lincoln."

Negroes noted that in this first of Lincoln's state papers he repeated that he had no intention of interfering with slavery. They noted also that he favored the proposed amendment denying Congress the right to touch slavery in the states. The inaugural address made it clear, too, that the Fugitive Slave Law should be enforced. To Negro critics it was bad enough that Lincoln apparently intended to assume the role of "National Kidnaper," but they were especially vexed about his assertion that the only substantial dispute between the North and the South was over the extension of slavery. Lectured the *Anglo-African:* "It is the *existence* not the *extension* of slavery that is the issue." This sheet had a bitter prediction for the new President to mull over: " 'The only substantial dispute' when the history of the contest is fairly written, will be found to be something more than a mere question of extension."

If by being soft on slavery Lincoln hoped to win over the South, he was soon set straight. United and determined, the secessionists of the recently formed Confederacy simply ignored Lincoln's olive-branch inaugural words. "Physically speaking, we cannot separate," Lincoln had said. But the people below the Potomac, believing that slavery was imperiled as never before, had become conditioned to leaving the Union.

If the new President believed that war could be avoided, he was not in office six weeks before he had to change his mind. On the day after he took the oath of office, Lincoln was presented with a report from Major Robert A. Anderson at Fort Sumter in the Charleston Harbor. Anderson sent word that his food supply was so low that his force of eighty-one men faced surrender to the Southern Confederacy. The beleaguered Sumter had become a symbol of federal authority, and Lincoln decided to send a relief expedition. Learning of Lincoln's intention, the Confederate Secretary of War wired the commander at Charleston to "reduce the fort." At daybreak on April 12 a bombardment was ordered. After forty hours under fire Anderson ran up the white flag. On the day of the fort's surrender Lincoln issued a call for 75,000 men to put down the rebellion.

The response gave him a lift. In the North the shock of the attack on Sumter was accompanied by a wave of excitement and enthusiasm. The dread of disorder which marked the winter of compromise now gave way to an outburst of patriotism. The martial spirit swept the North as recruits lined up at the enlistment centers, some expressing apprehension lest the war end before they were able to get in a blow of their own.

Sharing fully in the great enthusiasm were the Negroes. They reasoned that since slavery was the root of the conflict, freedom would be the result. In colored circles the call to arms was certain to fall on cocked ears. Four days before the firing on Fort Sumter, one Levin Tilmon of New York informed Lincoln that if he wished to have colored volunteers, he had only to signify by sending word to 70 East 13th Street. Tilmon's sentiment was echoed by an editorial squib in a Negro weekly: "Colored-American balls hereafter should be of a different mould. They must be leaden, not festive."

volunteering

Negroes throughout the North offered their s
thorities. Less than two days after Lincoln's call, a
Negroes, meeting in the Twelfth Baptist Church
President their lives and their fortunes. In Prov
company offered to march with the First Rhode 1
as it left for the front. New York's governor w
services of three regiments of colored men—their ar
and pay to be furnished by the Negroes of the state. Philadelphia
Negroes formed two regiments, which drilled at Masonic Hall, and
in Pittsburgh the Hannibal Guards offered their services, pointing
out that as American citizens they were anxious "to assist in any
honorable way or manner to sustain the present administration."

Negroes in Cleveland, meeting at National Hall, declared their
allegiance to the Lincoln government and offered to supply money,
prayers, and manpower to help with the war. At Detroit Captain
O.C. Wood and the thirty-five members of his Detroit Military
Guard sought to enlist. Another Michigander, Dr. G.P. Miller of
Battle Creek, asked War Department permission to raise "from
5,000 to 10,000 freemen." Among the last of the volunteering
letters was one to Lincoln from clergyman J. Sella Martin, who had
just returned to Boston after a lecturing tour in England. "If I can
be of any manner of service here, should your excellency ever think
it best to employ my people, I am ready to work or preach or fight
to put down this rebellion," wrote Martin, enclosing a personal
photograph and a batch of London newspaper clippings about
himself.

Nothing came of any of these proposals. Every city to which
Negroes offered their services adopted a thumbs-down attitude.
When five hundred Negroes in New York hired a hall to organize a
militia unit, the Eighth Precinct police captain suppressed the
meeting lest it lead to "unpleasantness." City fathers elsewhere
were more polite but no less definite in their refusals. The Negroes
met the same attitude at Washington. When Jacob Dodson, a
Senate attendant who had seen service with John C. Frémont in
crossing the Rockies, offered the services of three hundred Negroes

defense of the nation's capital, he was officially informed
the War Department had no intention of using colored
soldiers.

The turning down of colored volunteers sprang from a wish to
avoid anything resembling trouble in dealing with the Negro, North
or South. Popular sentiment in the North was reflected in a House
of Representatives resolution of July 22, 1861, declaring that the
war was being waged not for the overthrow of the established institutions of the Southern states, but for the upholding of the Constitution and the preservation of the Union. Three days later the
Senate adopted a similar resolution. The North was willing to let
the slave alone, but looming ominously was a fateful question:
Would the slave let the North alone?

"AFTER THE COMMENCEMENT of hostilities," wrote Lincoln in
January 1863 to one of his generals, "I struggled for nearly a year
and a half to get along without touching the 'institution.'" But
at the very outset of the war, this hands-off policy was undermined
by the slaves themselves. No sooner had the war begun than the
slaves began to sift into the Union lines. As the war brought federal
troops into the slaveholding regions, the freedom-minded bondman
no longer had to follow the North Star to a point above the Mason
and Dixon Line or the Ohio River. Now with the camps of the
Union armies on Southern soil, freedom beckoned more insistently.

The black population showed such great willingness to take leave
of the "dear old bandanna days" that a Union army unit moving
into the South was faced with an inundation of blacks. Many considerations prompted these Negroes to flee their masters, but Confederate President Jefferson Davis probably had the best explanation: "The tempter came, like the serpent in Eden, and decoyed
them with the magic word 'freedom.'"

These Negroes who had freed themselves presented a problem
to the military men into whose lines they came. Lincoln and his
War Department had formulated no policy on these black
refugees; hence each commander was forced to follow his own

inclinations. In making his own policy, one of the most inventive of the generals was Benjamin F. Butler, commanding at Fortress Monroe, located in Virginia at the tip of the peninsula between the James and the York rivers. Late in May 1861 three runaways paddled up to the fort and presented themselves to the picket guard. Butler had them put to work. When their owner tried to recover them, Butler, a lawyer turned soldier, ruled that they were "contraband of war." Hence, said he, they were not returnable, unless their master came to the fort and took an oath of allegiance to the Union. Butler's ruling gave an official name to these runaways: "contrabands."

The news of Butler's action spread quickly in slave circles. "Proclaim an edict in the hearing of a single slave on the Potomac, and in a few days it will be known by his brethren on the Gulf," wrote a man who knew the contrabands intimately. Within a week after his ruling on the three runaways, General Butler reported that more than $60,000 worth of slave property had delivered itself to Fortress Monroe.

As the slaves poured into the fort, Butler asked instructions from Washington. On May 30, Secretary of War Simon Cameron advised him to continue employing the Negroes and to keep accounts of their services and the expenses of their maintenance. The question of their final disposition, wrote Cameron, was yet to be decided. Two months later Butler had nearly a thousand contrabands—men, women, and children—within his lines, and again he wrote the Secretary of War for instructions.

This time Cameron was able to refer to an act of Congress passed on August 6—a measure declaring that slaves were forfeited if their masters permitted them to be used in the service of the Confederacy. Two days after this Confiscation Act was passed, Cameron informed Butler that it was Lincoln's desire to respect all existing rights in all states, and that in disloyal states the act of August 6 must be Butler's guide.

Lincoln signed this act with reluctance. He felt that he was the proper and most competent judge of questions relating to the status of slaves, and that the men on Capitol Hill should take their cues from him. In his opinion Congress had jumped the gun. But he did not withhold his signature, because he knew that a veto of the bill would have looked as if he were providing justification for the Confederacy to use its slave population for military purposes.

Although cool toward the Confiscation Act, Lincoln had no contraband policy of his own. On fugitives who came under the Union flag, the Secretaries of War and Navy could get no advice from the Secretary of State, who seemed to feel that if no one talked about the problem, it might solve itself. This look-the-other-way policy of Lincoln and his Cabinet left things in the hands of commanding officers, whose practices varied.

Some military officers permitted slaveholders, loyal or otherwise, to repossess their runaways. Eight fugitives who reached Fort Pickens were heartbroken when Commander A.J. Slemmer ordered them taken back to Pensacola and delivered to their masters. "I have raved and I have wept about that Fort Pickens affair," wrote abolitionist Lydia Maria Child.

Some officers forbade slaves to enter their lines. Prominent among these was Henry W. Halleck, commanding in the Department of Missouri, who ordered that no fugitive should come into his troops, while either encamped or on the march. Some officers seemed to go out of their way to preserve the status quo: George B. McClellan, of the Department of the Ohio, sent orders to subordinates in late May 1861 to "suppress all attempts at Negro insurrection." In early June, Robert Patterson issued a similar order in the Department of Pennsylvania: "Should occasion offer, at once suppress servile insurrection."

Not all officers were unsympathetic toward contrabands. At Ellicot Mills, Maryland, Colonel Alfred H. Terry of the Fourteenth New York supported his men in refusing to deliver six runaways to their masters. Possibly influenced by the abolitionist views of William Henry Johnson, a self-educated free Negro who had attached himself to the regiment, these New York volunteers took the position that no human being in their camp could be branded as a slave. An officer in a Massachusetts regiment replaced the rights-of-man approach with one of his own. Confronted by a master who asserted title to a Negro in his camp, this officer put both slave and master outside his lines, leaving the verdict in favor of the fleetest of foot.

Such whimsical decisions were invited by the silence of the Commander in Chief, and Lincoln was prepared to swallow them for the moment. But he drew the line when on August 30, 1861, John C. Frémont, in command of the Department of the West, took a bold and sweeping step. Proclaiming martial law in Missouri, Frémont decreed that the property of rebels was thereby confiscated and their slaves freed. Frémont's ruling was received with hosannas in Negro circles; it would make people "look the real cause of war in the face," said Frances E. W. Harper, and would inspire the Lincoln administration to lay the ax to the tree.

But if the proclamation pleased the Negro, it vexed the man in the White House. It was, in essence, the shifting of the war's emphasis from preserving the Union to liberating the slaves. And, just as bad from Lincoln's point of view, Frémont's action presumed to fix the permanent future condition of the slave—a power that belonged to civil authorities, not to the military. Losing no time, Lincoln suggested to Frémont that he backtrack on the proclamation, making it conform to existing law which freed only those slaves whom the rebels used for war purposes. When Frémont stubbornly refused to comply, Lincoln issued an open order that he do so.

In pro-Negro circles the reaction was predictable. Lincoln's letter to Frémont was "the saddest thing that has occurred since the defeat of Bull Run," mourned *Pine and Palm*, a weekly published at Boston and devoted exclusively to news about Negroes in the United States and Haiti.

As if the Frémont episode were not displeasing enough, Lincoln was soon confronted by another antislavery expression by an important public figure. This time it was a member of his official family, Simon Cameron, Secretary of War. By the end of 1861

Cameron had become an advocate of organizing Negro troops among the contrabands. A long-time hater of slavery, Cameron did not need much convincing about arming the Southern Negro. The abolitionist inclinations of the Secretary of War were strengthened by his close ties with the influential Republican bloc that was bent on controlling both Congress and the President. These "Radicals," as they came to be called, had a long-range plan to lay a heavy hand on the South, and one of the first steps toward this was arming the former slaves.

Without consulting the White House, Cameron drew up his annual report of 1861. In it he asserted the right and the duty of the government to arm slaves and employ them against the rebels. The report had been printed and advance copies put in the mails before the stunned Lincoln read it. Although it was a Sunday, Lincoln summoned Cameron to the Executive Mansion and laid down the law: the report must be revised, leaving out the passage on arming the slaves. Cameron, like Frémont, sought to justify his action. But, like Frémont, he had no choice but to obey.

Before Lincoln had fully made up his mind on the status and use of the slaves of rebels, he was forced for the third time to overrule an order of military liberation. In this instance the offender was a man for whom Lincoln had a personal regard. David Hunter had accompanied the President-elect on the trip from Springfield, and after the inauguration he had been in charge of the volunteer force guarding the White House. In March 1862 Hunter had become commander of the Department of the South, a region along the south Atlantic coast which initially had come under Union control in November 1861, following a massive, combined army-navy assault.

An abolitionist at heart, Hunter had no sooner arrived at his Sea Island headquarters at Hilton Head than he began to pass out certificates of freedom to overjoyed blacks; and within two weeks he issued a declaration freeing the slaves at Fort Pulaski and on Cockspur Island. In early May the general took a giant step without first asking, "May I?" He declared martial law in the territories under his command, and in the next breath he asserted that since slavery and martial law were incompatible in a free country, "the persons in these three states, Georgia, Florida and South Carolina, heretofore held as slaves are therefore declared forever free."

Sea Island Negroes were in raptures. When a Yankee schoolteacher asked one of them how he felt, she got the reply, "Most beautiful, missis; onspeakable."

"Unspeakable" also describes Lincoln's feelings when he read the Hunter order in a newspaper. To Salmon P. Chase, who asked him not to revoke it, Lincoln curtly replied that "no commanding general shall do such a thing, upon my responsibility, without consulting me." Not satisfied with merely asking Hunter to withdraw the order, Lincoln issued a formal public proclamation repudiating it as "altogether void." If, said Lincoln, as Commander in Chief he had the power to declare slaves free, he reserved such power to himself, not leaving it to be shared with officers in the field.

The Hunter episode was one of the last major imbroglios over the status of the Negro who had come within the Union lines—whether he was a slave, a free man, or a half-and-half character dwelling in a twilight zone conveniently labeled "contraband." But also confronting the Lincoln administration during the first twelve months of the war was a problem that was more down to earth than the legal status of the former slave—the problem of his employment and relief. What should be done with the men, women, and children whose sudden separation from their masters exposed them not only to the good things of freedom, but also to want, vagabondage, and crime? Here again the federal government was slow to act.

While Lincoln and Congress were tarrying, the plight of the former slaves attracted widespread attention in other quarters. Throughout the North, philanthropic associations and church groups formed freedmen's aid societies, whose first efforts were devoted to shipping southward bundles of shoes, clothes, bedding, and garden seeds and tools. These "contraband boxes" brought to

in the great swell of Christian charity private efforts to fill the void.

To a government overwhelmed with the supply and conduct of the war, there arose many of their grateful recipients the first articles they could really call their own.

But the needs of these newly freed families were not limited to what they would wear and eat. Born in states where it was illegal to teach a Negro to read or write, they needed instruction in the three R's. Gladly did the newly organized benevolent societies set out to recruit schoolteachers who could double as general counselors, guiding their charges aright in problems of family life, religious practices, and the social graces. From the North by the end of the summer of 1861 came the first flood of missionaries to the freedmen—young men from America's oldest colleges and divinity schools, and women of various ages with sound academic backgrounds. Much of their less formal education had come from a close reading of Garrison and Phillips. "We have come to do anti-slavery work, and we think it noble work and we mean to do it earnestly," wrote hard-working and high-minded Laura M. Towne upon her arrival in the Sea Islands.

The benevolent societies conducted their activities in cooperation with the military: the societies paid the salaries of the teachers, and the army commissariat furnished them with one ration a day. In most instances the commanding officers welcomed the agents from the relief organizations. In February 1862 Thomas W. Sherman invited the philanthropic groups to send him a corps of men and women "to teach the rudiments of civilization and Christianity" to the contrabands in the Department of the South. "Never," ran his appeal, "was there a nobler or more fitting opportunity."

General Sherman's plea came just at the time that the Lincoln administration began to bestir itself about the welfare of the colored refugees. Fortunately for the latter, this responsibility fell to Salmon P. Chase, an ardent and long-time drumbeater for Negro rights. It was Chase's duty as Secretary of the Treasury to take charge of the cotton, rice, and other produce that came into the hands of the invading Union forces. To harvest the crops and prepare them for market called for workers, who could be supplied by the former slaves. An order from the Secretary of War, dated February 13, 1862, notified army officers that they were to co-operate with treasury agents.

During the same month Chase appointed a kindred spirit, young Edward L. Pierce, as government agent in charge of cotton and Negroes at Port Royal in the Sea Islands. Pierce was not an inexperienced hand, since he had organized the contrabands who flocked to Fortress Monroe, and had spent a month in the Port Royal region making a study of the needs of its nearly ten thousand contrabands.

As Pierce prepared to return to Port Royal, his department chief, Secretary Chase, had an idea: Why not have him tell Lincoln about the Negroes along coastal South Carolina? Pierce was willing. To him the former slave was not an inferior, but an American who needed only a helping hand and a friendly word to become a useful citizen. A dedicated man, Pierce was anxious to share these views with the Chief Magistrate.

Armed with a letter of introduction from Chase, young Pierce presented himself at the White House. When his turn came, full-of-his-subject Pierce had not proceeded very far before Lincoln cut in, exclaiming that he ought not to be troubled with such details. According to Pierce, Lincoln spoke of "the itching to get niggers into our lives" and said that only recently the Senate had hesitated to confirm General Halleck because of his slave-exclusion order. When Lincoln paused for a moment, Pierce attempted to start again, this time giving a shorter account than he had first intended. Again Lincoln called a halt. This time there was nothing for Pierce to do but move toward the door. Noting his chagrin, Lincoln said, "I did not suppose you were a beggar. Wait a minute." Taking a card from his desk, the President penned a peace-offering line: "I shall be obliged if the Sec. of Treasury will in his discretion give Mr. Pierce such instructions in regard to Port Royal contrabands as may seem judicious." This gesture did not fully soothe Pierce's injured feelings, and he left the White House with a poor opinion of its occupant. But a quarter of a century later, in a letter to Jesse

Weik, Pierce recalled that at the time of his visit Lincoln's son was quite sick, and this may have had something to do with the President's mood.

Possibly Lincoln was in the right frame of mind when he was visited by another zealous worker among the contrabands—Vincent Colyer, of the New Bern region in North Carolina. Appointed in February 1862 by General Ambrose E. Burnside as Superintendent of the Poor, Colyer brought to his task all the dedication of one who thought of himself as a steward of the Lord. One of his first steps was to set up schools for illiterate poor whites and former slaves, using college-trained soldiers as teachers.

As schoolrooms for the former slaves, Colyer made use of the two African churches in New Bern. Here some of the teaching was done by Colyer himself, employing a technique of his own. Taking a cotton sheet and using black ink, clergyman Colyer would print some short Bible passage, such as "Love your enemy" or "Bless them that curse you." With a long pointer he would go over the letters, then the syllables, and then the whole sentence.

As his school entered the second month of operation, Colyer was pleased with the progress of his pupils and was joyful at the prospect of reaching other beginners. But late in May 1862 came a crushing blow: the military governor of North Carolina, Edward Stanly, ordered the colored schools closed.

Stanly, who had represented North Carolina as a five-term Congressman, had a ready explanation. Although his superiors had told him to say as little as possible about the Negro, they had told him "to restore the old order of things." This meant closing the schools, reasoned Stanly, since under North Carolina law it was a criminal offense to teach Negroes to read.

A well-intentioned man who had been kind to slaves, Stanly's eye was on the past. He soon learned, however, that the old order was changing, for Colyer saw to it that Stanly's directive was widely circulated in the North. Gladly responding to the ground swell of indignation, the Radicals in the House of Representatives pushed through a resolution on June 2, 1862, requesting Lincoln to report on Stanly's activities. Two days later Lincoln replied that the War Department had no official information on Stanly's school-closing order, but that the military governor was being requested to furnish a report.

On the following day, 5 June, Colyer arrived in Washington. Soon afterward, in company with Charles Sumner, Colyer called at the White House and told his story. After hearing him out, Lincoln remarked that Governor Stanly was under a misapprehension if he thought his instructions called for closing colored schools. In any event, added the President, such instructions were unlawful. Taking advantage of having the President's ear, Colyer hastened to mention another charge against Stanly: under his governorship former slaves were being returned to their masters.

Lincoln's comment on this delighted his visitors. He had always insisted, he told them, that a rebel-owned slave who came into Union lines should never be returned. A "thank the Lord for that," slipped through Colyer's lips. On the way out of the White House Sumner remarked to Colyer that he (Colyer) had seen more of the "real character" of Lincoln than could have been gleaned from a hundred interviews.

THE CONTRABANDS in the Union-held regions along the Atlantic were less of a problem to Lincoln than were those right at his doorstep. Shortly after the war broke out, the District of Columbia became a mecca for contrabands, hundreds of whom made their way across the Potomac and into the camps around the city. On July 16, 1861, Lincoln let it be known to General Irvin McDowell that he was disturbed by this influx of former slaves, and that he thought it might be well to allow their owners to come and get them. On the following day the Department of Washington issued a general order excluding the black refugees from its camps and quarters. By another order, issued three weeks later, no Negro could leave the city unless he could produce evidence of his freedom, a measure designed to prevent the contrabands from hurrying northward.

The passage, on August 6, of the act forbidding officers to return rebel-employed slaves made things much brighter for the contrabands who came to Washington. These Negroes could claim that they had been used for insurrectionary purposes, and hence were not returnable to their masters. Sometimes these claims were ignored by the authorities in Washington, but Secretary of State Seward, acting upon Lincoln's orders, soon had something to say on this. On December 4, 1861, he informed General McClellan, the mayor of Washington, and the marshal of the District that enemy-employed slaves were, by law, to be "received into the military protection of the United States," and that, if they were arrested as fugitives, the parties who made the seizures should themselves be placed under military arrest.

But Seward's order left untouched two troublesome questions: What of the contrabands in Washington whose masters were not disloyal? And in such cases who should enforce the Fugitive Slave Law—the civilian authorities in the District or the military commanders? The nation's capital presented a peculiar problem, since it was, in essence, half city and half camp.

Regardless of the loyalty of the master, the enforcement of the Fugitive Slave Law in wartime Washington was bound to arouse condemnation. Much of this ire was directed not at Lincoln but at his appointee as marshal of the District, Ward H. Lamon. Although unlike in disposition, Lamon having a boisterous manner and a love of the bottle, the two men were intimates. In a letter of recommendation of May 28, 1862, Lincoln referred to Lamon as "my particular friend," and on his thirty-fifth birthday, eight months later, Lamon received a Swiss watch from his former business associate.

As chief law-enforcement officer of the District, Lamon adopted the general policy of authorizing the arrest of contrabands. Pointing out that the Fugitive Slave Law was still on the books, Lamon operated on the theory that vagrant Negroes were the escaped chattels of loyal masters. While sanctioned by custom in times of peace, locking up out-of-town Negroes became impractical when a host of contrabands descended upon the city. The situation was complicated by unscrupulous men who—as they had been doing since before the war—seized Negroes indiscriminately, hoping that some of them would be claimed. Then their captors would receive the "apprehension fee" that an owner paid for the recovery of a runaway.

While waiting for the owners to show up, these fee-seeking slave procurers needed a lodging place for their prey. To their delight, the doors of the city jail were opened to them. Normally holding only fifty prisoners, the jail was soon badly overcrowded, and Lamon as its chief custodian found himself under further sharp attack. Calling the city jail the "Washington Slave Pen," Lamon's enemies charged him with trying to get rich off the allowance of twenty-one cents a day for the upkeep of the inmates.

A final charge against Lamon was that he permitted masters to use the city jail as an abode for their slaves. Some disloyal masters, so said Lamon's critics, were using the jail as a place of safekeeping for their bondmen and planned to keep them there for the duration. And the city jail, as Lamon's assailants pointed out, was scarcely a home away from home. Its dark corridors led to an enclosure into which the inmates were herded, each with his little bundle of belongings, with no chair or bed to grace the expanse of cold stone floor.

The clamor against Lamon reached Lincoln's official attention when the Senate, on December 9, 1861, directed the Marshal to state by what authority he took slaves into the jail at the request of their masters. Lamon got in touch with Lincoln, who worded a reply. Two points were made by the President: the practice of admitting a slave to the jail at his master's request was an old one, and Marshal Lamon had done so only in three instances. Lincoln's bland tone was typical of his handling of Congress; if he had to quicken his step in order to keep time to a tune called by the men on Capitol Hill, he would give them the old softshoe.

But the Lincoln-drafted letter was not destined to have a fair chance to soothe the Senate breast. Scarcely had the bellicose

79

Lamon sent the letter under his own signature when he issued an order requiring that anyone who wished to visit the jail must first secure a permit. This restriction included members of the District Committee of the Senate and was in fact aimed at them. Lamon resented the visits of congressmen who came to the jail for the sole purpose of interviewing, as he phrased it, "inmates whose color was not of orthodox Albino-Anglo American tint."

Lamon's order was certain to bring renewed cries for his scalp. But before the Senate could fire off another resolution, Lincoln stepped in. He had Seward send an official letter to Lamon ordering him not to receive into custody any alleged runaways unless the latter were charged with a specific crime. And when contrabands formally charged with crime were placed under arrest, they were not to be detained beyond thirty days.

Lamon's quarrel with Congress had scarcely simmered down when he found himself confronted by another critic of his contraband policy. Again his opponent was a formidable one—General James S. Wadsworth, military governor of the capital. Thin and erect, with white sidewhiskers flanking blue, deep-set eyes, Wadsworth owned extensive farmlands in New York's fertile Genesee valley. But unlike most men of immense wealth, Wadsworth held abolitionist views.

It was Wadsworth's job, as commanding officer of the Military District of Washington, to interrogate the contrabands entering the city in order to ascertain whether they were returnable to slavery. If they came from Virginia, Wadsworth assumed that they had been used for military purposes by the rebels. In such cases, therefore, he invariably issued "official protections," certificates stating that "the bearer, A—— B——, colored, is under the protection of the military authorities of the District."

Lamon could voice no objection to this procedure. But he claimed the right to apprehend a "protection-bearing" contraband in order to satisfy himself about the loyalty of the master. On May 22, 1862, Lamon's deputies seized two contrabands who were servants to officers of a New York regiment. Wadsworth's indignation changed to fury when later that day he learned that his mulatto Althea Lynch, had also been picked up and was in city jail awaiting examination the following day.

Wadsworth lost no time in sending a lieutenant to demand the release of Althea. When this demand was turned down by Lamon's deputies, Wadsworth summoned a dozen soldiers. This detail proceeded to seize the jail and to release Althea and the other inmates.

When the news reached Lamon that the jail was in the possession of the soldiers, he hastened to the White House to procure authority for the arrest of Wadsworth's men. But his midnight mission was in vain: Lincoln was out of town. Later the next day Lamon and Wadsworth came to an uneasy truce, with Althea remaining at liberty.

Lincoln kept Lamon in office, despite the Marshal's many critics. Lamon charged that his enemies were really striking at Lincoln through him, and Lamon seems to have succeeded in winning Lincoln over to this point of view.

If the President avoided a showdown between Lamon and Wadsworth by being luckily unavailable, he showed some skill in verbal evasion in another case involving the abolitionist military governor. During the same week of the Althea Lynch affair, a committee came to the White House representing one hundred slaveowners of Maryland's Prince George's County, who complained that Wadsworth was preventing them from recapturing runaways who had fled to Washington. The Prince George's County masters alleged that Wadsworth was guilty of a double affront to them: he required that they submit proof that they were loyal, and he then made his decision on the basis of evidence submitted by the runaways themselves.

Obviously Wadsworth was reluctant to return a single runaway, being more than eager to believe a slave's story about his master's secessionist sympathies. This Lincoln knew. But he was also aware that Wadsworth was devoted to the Union cause, and that he had close friends in the Radical Republican ranks. Without criticizing

ncoln attempted to placate the slaveowners' com-
itary governor, said he, was able and well inten-
same breath Lincoln assured the committee that
o the matter and see to it that no injustice was

LINCOLN'S DIFFICULTIES with military commanders and civilian officials over the contrabands showed one thing above all else. There was no single fountainhead for the administration's "contrabands policy" during the first year of the war. The official policy had to be reduced from a combination of wellsprings, including the President's own stated views, the directives of his Cabinet officers, and the proclamations of his military commanders.

This lack of a clear-cut presidential policy was the result of design. On questions relating to the Southern Negro, Lincoln deliberately took his time. Tomorrow was good enough for him. His "make haste slowly" policy on Negro matters had various roots, among them his own mental make-up and his political sensitivity to public opinion.

To have congratulated Lincoln on never being rash would perhaps have brought him more inner pleasure than most compliments. Lincoln was not a man to act until after much winnowing and sifting, until he had taken time to view a question from all sides. He knew that in public life a reflective man was often considered weak-willed, but this risk he was prepared to run.

On matters relating to the Negro, Lincoln appeared to be slow because he was not an extremist. Essentially he was a man of the middle way, a moderate, one might almost say an extreme moderate. Lincoln thought of himself as an agent of reconciliation, an executive whose true function was to bring together conflicting parties in the hope that they could reach a common ground. Lincoln made policy only when other actions were exhausted.

The Lincoln of the White House years had deep convictions about the wrongness of slavery. But as Chief Magistrate he made a sharp distinction between his personal beliefs and his official actions. Whatever was constitutional he must support regardless of his private feelings. If the states, under the rights reserved to them, persisted in clinging to practices that he regarded as outmoded, he had no right to interfere. His job was to uphold the Constitution, not to impose his own standards of public morality.

As a constitutionalist Lincoln was dedicated to the preservation of the Union. If Lincoln had a ruling passion, it was to show the world that a government based on the principles of liberty and equality was not a passing, short-lived experiment. Up to the time of the Civil War many people, particularly in the Old World, were skeptical about the staying power of America. These doubters believed that a kingless government carried the seeds of its own destruction. Lincoln believed otherwise. He was determined that the American experiment in democracy must not fail, and that such a government by the people "can long endure."

Lincoln's behavior on Negro questions not only was a product of his temperament but also reflected his sensitivity to public opinion. Lincoln always had his ear to the ground, trying to sense the mood of America, the things for which men would fight and die. He was a practical politician with a coldly logical mind which impelled him to accommodate himself to the prevailing currents. He did not propose to buck the tide; in Herndon's words, he "never ran in advance of his age." Congressman James G. Blaine noted that President Lincoln preferred "to keep somewhat in the rear rather than too far in advance of public judgment."

To C. Edwards Lester, an abolitionist who had been a delegate to the first World's Anti-Slavery Convention, held in London in 1840, Lincoln explained that "it would do no good to go ahead any faster than the country would follow." He thought, continued the President, that reformers like Lester "would upset our apple-cart altogether, if you had your way." On slave emancipation Lincoln was prepared to wait for public opinion to ripen, pointing out that "the powder in this bombshell will keep."

Lincoln's habitual caution was reinforced by his belief that the nation's security was endangered by too early action on matters relating to the Negro. Looming large in Lincoln's thinking were the slaveholding states on the side of the North. These border states of Missouri, Kentucky, Maryland, and Delaware would fight to restore the Union. But as for slavery, they wanted it left alone, and they would almost rather lay down their arms than see it done away with. Their point of view was expressed by the *Louisville Journal* of April 9, 1862: "Abolitionism should be abolished and secession seceded from."

Kentucky-born Lincoln was aware of the attitude of the whites in the border states. He knew that to them it was an article of faith that any change in the status of the Negro would bring in its train all kinds of calamity. Lincoln knew that slaveholding communities lived in fear of the servile population running amok, and that in wartime the horrors of slave insurrection would become especially vivid. Lincoln did not want the border states to become alarmed about the loss or the behavior of their bondmen. Such fears might impel these states to join the Confederacy, and thus prolong the war.

This would never happen if Lincoln could prevent it. "I think to lose Kentucky is nearly the same as to lose the whole game," wrote he to Illinois Senator Orville H. Browning. "Kentucky gone, we can not hold Missouri, nor, as I think, Maryland." Not too wide of the mark was a current witticism: "Lincoln would like to have God on his side, but he must have Kentucky." A less subtle observation came from slavery-hating Horace Greeley, editor of the *New York Tribune*: "We think," he wrote in an open letter to the President, "that you are unduly influenced by the counsels, the representations, the menaces, of certain fossil politicians hailing from the Border States."

In coping with an unfriendly attitude toward the Negro, Lincoln's difficulties were not limited to border-state inhabitants. In the large Northern cities the foreign-born, particularly the Irish-Americans and the German-Americans, lived in fear that the slaves, if freed, would leave the South and flood the manpower market with cheap black labor. In the Midwestern states there was a sizable number of immigrants from the Southern states, people who had brought with them the conviction that to be a Negro was to carry an inborn defect of race. To such persons any attempt to upgrade the Negro was contrary to the best interests of all concerned, including the black man himself.

In moving slowly on the Negro question, Lincoln was also influenced by his friendly feeling for the people of the Confederacy. He believed that many of them were really loyal to the Union, but that they had permitted themselves to be carried into the war. To free the Negro would be to punish these many well-intentioned Southerners whose only fault was a temporary lapse of judgment. Lincoln's sympathetic attitude toward the people below the Potomac, loyal or otherwise, made him hesitate to take any step that would widen the breach between the North and the South. If Lincoln hated slavery, he did not hate slaveowners; if he condemned the former, he refrained from abusing the latter. He wanted the South to free its slaves, but he felt that people outside the South should urge the measure "persuasively, and not menacingly."

Lincoln made no fetish of consistency. Hence his policy of "masterly inactivity" on Negro questions, like all of his policies, was subject to change. The influences that prompted him to go slow ran head on into counter influences. And as the war entered its second year, these forces for change began to gain strength and momentum.

Loudest of the voices for changing the status of the Negro were those of the abolitionists. In private life Lincoln had carefully side-stepped contacts with antislavery zealots, never even taking part in their war of words. But immunity from abolitionists was forfeited when one took high public office. No sooner was Lincoln sworn in as Chief Magistrate than he found himself beset by reformers who had descended upon the nation's capital. Elizabeth Todd Grimsley, a favorite cousin of Lincoln's wife who spent six months in the White House, observed that during the first year of the war Lincoln bore no greater "affliction" than "the importunities, meddlesomeness, impatient censure, and arrogance of preachers, politicians, newspaper writers and cranks who virtually dogged his footsteps, demanding that he should 'free the slaves,' 'arm the slaves,' and 'emancipate the slaves and give them the ballot.' "

Lincoln knew that these men of the Garrison-Phillips stripe had deep convictions about human brotherhood, and that they had no political favors to beg. But he also viewed them as men whose zeal outran their judgment. In running the country, as Lincoln knew, the give-and-take of compromise was essential. But to the reformer, compromise was a sin. Daily the Lincoln of the White House had to make choices between unpleasant alternatives. Perfectionism could be practiced only by men not burdened with the responsibilities of getting things done in government.

Ignoring the practical considerations that influenced Lincoln's course of action, the Negro and his friends besought the President to get on the freedom track. God's timetable, said Harriet Tubman, was faster than Lincoln's, and she predicted that "God won't let Massa Linkum beat de South till he do de right ting."

Less theological was the language of two men of the cloth. "It is impossible for Abraham Lincoln to move faster than a tortoise," orated the Unitarian clergyman Moncure D. Conway at a West India Emancipation Day celebration at Arlington, Massachusetts, on August 1, 1862. Lincoln had "a heavy shell on his back," which he got at his birth, "for that is the kind of animal that is grown in Kentucky." A week later the Reverend Henry Ward Beecher informed the readers of the *Anti-Slavery Standard* that there was not a single line in any of Lincoln's messages or state papers "that might not have been issued by Czars, by Louis Napoleon, or by Jeff Davis."

But if the abolitionists were critical of Lincoln, they were resigned to the necessity of winning him over. As Lydia Maria Child pointed out, "Providence sometimes used men as instruments whom she would not touch with a ten-foot pole."

Lincoln did not lack advice from critics of reformers. "Abolitionism and the republic cannot both live," wrote Anna Ella Carroll of Baltimore, who was fashioning a career out of counseling the occupant of the White House. But abolitionism found support among men whom Lincoln respected. His minister to Spain, Carl Schurz, returned to America to become one of the founders of the Emancipation League, organized early in 1862. Schurz's love of liberty had been tested in the German revolutionary movement of 1848, but in his discussions with Lincoln he hammered on the point that freeing the slave would win European support for the administration.

This point of view was strongly echoed by Cassius Marcellus Clay, another Lincoln friend and short-time foreign minister. A Kentuckian like Lincoln and an old friend of Lincoln's wife's family, Clay was nonetheless staunchly antislavery. Returning from his post as ambassador to Russia in August 1862, he urged Lincoln to free the slaves in the seceded states.

Another student of international affairs, George Bancroft, formerly minister to the Court of St. James, informed Lincoln that "civil war is the instrument of Divine Providence to root out social slavery." Likewise, said the letter from this most eminent of American historians, Lincoln's administration was destined to be remembered as long as human events found a record. Lincoln's reply was a typical mixture of the courteous and the noncommittal. He esteemed it a high honor to have a letter from Mr. Bancroft, wrote he, adding that he would deal with slavery "in all due caution" and would bring to bear his best judgment.

In allying Providence with abolitionism, Bancroft struck a note that already had become familiar to the President. Church groups were constantly petitioning him or seeking a White House hearing. Less than two months after the war's beginning, a group of twenty-six Congregationalists—including Lewis Tappan, the New York reformer and merchant; Jonathan Blanchard, president of Wheaton College; and John G. Fee, a founder of Berea College— met at Boston and prepared a document for the President's edification. These earnest men informed Lincoln that it was of the utmost importance that the Negro, slave and free, be made to understand that the North was their friend. Lincoln should proclaim liberty by his war powers, for it was their conviction that the war was God's judgment on slavery, and that the Lincoln government was in for a terrible awakening if it presumed that success was possible if Jehovah's laws were not heeded.

Church groups and delegations could be turned away with a soft answer. But this technique was lost on Lincoln's critics in Congress. These Radical Republicans, staunch enemies of slavery, were not to be put off, and their pressure never let up.

A handful of these emancipation-minded Congressmen were personally friendly to Lincoln and were inclined to give him public support whenever they could. One of these Lincoln supporters was the Illinois Republican, Owen Lovejoy, whose abolitionism was indelibly confirmed that dread night in Alton when he looked down on the dead form of his brother Elijah. In Illinois, Owen Lovejoy had often courted a jail sentence for harboring runaways. Elected to the House in 1856, he could be counted on as an ardent supporter of emancipation measures. Nonetheless he never joined the legion of Lincoln critics, believing always that the President needed just a little more time to see the light. Lincoln was grateful. Over the years of his presidency he counted Lovejoy as "my most generous friend," as he wrote in heartfelt eulogy upon Lovejoy's death in March 1864.

Of the small coterie of Radical Republicans who championed Lincoln, the most influential was Charles Sumner. Their friendship had an odd quality, for Lincoln was no dealer in absolutes, whereas Sumner was. A hard-shell abolitionist, Sumner was unwearying in his advocacy of measures against slavery and racial discrimination. "Please accept my sincere thanks for your efforts to remove the disqualification of color in mail-carrying," wrote Negro William C. Nell on May 20, 1862, after Sumner had pushed through the Senate a bill to abolish the law requiring that mail handlers be free whites.

Sometimes even Sumner's supporters questioned his practice of forever forcing the Negro question on the Senate's attention. After listening to Sumner plead for the repeal of the Fugitive Slave Law, one colleague expressed the hope that the Senate might be granted "one day without the nigger." More pointed were Sumner's many critics: "I beg you," wrote Maryland Governor Thomas H. Hicks to Lincoln on May 26, 1862, "to prevent as far as you can the mad doings of Sumner. . . ."

While Sumner could not regard Lincoln as a kindred spirit, he thought of the President as one whose heart was in the right place. Sumner believed that Lincoln was in favor of Negro freedom, and he was willing to forgive him if he was six weeks, or even six months, behind the Sumner schedule. As in the case of his Senate associates, Sumner was incessantly urging Lincoln to take steps to help the slave and to strike at his master.

Having Sumner always at his elbow seems not to have irked the President. Possibly he felt that Sumner's views deserved respect and attention; he may have felt that Sumner was doing a service in preparing the public mind for the inevitable. Thus, although never a spokesman for the White House, Sumner might be a good expediter, forcing people to come to grips with the problem of freedom and equality for the colored American.

Personal friendship was a factor enabling Lincoln and the foremost pro-Negro Congressman to bear with each other in politics. Sumner was often invited to theater parties arranged by Mrs. Lincoln, who was fond of the bachelor with the Byronic head. Sumner managed to look like a Senator while at the same time affecting what a contemporary referred to as "a picturesque style of dress." His customary attire was "a brown coat and light waistcoat, lavender-colored or checked trousers, and shoes with English gaiters." Mrs. Lincoln may have shared her cousin Elizabeth's opinion that Sumner was "the very embodiment of elegance, culture and 'farawayness.'"

As a nonworshiper Lincoln would not have objected to Sumner being "far away." But the President seems to have found Sumner an interesting, even a stimulating conversationalist—not a boresome pedant, as some found him. The two public figures were to remain friends, although Lincoln was never to speed up to the Sumner pace.

Unlike Sumner, most of the members of the radical wing of the Republican party were not so charitable toward Lincoln. Men with programs and ambitions of their own, they found that the long shadow cast by the White House made it difficult for them to reach their places in the sun. Those, like Thaddeus Stevens, who believed in equal rights for all, felt that Lincoln did not share their concern for the downtrodden and the oppressed, and that he was tender toward the South, to boot. Those Republican politicians who had economic axes to grind—high tariff, internal improvements, a national banking system, and free homesteads in the West—were anxious to get these aims translated into the law of the land as quickly as possible, with no threat of a veto by a President who was not one hundred per cent sold on the philosophy of the spoils belonging to the victors. Concerned primarily with the interests of their own section of the country, many Republican congressmen were cool toward Lincoln's tendency "to look over the whole land." And all Republicans of the left, whatever their motivation, shared a deep suspicion of the great concentration of wartime power that had found its way into the hands of the Chief Executive. Having no taste for playing second fiddle, they looked with disfavor on any encroachments upon the powers and the prestige of Congress.

Lincoln knew that he would have to get along with the Radical Republicans, since they were members of his own party. Moreover, their influence seemed to be waxing, rather than waning, from month to month; particularly did their point of view on slavery seem to be making headway. The full extent of their power became evident when, on July 17, 1862, Congress passed a second confiscation act. The product of six months of debate on Capitol Hill, this sweeping measure declared free all slaves of rebels and of anyone who committed treason.

Lincoln signed this act with reluctance. He felt that
was operating in a field that better belonged to the Chi
tive. He believed that the President was the best judge i
of slave confiscation: he had a better grasp of the militar
of the moment, a better sense of timing.

However distasteful it was to him, the passage of the second
confiscation act confirmed Lincoln's belief that the time had come
for him to speed up on the Negro question. He could see that the
stresses of the war were uprooting old beliefs. "The American
people," wrote C.C. Hazewell in the fall of 1862, "are capable of
conquering their prejudices, provided that their schooling shall be
sufficiently severe and costly."

In its attitude toward slavery the North of midsummer 1862 was
not the North of a short twelvemonth ago. Events were exerting
a mounting pressure of their own. Lincoln, sitting in the eye of the
storm, was not blind. He knew that the time had come to broaden
the base of the war. No longer limited to preserving the Union,
the main issue had become double-pronged, "a perplexing com-
pound—Union and Slavery," as Lincoln put it.

IN THE LATE STAGES of the war, in writing to a fellow Kentuckian
about the problem of the Negro slave, Lincoln confessed that he
had not controlled events, but that events had controlled him. His
own severest critic, Lincoln was something less than fair to himself. For he had not sat idly in the White House waiting for fate
to work its purposes without a presidential assist. Lincoln's tactics,
said his friend Leonard Swett, were to get himself in the right
place and remain there until the event would find him in that
place.

A reflective man, Lincoln felt that he had a grave responsibility
both to his own generation and to the future. "We cannot escape
history," he wrote to Congress on December 1, 1862. As one who
had grasped that hard fact, the Lincoln of the second year of the
war was prepared to come to grips with the problems relating to

e colored American. There would be no easy solutions. "The Negro question is a tough customer," wrote J. Wilson Shafer, chief quartermaster in the Department of the South, to Lincoln on April 13, 1862. That the Negro problem was a tough one, Lincoln knew. How tough it was, he was to learn.

5

"I MAY ADVANCE SLOWLY"

THE MAIN EVENT was Lincoln versus slavery, a fact the President sensed from the moment he took office. Therefore, when the final test came, he did not enter the ring a novice. In a number of preliminaries Lincoln had had his rounds with the Negro problem in its various forms. In these tune-ups, he had suffered a few defeats. But on the whole his average was good, although his victories, in most instances, came on points.

In matters relating to the Negro one of Lincoln's earliest and most clear-cut victories was the suppression of the foreign slave trade. Although outlawed since January 1, 1808, the importation of black cargoes from Africa and the West Indies had proved hard to stamp out. Indeed, the volume of trade reached its highest peak in the two decades preceding Lincoln's election, and the fitting out of slavers had become a flourishing business in the seaport cities of New York, Boston, and Portland, Maine.

The apathy of the federal authorities toward the illicit trade in human beings ceased almost as soon as Lincoln moved into the White House. The new President took a major step by consolidating under one department all of the activities relating to the foreign slave trade. A presidential order of May 2, 1861, informed Caleb B. Smith, the Secretary of the Interior, that henceforth his office would be in charge of executing the laws against the slave trade which Congress had been putting on the books since 1819. Thus, in a message of one sentence Lincoln was abolishing the system of divided and poorly defined responsibility in which the Interior shared power with four other departments—Treasury, State, War, and Navy.

Secretary Smith, sensing Lincoln's keen interest, set about enlisting a corps of able assistants, foremost of whom was Chief Clerk George C. Whiting. The two Interior executives were able to lure the men they wanted, as Congress had appropriated $900,000 for the compensation of district attorneys and marshals engaged in suppressing the trade. By mid-August, Smith and Whiting were ready to stage a meeting of the United States marshals stationed in the loyal seaboard states. Held in New York, this meeting was devoted to giving marshals of ten states an on-the-spot training in how to detect a slave ship and how to inspect a vessel suspected of being one.

Smith and Whiting were pleased about their work. "The most vigorous measures are being put into execution for the suppression of this odious trade, and to bring those who may be found in it to condign punishment," wrote Smith to a subordinate in Liberia —John Seys, United States Agent for Liberated Africans. Whiting was no less optimistic: "We feel that we are giving the slave trade some good knocks," he wrote on October 1, 1861, to the marshal of Boston.

The Interior officials had reason to feel satisfied. In his first annual report, dated November 30, 1861, Smith was able to inform Lincoln that five slavers had been seized and condemned. Moreover, the recaptured Africans aboard these vessels had been sent to Liberia where for a year John Seys would provide for them.

Lincoln found the Smith report good reading. Three days after it came across his desk, the President, in his first annual message to Congress, called attention to the African slave trade: "It is a subject of gratulation that the efforts which have been made for the suppression of this inhuman traffic have been recently attended with unusual success." With unmistakable relish Lincoln added a few details: two mates of slavers and a builder of such a vessel had been found guilty, and a captain, caught with a cargo of Negroes, had been convicted.

The captain to whom Lincoln referred was Nathaniel P. Gordon, of Portland, Maine. Within fifty miles of the West African coast, Gordon's ship *Erie*, with 893 slaves aboard, had been captured by a United States war vessel. The court had sentenced Gordon to death by hanging and set the date for February 7, 1862. However, not everyone believed that Gordon would swing. The death penalty was on the books, true enough, but it had never been enforced.

There was much public sympathy for the luckless Gordon, his young and pretty wife, and their little boy. To the White House came many petitions to commute Gordon's sentence to life imprisonment. But no pardon went out over the President's signature. The clamor had been so loud, however, that Lincoln did grant Gordon a two weeks' respite, which pushed the hanging day back to February 21. Lincoln wanted to give Gordon time enough to make "the necessary preparation for the awful change that awaits him"—a preparation Lincoln felt Gordon had been putting off in the vain hope that it would not be necessary. It was his painful duty, continued Lincoln, to admonish the prisoner to take refuge in God's mercy, "relinquishing all expectation of pardon by Human Authority." Lincoln's stand was approved by Charles Sumner, who took it upon himself to coin a word befitting the enormity of the crime: "English lawyers dwell upon treason to the King, which they denounced in a term borrowed from the ancient Romans—*lèse*-majesty; but the Slave-trade is treason to man, being nothing less than *lèse*-humanity."

Gordon died on schedule. But the manner of his passing only filled to overflowing the well of sympathy. The newspapers described the tearful scene when he saw his family for the last time, and his last-minute attempts to cheat the hangman by smoking a cigar saturated with strychnine. Lincoln's refusal to commute Gordon's sentence was not popular. But it succeeded in getting across the message that the administration was determined to live up to its pledge to stop the slave traffic.

While the furor over Gordon was going on, Lincoln and his Secretary of State had been quietly taking a decisive step against the foreign slave trade—the negotiation of a treaty with England. Her Majesty's government had long sought such a treaty. But senators from the cotton states had been lukewarm, if not openly hostile. And many Americans, North and South, had balked at the, so-called "right of search"—the right permitting a British captain to stop and search a ship that he believed might be illegally flying the American flag in order to cloak its slave operations.

With no senators from the eleven seceded states of the South to deal with, and with public attention focused on battlefield events, Lincoln felt that the time was favorable to negotiate an antislave trade treaty with the world's most formidable sea power. On March 22, 1862, Secretary of State Seward sounded out the British ambassador at Washington, Richard Bickerton Pemell, Lord Lyons. The delighted Lyons, not bothering to get in touch with London, responded immediately, bespeaking his government's interest.

Not wishing to invoke memories of the War of 1812, Seward held no press conferences about his negotiations with Lord Lyons. So quietly did the work on the treaty proceed that an important figure like the Secretary of the Navy knew nothing of it until it came up for ratification. On April 10, 1862, Lincoln sent it to the Senate, which, two weeks later to the day, took favorable action without a dissenting vote.

Within ten minutes after ratification, the Senate's chairman of the Committee on Foreign Relations, Charles Sumner, was on his way to the State Department office to bring the good news to the Secretary. Seward had been stretching out on a sofa, but Sumner's words brought him to his feet. Soon the Secretary was reaching for the inkstand, and a letter, addressed to "My dear President," was speeded to the White House: "I congratulate you upon the unanimous ratification by the Senate, of the Treaty to suppress the African Slave Trade—the most important act of your life and mine."

The contents of Seward's note pleased Lincoln, a pleasure that was soon increased by the generally favorable public reaction. "The Slave Trade Treaty has met with more general approval than I expected," wrote Lyons to Lord John Russell on 25 April. "It has excited quite an enthusiasm among the Anti-Slavery party."

Following the exchange of ratifications with the British, Lincoln requested Congress to pass laws putting the Seward-Lyons treaty into effect. This Congress did on July 11, 1862. Henceforth the way of the "blackbirder" would be hard, for now the war vessels of either country were authorized to patrol the high seas in search of slavers. And if a merchantman had a reasonably suspicious appearance in construction or equipment, it would find itself headed for one of the courts of judges and arbitrators established at New York, Sierra Leone, and the Cape of Good Hope. From the judgment of these courts there was to be no appeal; the culprit would receive the punishment prescribed by his respective country.

The importation of slaves quickly came to a halt. "It is believed," said Lincoln in his annual message of 1863, "that, so far as American citizens are concerned, that inhuman and odious traffic has been brought to an end." For this accomplishment no man deserved more credit than the President himself. His zeal for the suppression of the foreign slave trade had been second to none. Those whose job it was to ferret out offenders had always received his staunch support. In one instance, for example, he had not hesitated to issue an order approving payment to the United States Marshal for the Southern District of New York, Robert Murray, who had obtained evidence by bribing captain, masters, sailors, stevedores who loaded vessels, and deckhands employed by mercantile firms, but who, by the very nature of his operations, had been unable to furnish vouchers for his expenditures and thus had been threatened with a financial loss before Lincoln stepped in.

Lincoln's action against the slave trade seems not to have been inspired only by considerations of foreign diplomacy. Unlike

Seward, whose primary interest in the treaty was its presumable influence on British and Continental opinion, Lincoln's principal motive was his detestation of the traffic in human beings. Highly pleasing to Negroes was Lincoln's role in the stifling of the foreign slave trade—a President doing the right thing for the right reasons.

THE SPRING of 1862 was notable for another bill signed by Lincoln which dealt with the Negro outside the United States. This was the measure establishing diplomatic ties with Haiti and Liberia. Down to the time of the Civil War the attitude of Congress toward these black countries had not been friendly. Here again American policy had reflected the influence of the cotton states. Southerners looked with disfavor on an independent Negro nation, particularly one that, like Haiti, had come into existence through a mass insurrection of rebellious slaves.

The secession of the eleven states of the Confederacy removed the chief barrier to official recognition of Haiti and Liberia. Lincoln might have proceeded on his own initiative. But he regarded the establishing of diplomatic relations with the two Negro countries as "a novel policy," and hence a step he did not wish to take without the approval of Congress. This he sought on December 3, 1861, when his first annual message afforded a convenient opportunity. Recognition of the two countries might bring "important commercial advantages," said the President.

The Lincoln administration felt better about its case after receiving a report from the American agent in Liberia, John Seys. Asked by Secretary Smith whether it was advisable to establish diplomatic relations with Liberia, Seys sent word that it was one of the wonders of the Christian world that the step had not been taken. American-born Negroes ran Liberia, yet the United States was almost the last major power to withhold its recognition of the West African republic. Moreover, continued Seys, Liberia had demonstrated "that the Black Man is capable of self-government, that a Christian Republic of Black and colored men has been established on this coast, the admiration of the civilized world, the hope of Africa."

The glowing opinion of Seys was not shared by congressmen from the border states. Senator Garrett Davis of Kentucky expressed the fear that the two black republics might send as their representatives full-blooded Negroes who, with their wives and daughters, would expect to be invited to presidential receptions given for the diplomatic corps. This point of view was voiced in the House by S.S. Cox of Ohio: "How fine it will look to welcome here at the White House an African, full-blooded, all gilded and be-laced, dressed in court style, with wig and sword and tights and shoe-buckles, and ribbons and spangles, and many other adorn-ments which African vanity will suggest."

Such attacks often provoked merriment on Capitol Hill and in Washington drawing rooms, but they did little to change the results. With Charles Sumner heading the Committee on Foreign Relations, a measure authorizing the President to appoint diplo-matic representatives to the two Negro nations was certain to receive powerful backing. The Senate vote, taken on April 24, 1862, was a one-sided 32 to 7. Less than two weeks later, the House passed a concurring act. Lincoln's quick assent was a fore-gone conclusion.

In mid-July the Lincoln administration named Benjamin F. Whitten of New Hampshire as this country's first diplomatic representative to Haiti. Less than a month after he had taken resi-dence at Port-au-Prince, Whitten requested the State Depart-ment to upgrade him to the rank of minister. As United States commissioner and consul general he was outranked by several European diplomats; moreover, he wished to exercise broader functions than those of a predominantly commercial nature. But Lincoln, as Whitten soon learned, had gone as far as he proposed to go.

Although the representative sent to Haiti was a white man, Lincoln had no objection to a Negro's being sent to Washington. So he told an interested inquirer, James Redpath, who was a close acquaintance of President Fabre Geffrard of Haiti. Redpath brought word to Lincoln that the Negro republic would not object to sending a white man as its representative if he so desired. Drawled Lincoln, "You can tell the President of Haiti that I shan't tear my shirt if he does send a nigger here!"

Negroes liked the content, if not the wording, of this reply. An associate of John Brown, Redpath had been picked by the martyred abolitionist's wife to write his official biography, and he stood high in the esteem of Negroes. But they felt that in this instance he had acted in his own interests; he had gone fishing for the job himself, and Old Abe had seen through the dodge. Black-skinned Martin R. Delany wrote to brown-skinned Frederick Douglass expressing pleasure that Lincoln apparently recognized the fact that in matters relating to the Negro a second- or third-rate white appointee was not as desirable as someone "from among ourselves."

Testing Lincoln's shirt-tearing abstinence, the Haitian government sent to Washington a richly pigmented diplomat, Ernest Roumain, formerly private secretary and aide-de-camp to President Geffrard. Arriving in February 1863, the twenty-seven-year-old colonel was received at the Department of State upon presenting his credentials as chargé d'affaires.

Within a month after his arrival in Washington, young Roumain and his secretary were honored guests at a party held "at the home of an aristocratic Boston Member" of Congress, an affair attended by high-ranking military officers, Cabinet members, and Embassy Row notables, headed by Lord Lyons. Present also was socialite Mrs. John A. Kasson of Iowa, who found it hard to keep from staring at the two Negroes. It was not every day that she saw "two elegant colored gentlemen, white kid gloves, Parisian toilet, conversing in Spanish, French and English, yet unmistakably darkey." To Mrs. Kasson, Roumain's presence was not wholly incongruous—he was "very fine looking and bright copper colored," with hair like that of an Indian, and "his features Spanish." But his secretary was a Haitian of another color. He was, wrote Mrs.

Kasson, "a regular colored representative and no m.
hair of this gentleman kinks!" Although it was "droll to
in society," Mrs. Kasson noted that they were modest,
and dignified.

Mrs. Kasson's opinion of Roumain's *savoir-faire* was sha\
C. Edwards Lester. Abolitionist Lester found in the Haitian a.plo-
mat a man of parts, one whose "acquaintance is a real acquisition
in the dreadful rowdyism of this city, which has become disgusting
during the war." A Charles Sumner enthusiast, Lester may have
been predisposed toward Roumain after the latter had spoken
words of deepest praise for the Massachusetts senator, his host at
the party. Roumain also told Lester of his respect and admiration
for Lincoln; if the tribute to Lincoln was somewhat less warm
than that to Sumner, it was no less sincere.

Lincoln had no occasion to regret the step that brought minister
Roumain to these shores; the recognition of the two black republics created no problems at home or abroad. In his last annual
message to Congress, Lincoln reported that this country's relations
with seven Latin American nations, Haiti among them, were of
the most friendly nature. As for Liberia, the United States was
pleased by her progress, continued Lincoln, adding that he solic-
ited the authorization of Congress to sell her a gunboat, moderately priced and to be paid for in installments.

OF ALL THE MEASURES relating to the Negro, the one that was
closest to Lincoln's heart was that of compensated emancipation.
In his belief in the efficacy of the "pay-for-slaves" policy, Lincoln
stood in a class by himself among the public men of his day. In his
program for the solution of slavery, paying the owners was the
first and foremost step. That compensated emancipation was both
fair and sound he had no doubts.

Particularly was he anxious that the border states adopt such a
policy. Lincoln felt that as long as slavery existed in these states,
their citizens would have much latent sympathy for the Confederacy, thus giving hope to the Richmond government. To do away

,nth slavery in these loyal states would strengthen their allegiance to the Union and at the same time weaken the Southern will to resist.

In promoting compensated emancipation, Lincoln's first step was to select one state which, if all went well, would furnish a shining example to its sisters. His choice fell on Delaware. True, that commonwealth had fewer than 2000 bondmen. But Lincoln reasoned that if any border state, whatever the size of its slave population, took the step, the others would soon follow suit. In late November 1861 Lincoln wrote out drafts of two separate bills: both would pay $719,000 to Delaware out of the national treasury, or approximately $400 for each slave. One bill would terminate slavery in 1867; the other, in 1893. But neither got anywhere: the Delaware legislature was opposed to emancipation with or without compensation. Indeed, Lincoln's handful of followers in the legislature, sensing a humiliating defeat, never formally introduced the proposal.

Lincoln was disappointed but not discouraged. To him the Delaware setback simply meant that he must broaden his base of operations: he would lay his proposal before Congress. One preliminary step must be taken—to prevent Charles Sumner from raising his powerful voice against the measure. On the morning of March 6, 1862, Sumner received a message asking him to come to the White House as soon as he could. Leaving the breakfast table, the senator from Massachusetts hurried over. He listened while Lincoln read from a manuscript the draft of a special message to Congress recommending federal financial aid to states that freed their slaves. Reaching for the draft, Sumner read it over slowly, far too slowly for Lincoln, whose private secretaries were waiting in readiness to copy the bill and speed it to Capitol Hill. Sumner's reaction proved to be worth a little delay for secretaries Nicolay and Hay. The abolitionist Senator informed Lincoln that he himself would not sponsor the measure, since he was opposed on principle to anything except immediate and uncompensated emancipation. But, he added, he would say nothing against the proposal since it was a step in the right direction. This promise of benevolent neutrality was all Lincoln needed; within a few hours his special message on compensated emancipation was on its way to Congress.

Lincoln's recommendation was quite favorably received by Negroes and by others with abolitionist leanings. "The first era of the supremacy of the rights of man in this country dates from the Declaration of Independence," exclaimed the *New York Tribune;* "the second began on the 6th of March, 1862, with the Emancipation Message of President Lincoln." The Massachusetts legislature sent to Lincoln a joint resolution, dated April 2, 1862, expressing its approval. Even the nonabolitionist Henry J. Raymond, editor of the *New York Times,* came around, writing to Lincoln on March 15 that he regarded the message "as a master-piece of practical wisdom and sound policy...."

But silence, ominous silence, came from the one quarter Lincoln wanted most to win over, the border state congressmen. On March 10 Lincoln invited these legislators to the White House. He assured them that he was not hostile to their interests. But in the border states, said he, runaway slaves were creating serious problems, and if the complaints of their loyal masters were not quieted, the Confederacy would take renewed hope. He urged his listeners to give serious consideration to compensated emancipation. The border state men listened politely, saying little.

One month after the interview Congress, by a joint resolution, passed Lincoln's proposal exactly as he had worded it. But not a single assenting vote came from any Democrat from the slaveholding states.

ALMOST AS IF TO SHARPEN Lincoln's disappointment over the refusal of border state congressmen to approve compensated emancipation, Congress, on April 11, 1862, passed the District of Columbia Emancipation Act. This measure would abolish slavery in the national capital and would appropriate one million dollars to pay loyal masters.

Lincoln was glad to see slavery abolished anywhere, but in this instance he was a little "uneasy," he informed Horace Greeley, "as to the time and manner of doing it." The act had two features Lincoln liked—gradualism and compensation—but it had one feature he disliked: it originated with Congress rather than with the voters of the District. More important, however, Lincoln greatly preferred that the border states, rather than the District, lead the emancipation procession.

For nearly a week Lincoln kept the bill on his desk. Negroes became apprehensive. To the White House went Bishop Daniel A. Payne of the African Methodist Episcopal Church. Thin, emaciated, with mixed gray chinwhiskers, Payne looked as though he had been fasting in the wilderness, and he carried himself like a man sent from God. "I am here," he began in a voice as high-pitched as Lincoln's, "to learn whether or not you intend to sign the bill of emancipation." Taken aback but courteous, Lincoln said that a group asking him not to sign the bill had been in earlier that day. In the forty-five minutes he stayed at the Executive Mansion, the Negro clergyman could get no positive assurances from Lincoln.

A pastor who could not get down to Washington for a personal audience sent a telegram to Lincoln on April 16: "The *Independent* goes to press at 2 p.m., today, Wednesday," wired Henry Ward Beecher from New York. "May I say that the District of Columbia is free territory?" Beecher received no direct reply, but his instinct was good: on that day Lincoln signed the bill.

Doubtless it had occurred to Lincoln that a presidential veto of the bill might be overridden, since the bill had passed both House and Senate by two-thirds majorities. But, despite his reservations about the measure and despite the political considerations that could have made him withhold his veto, there is little reason to believe that Lincoln was not content to see the bill become law. As he pointed out in the message that accompanied his signature, he had "ever desired to see the national capital freed from the institution in some satisfactory way."

Whatever the degree of gratification Lincoln felt, it was scarcely to be measured against the joy of the colored American. To Negroes the act was a blow to slavery everywhere; hence the public celebrations were nation-wide. In Washington itself on Sunday, April 20, every Negro church in the city held special services of prayer and thanksgiving. The proceedings did not always conform to the established rites for public worship, as church members were singing, shouting, praying, weeping, or jumping, all without direction from the pulpit.

Negroes outside the nation's capital were more restrained but scarcely less celebration-minded. In near-by Baltimore they set aside May 1 as a day of praise and prayer. Some whites attended the city-wide meetings. "The jubilee and thanksgiving of the colored people today, because of the emancipation of the slaves in the District, attracted some attention," observed the *Sun*.

Matching their fellows in Baltimore, the Negroes in New York City held a day-long celebration on May 5. The activities began at five in the morning with a public prayer meeting at Shiloh Church. The afternoon feature was a flag-raising ceremony, with thirteen Virginia contrabands sharing the speaker's platform with Henry Highland Garnet. At night the scene shifted to Cooper Union. Here a large roster of speakers, including George T. Downing, Stephen Myers, and J. McCune Smith, appeared before an overflow audience of 3500, in part made up of delegations from nearly two dozen cities, some from as far as Troy and Ossining.

At the Cooper Union meeting, speaker Garnet paid "a lofty tribute to the worth and honesty of the President of the United States." This was not an unusual note. In the many celebrations held by Negroes throughout the nation, the dominant theme was to give God the glory. But if any mortal came in for a meed of praise, it was likely to be Lincoln. At the meeting in Boston, wrote William C. Nell, "there gushed forth from the grateful hearts of colored men and women their expressions of joy and thanksgiving for this inauguration of emancipation by President Lincoln, destined, as they humbly trust, to spread out, and insure the healing

of the nation." At a celebration in Terre Haute, Indiana, a resolution was passed asking God's blessing on Lincoln and characterizing him as one "aiming to do what is just and right to all men."
At Buffalo, where the celebration ceremonies were held on a Sunday at the court house, Mrs. Nancy M. Weir led the audience in
the singing of a hymn she had composed:

> God bless the Nation's honored chief!
> Thy servant may he be,
> Who wisely has advised relief
> Columbia's soil to free.

While Negroes were holding their series of celebration meetings,
a three-man commission began its task of carrying out the provisions of the District Emancipation Act. Assisted by B.M. Campbell of Baltimore, the best known of the Maryland slave traders in
the ante-bellum New Orleans market, the commissioners determined the amounts to be paid to masters. Of the 979 owners, 9
were Negroes, one of whom was awarded $2168.10 for his 10
slaves.

With compensated emancipation in the District going
smoothly, Lincoln hoped that people in the border states would
see the light. In May he reminded them of the congressional resolution authorizing payment for their slaves; at the same time he
warned them not to be blind to the signs of the times, and assured them that compensated emancipation "would come gently
as the dews of heaven, not rending or wrecking anything." Continued silence was the only response to this plea.

In midsummer, with the adjournment of Congress imminent,
Lincoln made another move. Summoning the border state legislators to the White House on the Saturday morning of July 12,
he read a statement on the necessity for compensated emancipation. If they had taken this step four months earlier, said he, "the
war would now be substantially ended." Again he reminded them
that the war had made all slave property uncertain. Tactfully, however, he did not mention the congressional act, signed by him

three weeks earlier, that abolished slavery in the territories with no compensation to owners.

The argument that Lincoln stressed most in this second meeting with the border state men was a new one. He tried to drive home the point that there was great pressure on him to do something about slavery, that that pressure was increasing, and that much of it was now coming from those whose support the country could not afford to lose. Lincoln brought his plea to a close by asking the congressmen to discuss the matter among themselves before leaving Washington. Promising a reply, but betraying little enthusiasm, the visitors trooped out.

In quick succession came three reports from the men who had listened to Lincoln's earnest words. One of these statements bore the lone signature of Tennessee's Horace Maynard. (Tennessee legislators considered themselves border state men and attended their meetings and caucuses.) Written in support of the compensated-emancipation proposal, Maynard's letter is notable for its accurate appraisal of the Lincoln of the summer of 1862:

> Your whole administration gives the highest assurance that you are moved, not so much from a desire to see all men everywhere made free, as from a desire to preserve free institutions for the benefit of men already free; not to make slaves freemen, but to prevent freemen from being made slaves, not to destroy an institution which a portion of us only consider bad, but to save institutions which we all consider good.

Another minority report, signed by seven congressmen, was not as laudatory as Maynard's, but its drafters assured Lincoln that they would place his proposal before their constituents.

The majority report was far less cooperative. Its twenty-one signers pointed out that they had originally opposed Lincoln's compensated-emancipation proposal because it was too costly, it was an invasion of states' rights, and it involved a change in the social order. But their main reservation now, they said, centered on the uncertainty whether Congress would by legislative act, rather than by mere resolution, provide sufficient funds. If the necessary monies were set aside in advance, concluded the congressmen, then they would lay the matter before the voters.

This was not a hopeful statement, but the ever hopeful Lincoln took it at face value. As soon as he had read it through, he hurried over to Thomas T. Eckert's military telegraph office, where he could work without interruption. Within an hour or two he formulated a bill to compensate any state that abolished slavery; such a state would receive interest-bearing bonds for all its slaves as reported in the census of 1860. Before the afternoon was over, the draft was on its way to Capitol Hill. But Lincoln's hastily formulated bill was stillborn in a Congress bent on immediate adjournment.

THE COOLNESS of the border states toward compensated emancipation was particularly grievous to Lincoln, because it threw cold water on his other pet plan for the Negroes—to send them out of the country. Lincoln's plan of compensated emancipation rested on the assumption that the liberated slaves would not remain in America. It was not his intention to swell the free Negro population. In Lincoln's thinking, compensated emancipation was doomed unless it could be tied in with deportation. Such a tie-in was necessary to quiet the fears of the people in the North that their states would be "Africanized"—swamped by Negroes made free by the war.

Lincoln held the strong belief that colonization would accomplish a dual purpose: rid the South of human bondage and rid the country of the colored man. Slavery and the race problem would thus vanish simultaneously.

Lincoln's belief in Negro deportation was rooted in his reverence for Thomas Jefferson and his deep admiration for Henry Clay, both of whom held similar views. The Lincoln of the 1850's had come to believe that it was to "our national interest to transfer the African to his native clime." He admitted that the task would not be easy, but he held that what colonization needed most was "a hearty will."

His election to the presidency and the outbreak of the war gave Lincoln the opportunity to supply a substantial quota of hearty will. His first annual message to Congress contained a proposal to colonize rebel slaves made free by the war. Free Negroes who desired to leave the country might also be included. If, continued Lincoln's message, colonization involved the acquiring of territory, there was ample constitutional warrant, going back to Jefferson's purchase of Louisiana.

Lincoln's support of colonization succeeded in breathing a little life into the long-ailing movement. Taking note of the rise in interest, Congress bestirred itself. On April 7, 1862, the House appointed a nine-member Select Committee on Emancipation and Colonization, authorized to examine the various deportation plans and to recommend whether the United States should appropriate funds to further such ventures. A few days later Congress passed the District Emancipation Act which, in addition to freeing the Washington slaves, appropriated $100,000 "to be expended under the direction of the President of the United States, to aid in the colonization and settlement of such free persons of African descent now residing in said District, including those liberated by this act, as may desire to emigrate to the Republic of Hayti or Liberia, or such other country beyond the limits of the United States as the President may determine." Lincoln now had both the sanction of Congress and an appropriation.

But Congress was not done with its giving. Two months later, on July 16, the legislators placed at Lincoln's disposal half a million dollars "to carry out the Act of Congress for the emancipation of the slaves in the District of Columbia, and to colonize those to be made free by the probable passage of a confiscation bill." Such a confiscation bill, passed the very next day, authorized Lincoln to colonize Negroes made free by its provisions.

During the same fruitful mid-July days Congress gave Lincoln another assist. The House committee on colonization reported its conclusion that the highest interests of the white race—Anglo-Saxon, Celt, or Scandinavian—made it imperative that the United

States be occupied by no one else. This country held no hope for the Negro within its borders; he would always be remembered as a slave—a memory kept alive "by the changeless color of the Ethiope's skin." But the committee was sure that if the American Negro went to the tropics, he would prove to be an asset: "Our American negroes surpass in skill and intelligence all the other colored of the world," stated the committee, recurring to the "redemption of Africa" colonization theme so prominent in the early decades of the movement.

With this moral support from the House committee and with $600,000 of which he was sole trustee, Lincoln was now ready to tackle the two final hurdles: finding somewhere for the Negro to go and persuading him to go there.

Finding a place to colonize the Negro proved to be far more of a problem than Lincoln had anticipated. He knew that Liberia would welcome American Negroes. The black republic had sent to the United States two commissioners of emigration, one of whom was the distinguished clergyman-scholar-literary light, Alexander Crummell. The two commissioners had spent the early months of 1862 interviewing people who might be interested in going to Liberia, and trying to win the support of government officials like Caleb B. Smith, Secretary of the Interior, and his able assistant, George C. Whiting.

Lincoln did not meet the two commissioners, but he had first-hand information about Liberia from Joseph Jenkins Roberts, who visited the White House in August 1862. Nobody was better equipped to give a briefing on Liberia. Roberts had capped two decades of able service by becoming, in 1848, the new republic's first president. Later, after leaving politics, Roberts was persuaded to become president and professor of jurisprudence and international law at Liberia College, the position he held at the time he called at the White House. The President listened carefully as the distinguished-looking and smooth-talking Negro painted a glowing picture of the West Coast republic. Some of the figures he gave took root in Lincoln's mind: that the total population of the country was between 200,000 and 300,000, of whom some 12,000 were Negroes of American descent.

Roberts himself may have made a favorable impression on Lincoln, but he did not succeed in winning him over to Liberian colonization. For neither the Roberts eloquence nor his geniality could charm away Lincoln's two major objections to his country as the place for the mass migration of Negroes: it was too far away, and it was not located "on a great line of travel." Doubtless, too, in Lincoln's mind were the three objections stated by Secretary Smith in a long letter of May 9, 1862: colonization of Liberia would call for enormous expenditures; the country's climate was unhealthy; and migration-minded Negroes preferred a site on this side of the Atlantic.

Lincoln, too, wanted a spot nearer to the United States, and he had his eye on what he thought was just the place. It was Chiriqui, a province in Panama, then a part of the republic of Colombia. The man who had influenced Lincoln's thinking was Ambrose W. Thompson, chief owner of the Chiriqui Improvement Company, a speculating group made up primarily of United States investors. Thompson succeeded in convincing Lincoln and Secretary of the Interior Smith that Chiriqui had rich coal deposits and that his company had the legal authority to convey title to lands in the province.

The eager Lincoln was not hard to persuade. On September 11, 1862, he authorized the signing of a contract between the United States and the Chiriqui Improvement Company which, among other features, stipulated that the company's lands would be open to Negro immigrants. A day later Lincoln named Senator Samuel C. Pomeroy of Kansas as agent for Chiriqui colonization.

Lincoln's willingness to deal with Ambrose Thompson's outfit reveals as does nothing else the extent of his desire to get moving on Negro colonization. In negotiating with the Chiriqui Company, Lincoln had to close his eyes to many things. He had to abandon the sound legal instincts that would have prompted him to examine the Thompson title. He had to ignore the wishes of the govern-

ment of Colombia and to act as if he did not know that part of the
Chiriqui lands were the subject of a title dispute between Colombia
and Costa Rica. He had to pay no attention to the sound advice
from Secretary of the Navy Gideon Welles, who from the beginning had expressed his distrust of the slippery Thompson and his
corps of "scheming jobbers." And, finally, Lincoln had to ignore
a scientific report from Professor Joseph Henry of the Smithsonian
Institution, who, after examining a boxful of Chiriqui coal, pronounced that it had "slacked down to a boxful of coal dirt."

But there was one thing Lincoln could not ignore. This was the
opposition of the neighboring Central American countries. Through
their diplomatic representatives at Washington, the governments
of Costa Rica, Honduras, Nicaragua, Guatemala, and El Salvador
protested vigorously, if not bitterly, against the Chiriqui project.
It was, stated the indignant republics, a violation of the Monroe
Doctrine and a grave threat to their amicable relations with the
United States.

This chorus of disapproval had its effect on Seward; the good
will of Latin America was a key factor in his foreign policy. The
Secretary advised his chief to call a halt. Lincoln yielded, feeling
that the odds against the Chiriqui gamble had now become too
great. Within a month after his authorization of the project Lincoln
had to give his approval to a counter order "temporarily suspend-
ing the proposed emigration to the tropics."

Lincoln was not ready to give up. His next move was to sound
out European powers who owned territories in Latin America. On
September 30, 1862, Seward sent a circular dispatch to the governments of England, France, the Netherlands, and Denmark, informing them of Lincoln's wish to colonize Negroes and offering to
make ten-year treaties to that end. Seward made it clear that the
Negroes who migrated would be doing so of their own free will,
and that they were to be guaranteed perpetual freedom and equal
rights with others.

Aside from a few feelers, nothing came of this circular letter to
the four nations. The British colony of Guiana showed some inter-

est, appointing an agent of emigration with offices in New York. Denmark offered to transport Negroes to St. Croix if they would contract to work on the sugar plantations for three years. A somewhat similar offer came from the Dutch government, which stated that Negroes would be welcome to Surinam if they would agree to remain "for a certain number of years (five, for example)."

This response was not all that Lincoln had hoped for, but it was far more than he received from the Central American republics. These nations would have nothing to do with Negro emigration to their lands. They regarded Lincoln's proposals as an affront, an attempt by the United States to use them as a dumping ground for its own problem children. Even the hopeful Lincoln could not pretend that his Negro deportation proposals met with any favor below the Rio Grande. In his message to Congress of December 1, 1862, he had to admit that "several of the Spanish-American republics have protested against the sending of such colonies to their respective territories."

The coldness of these countries plus the lukewarmness of the European powers left Lincoln only one colonizing spot in the Western Hemisphere. This was Haiti But again Lincoln made the mistake of dealing with a go-between, rather than trying to make direct contact with the government itself. In this instance the intermediary was Bernard Kock.

This enterprising adventurer had come to Washington in September 1862, armed with a long-term lease on Cow Island, a Haitian possession a few miles below the country's southern peninsula. After sounding out Secretaries Seward and Smith, the not-to-be-discouraged Kock wrote Lincoln a long letter, dated October 1, 1862, offering to provide immediate employment and permanent homes for 5000 Negroes. Describing Cow Island as having a healthy climate and no reptiles, Kock assured Lincoln that each Negro family going there would be provided with a comfortable home. Moreover, hospital and medical attention would be readily available, as would a church with a New England minister and a schoolhouse with a New England teacher.

Lincoln, anxious to avoid another Chiriqui, decided to have Kock investigated. This job was given to Senator Pomeroy, who seemed hardly to be a sound choice, as his enthusiasm for colonization was likely to affect his judgment. Pomeroy's report, however, was reserved; he favored the project but only on condition that "Kock's pecuniary responsibility could be established."

On the face of it Pomeroy's report was inconclusive, but actually it should have deepened Lincoln's distrust of Kock. Lincoln should have sensed that Pomeroy was trying to do two contradictory things: to tell Lincoln what he felt the President wanted to hear, and at the same time to warn him.

But when it came to colonization, the wishful-thinking Lincoln was slow to put up his guard. On December 31 the eager Kock came to the White House accompanied by James R. Doolittle of Wisconsin, one of the Senate's most ardent supporters of colonization. The two visitors took seats, while Lincoln read over the contract that Kock had prepared. According to its terms Kock agreed to colonize 5000 Negroes on Cow Island and to provide them with adequate housing and suitable jobs at money wages. Lincoln placed his signature on the contract, and Kock left the Executive Mansion walking on air.

But Kock reckoned without Secretary Seward, who had become highly suspicious of his honesty. Kock had to leave the contract at the State Department so that it might be properly certified and stamped with the United States seal. But when he returned to pick up the contract, Seward refused to see him. Instead of processing the contract, Seward had sent a little note to Lincoln: "I think it necessary to have a few precautions before I certify the contract of Bernard Kock, and I will speak to you on the subject when we meet." Three days later a formal letter came from the White House to the State Department ordering the Secretary not to countersign the Kock contract, "but to retain the instrument under advisement." Again Lincoln had come to his senses, again thanks to Seward.

DURING THE SAME MONTHS Lincoln was seeking a colonization site, he was also trying to persuade the Negro to leave the United States. Lincoln was opposed to compulsory measures; he wanted to get the Negro to leave of his own accord. This required a "selling" job. Equal to the occasion, Lincoln hit upon a plan that bespoke his political skill. He would get his point of view before the colored America by having a White House "interview" with a selected group of Negroes. Lincoln put the arrangement of the details of the meeting into the hands of the Reverend James Mitchell, a white man whom he had recently named Commissioner of Emigration, operating under the Interior Department.

If the basis for Lincoln's choice was the appointee's knowledge of colonization, it was a good pick. Mitchell's interest in Negro deportation spanned some fifteen years, many of which were spent as secretary of the Indiana Colonization Board. Mitchell followed Lincoln to Washington, and on October 3, 1861, the President wrote to Secretary Seward asking that Mitchell "be cared for" as one "I know, and like." By the spring of the following year Mitchell had become African Officer in the Interior. He wrote to Lincoln on April 18, 1862, giving a historical sketch of the office he held, and offering to take over the execution of the law that set aside the $100,000 for colonization of District Negroes. A month later to the day, Mitchell issued a twenty-eight-page pamphlet, printed at government expense and addressed to Lincoln. Bearing a lengthy title, *Letter on the Relation of the White and African Races in the United States, Showing the Necessity of the Colonization of the Latter*, the pamphlet described the evils resulting from the presence of the Negro, the foremost of which was "the license of the races, which is giving to this continent a nation of bastards."

As Commissioner of Emigration, Mitchell proceeded to round up the Negro delegation. On August 14, 1862, all was ready for the historic interview—the first time a group of Negroes ever met with a Chief Magistrate on a matter of public interest. Upon reaching the Executive Mansion, Mitchell presented the five-man delegation. The men whom Lincoln greeted were not Negro leaders, four of them being recently freed slaves. However, they suited his purpose far better than a contingent of outspoken Negroes of an argumentative turn of mind. For what Lincoln wanted was not to find out what the Negro was thinking, but to let the Negro know what he had in mind.

Lincoln launched into his monologue by informing the delegation that government funds had been made available for colonizing people of African descent, and that it was both his duty and his inclination to pursue such a policy. The racial differences between whites and blacks, explained Lincoln, operated to the disadvantage of both groups; indeed, white men were now cutting one another's throats because of the colored man. Moreover, American Negroes should be willing to go to other lands to help people who were not so fortunate as they, people "who had been subject to the hard usage of the world." As to the specific place to go, added Lincoln, his choice would be a site in Central America, where there were fine harbors and rich coal mines. It was in these coal mines, said Lincoln, that "I think I see the means made available for your self-reliance." Finally, added the President, it was not necessary to have a large migration at the outset; a successful beginning could be made by as few as twenty-five men with their families.

The chairman of the Negro group, Edward M. Thomas, told Lincoln that they would hold a meeting and give him an answer in good time. "No hurry at all," said Lincoln as Mitchell and the colored men moved toward the door.

The interview was widely published, as Lincoln had intended, and was widely read by Negroes, as Lincoln had hoped. "The President's address to the colored people of the District is being discussed in political Anglo-African circles," wrote Philadelphian Jacob C. White, on August 19, to his cousin, "and a diversity of opinion, of course, exists."

Colonization was a topic on which most Negroes had an opinion, for it was one they had been debating for fifty years. In the colored conventions held periodically since 1831, no issue was more

The Freedmen's Memorial Monument to Abraham Lincoln, by Thomas Ball
Courtesy of the National Archives

William de Fleurville,
Lincoln's closest Negro acquaintance
Courtesy of Dr. John E. Washington

Elizabeth Keckley
Courtesy of Dr. John E. Washington

certain to be on the agenda. Generally at these interstate meetings of Negro leaders, colonization came in for resolutions of condemnation. But generally, too, such resolutions fell far short of unanimous support.

The Negro reaction to Lincoln's colonization proposal was mixed, but its opponents were more numerous and certainly more vocal. The most common and the most dramatic expression of their condemnation of Lincolnian colonization was the holding of protest meetings. In Washington the five-man delegation that had visited Lincoln made it a point to be absent from an indignation meeting scheduled for Union Bethel Church; they sensed that they might be hooted at as betrayers. A white reporter who did attend found himself the object of hostile stares.

A meeting of Philadelphia Negroes resulted in the formulation and printing of "An Appeal from the Colored Men of Philadelphia to the President of the United States." This document first directed Lincoln's attention to the moral aspects of his proposal. "We can find nothing in the religion of our Lord and Master, teaching us that color is the standard by which He judges his creatures." The Appeal then discussed "pecuniary and political matters," stressing the Negro's role in producing the wealth of the United States, and noting the manner in which the slaveowning class of the South had corrupted American political life before capping their behavior by taking arms against their own government. The Appeal ended on a friendly note, as befitted a communication from the City of Brotherly Love: "In the President of the United States we feel and believe that we have a champion."

The Negroes of Queens County, New York, at a mass meeting held at Newtown, bluntly told Lincoln that his policy was a mistaken one. They would have him know that the United States was their country, that they loved it, and that they were less disposed than ever to leave at a time like this when their country needed them most.

Some Negroes wrote individual letters of protest. One of these came from George B. Vashon, an Oberlin College graduate who had passed examinations for the bar but had become a school-teacher instead. Negroes preferred to remain in America, wrote Vashon, not because they lacked the spirit of sacrifice or of daring, but because they expected their lot in this country to take a turn for the better. Another correspondent, A.P. Smith of Saddle River, New Jersey, informed Lincoln that Negroes had made this their homeland by shedding their blood on its behalf. Smith mentioned the military role of the Negro in the American Revolution and the naval role of the Negro in the War of 1812. Smith could not hold back a barbed appraisal of Lincoln's coal mine statement made to the White House visitors:

> "Coal land," you say, "is the best thing I know of to begin an enterprise." Astounding discovery! Worthy to be recorded in golden letters like the Lunar Cycle in the Temple of Minerva . . . Twenty-five Negroes digging coal land in Central America! Mighty plan! Equal to about twenty-five Negroes splitting rails in Sangamon.

Perhaps the one thing that most provoked the Negroes about the interview, as it was reported in the newspapers, was Lincoln's assertion that their presence in America was the cause of the present war. Said the *New Orleans Tribune* in sarcastic tones, "Pleasant, instructive, deep-meaning words." Blaming the Negro for the war drew equally sharp tones from Frederick Douglass: "A horse thief pleading that the existence of the horse as the apology for his theft, or a highwayman contending that the money in the traveler's pocket is the sole first cause of his robbery are about as much entitled to respect as is the President's reasoning at this point." Shifting from the content of the interview to its style, Douglass found Lincoln's language "exceedingly plain and coarse-threaded," but this was hardly surprising "since Mr. Lincoln in all his writings has manifested a decided awkwardness in the management of the English language." Douglass also had an acid comment on Lincoln's reported graciousness to the five Negro visitors: it reminded Douglass of the "politeness which a man might try to bow out of his house some troublesome creditor or the witness of some old guilt."

Perhaps the tersest criticism came from the *Liberator:* "Can anything be more puerile, absurd, illogical, impertinent, and untimely!" Perhaps the cleverest criticism came from humorist Orpheus C. Kerr ("Office-seeker"), who evoked the island of Nova Zembla and had Lincoln trying to talk the Negroes into going there:

> The festive island of Nova Zembla has been in existence for some time, and is larger than any smaller place I know of. A trip on your part to Nova Zembla will benefit both races. I cannot promise you much bliss right away. You may starve at first, or die on the passage; but in the Revolutionary War George Washington lived exclusively on futures.

Although they were in a minority, Lincoln's colonization proposal had its Negro supporters. For half a century some Negroes had been drawn by the lure of other lands. Emigration sentiment took a spurt in the late eighteen fifties, as Southern states tightened their restrictions on the free Negro; and 1860 was a banner year for leaving Dixie, and many of the more than six hundred Negro emigrants found their way to Haiti. They came in response to the outstretched hand of the island's President Geffrard. With James Redpath as general agent, Geffrard had established a "Haytian Bureau of Emigration." Appointed to work with Redpath was clergyman James Theodore Holly, a long-time leader of the minority wing of Negroes who favored colonization.

In a series of seven articles appearing in the *Anglo-African Magazine* (September 1859 to January 1860), Holly described Haiti in ecstatic terms and assured American Negroes that they would go there "with benefit to themselves and profit to their adopted country." In a talk at the colored pupil's schoolhouse in Toledo, Ohio, William J. Watkins, the Haytian Bureau of Emigration's "General Agent for the Northwest," went into some detail concerning the generosity of the black republic. Prospective settlers would receive free passage, free land, and, for eight days, free food.

On the eve of the Civil War, Holly and Redpath signed up a number of Negroes. Philadelphia's "colored population is moving to Haiti," wrote a *New York Tribune* reporter on February 16, 1861: "Most of the emigrants come from the South, free men driven out by the renewal of old laws or the enactment of new ones." During that month nineteen Negroes from South Carolina's capital city left for Haiti, among them "Captain Graddick, a well-known pilot of Charleston, who left behind considerable property he could not dispose of." At New Orleans a regular steamship line to Port-au-Prince was established for the express purpose of carrying Negroes to Haiti.

With the outbreak of the war the hard-working Redpath redoubled his efforts. He brought out a newspaper, *Pine and Palm*, and from his Boston headquarters he distributed Haitian journals and maps and specimens of the country's ores and staples. He hired ten recruiting agents, including John Brown, Jr., and Negroes of such note as William Wells Brown and H. Ford Douglas. Such efforts were not wasted. During the first months of the war Redpath could not provide transportation for all who signed up to go. By the middle of November 1861 some 1200 Negroes had taken ship to Haiti.

But before the end of the year Haitian emigration had gone into a marked and rapid decline. Word had gone around that the settlers were faring miserably, that the promises made to them were not being kept, and that they were in danger of becoming slaves to men of their own color. These adverse reports took firmer hold with the return of many of the emigrants, bringing stories of their own. Redpath attributed the decline of applicants primarily to the influence of the Negro clergy, who were fearful of losing their congregations. But whatever the cause, the flow of Negroes to the black republic slowed down to a trickle. "Emigration to Haiti does not appear to be in a flourishing condition of late," observed the *Baltimore Sun* of March 21, 1862.

The decline of the Haytian Bureau of Emigration did not mark the end of colonization sentiment among Negroes. The torch was kept high by the African Civilization Society, organized in the summer of 1858, with Henry Highland Garnet as president. The society's goals were the Christianization of Africa and the elevation of the American Negro. At the society's meeting in March 1861, Garnet proposed that $10,000 be raised to send a select group to Yoruba in Africa for permanent settlement. Among the thirty-eight signatures approving this recommendation were those of Horace Greeley and Henry Ward Beecher.

The highlight of the society's meeting of November 4, 1861, was a report of its secretary, Martin R. Delany, an able Negro who had given his daughter the name of Ethiopia, and whose five sons bore names equally race-conscious. Delany reported that he and Robert Campbell, another Negro explorer of Africa, had made favorable treaties of settlement with Yoruba chiefs, and that he was now ready to receive applications from carefully selected and well-recommended colored Americans.

The African Civilization Society was never able to fulfill its treaty with the Yoruba chiefs. The society lacked one vital thing—money. It could not expect large contributions from Negroes, few of whom were well-to-do. As it was a Negro-controlled organization, its officers had few contacts with white men of means. And the society could not appeal to those who wished to get rid of newly emancipated slaves, since its avowed purpose was to send to Africa only the cream of the crop and not "a mass of much crude material." Without funds the African Civilization Society had to yield its brief role as pacesetter for emigration. By the summer of 1862 leadership in the colonization movement had come to center on the man with the $600,000, Abraham Lincoln.

Prominent among those gravitating toward the President was the chairman of the Negro delegation that had visited him on August 14, 1862. Two days after the interview Edward M. Thomas wrote to Lincoln suggesting that two members of the delegation be authorized to make a trip to the larger cities of the North to present the President's views to the leading colored men. Thomas, seeing himself as one of the two selected for the trip, assured Lincoln that he desired no formal appointment. All he wanted was a letter from Lincoln's hand and an expense account. He concluded by asking for a personal interview of four minutes "on Monday morning at 8½ or 9."

Working up his case, Thomas went to see J.R.S. Van Vleet, associate editor of the *National Republican,* and had him write a strong letter of recommendation. Van Vleet informed Lincoln that Thomas was intelligent, respectable, and worthy of his confidence. To show Lincoln how influential Thomas was among Negroes, Van Vleet enclosed a printed program which revealed that "Edward M. Thomas, esquire," was president of the "Anglo-African Institute for the Encouragement of Industry and Art," scheduled to hold its first annual exhibition in New York in October.

Lincoln did not reply to Thomas and Van Vleet. Doubtless their letters were passed on to Commissioner of Emigration Mitchell. A Negro, J.W. Menard, who in May 1862 had written to Lincoln asking his help to get to Liberia, wound up as a clerk in the emigration office. This suggests that doubtless Lincoln preferred to have all deportation requests channeled directly to the chief officer of emigration.

For some two months—September and October 1862—this key officer was Senator Pomeroy. "Everything was in the hands of Pomeroy," was the message sent by Lincoln, via his private secretary, to a group of Negroes who had anxiously gathered in front of the White House and whose desire to emigrate had a certain urgency, for they had moved out of their dwellings and sold their furniture.

During the five weeks he was agent for the Chiriqui project, Pomeroy worked energetically. He sent releases to the newspapers, made speeches to Negro groups, and interviewed United States marshals at seaport cities in an effort to obtain ships to transport the prospective voyagers. "I confess the project seems to me one of insanity," wrote Negro abolitionist Robert Purvis, giving Pomeroy an unsolicited piece of his mind. But the Senator from Kansas was untouched by such barbs. He had received, he said, 13,700 applications from Negroes.

But Pomeroy was not destined to process these applications. Just when he was most hopeful, the Chiriqui project was brought to an abrupt halt. The somewhat bitter Pomeroy could do little more than send a last-ditch letter to sympathetic but helpless Senator Doolittle. In the waning weeks of the year the recruiting of Negro colonizers slowed down to a standstill.

Despite a succession of setbacks the sanguine Lincoln, in his congressional message of December 1, 1862, could express the belief that the attitude of the Negro toward colonization was improving. But, paradoxically enough, the man most responsible for the failure of Negro emigration was Lincoln himself. It was he who gave the Negroes the feeling that they could make their way in America, that this country was ready to take its first big steps in granting to its Negro sons and daughters their long-overdue rights. Lincoln gave hope to the Negro, and hopeful people are not minded to emigrate.

Five weeks after Lincoln had interviewed the colored delegation, he took a step that doomed his colonization plans. On September 22, 1862, he raised the hopes of the Negro as they had never been raised before: he issued a preliminary emancipation proclamation, warning the rebellious states that if they did not lay down their arms by January 1, 1863, he would declare their slaves free.

"I MAY ADVANCE SLOWLY," said Lincoln, "but I don't walk backward." On this latter point Lincoln's behavior on matters relating to the Negro had been reassuring. But in threatening to free the slaves, Lincoln was threatening to take a step without parallel in the American presidency, a step of far-reaching and revolutionary proportions. For a man of Lincoln's cautious temperament it would be a move almost out of character. Who could say for sure there would be no backward walking this time?

6

"THEN, THENCEFORWARD, AND FOREVER FREE"

On June 20, 1862, a delegation of six Quakers, representing the annual meeting of the Progressive Friends, came to the White House. Lincoln told them he was relieved to learn that they were not office seekers, "for his chief trouble was from that class of persons." Sensing their mission, Lincoln informed his visitors that his "next most troublesome subject was Slavery." In the discussion that followed, Lincoln matched his visitors in earnestness, but he did not promise them that he would issue a proclamation of freedom, as they wished.

Sometime within the space of the next three weeks, however, the President decided that the time had come for an edict of emancipation. Lincoln did not take lightly the wishes of religious groups, but more important in shaping his determination was the military situation. Things were not going well on the war front. In late June and early July 1862 Richmond, the Confederate capital, had withstood a bloody siege, thus sending a-glimmering the hope that the South would soon sue for peace. A prolonged war now became inevitable, which meant calling up additional troops and evoking a fresh source of inspiration. For this latter, morale-building component, Lincoln took the course that had been urged upon him for so many months by church groups, abolitionists, and Negroes—a presidential decree of freedom.

During the first days of July, Lincoln began to put together the first draft of an emancipation proclamation. The writing was done in the cipher room of the Military Telegraph Office at the desk of Superintendent Thomas T. Eckert. Here Lincoln could "command his thoughts" better than would have been possible at the White House, with its unfastened latchstring. Daily, over a span of two or three weeks, Lincoln would arrive at Eckert's office, obtain his papers, and review what he had previously written. This done, he would proceed to make corrections. He then wrote his next sentences, pausing now and then to glance out the window. When he had finished for the day, the long foolscap pages were carefully put under lock and key; only after he had completed the entire draft did Lincoln inform the curious Eckert of its nature.

It was on a day in mid-July that Lincoln first divulged his positive intentions to anyone. Twenty-four hours earlier he had been closeted with the border state congressmen in the unsatisfactory interview over compensated emancipation. With the reports from the battlefields not promising and with voluntary emancipation by the states at a stalemate, Lincoln felt that the time had come to summon whatever reserves he could.

Riding to the funeral exercises of Stanton's baby on Sunday, July 13, Lincoln turned to his carriage mates, Secretaries Seward and Welles, and told them that he had decided to make use of the "slave element" by issuing a proclamation of emancipation. The secretaries listened in quiet, saying nothing until Lincoln invited their comments. Both men were unprepared for such a presidential break with the past; to them this step was, as Welles phrased it in his diary, "a new departure" by Lincoln, who up to that time had regarded slavery as a "local domestic question."

But the Cabinet officers were not prepared to disapprove of the proposal, especially after Lincoln made it clear that his mind was made up, and that he was, in essence, just giving them advance information. Seward, skilled in the language of diplomacy, told Lincoln that such a step was doubtless necessary, but that it "involved consequences so vast and momentous that he should wish to bestow on it mature reflection before giving a decisive answer." Welles said that he shared Seward's views. On the return ride from the burial ground, Lincoln asked his Secretaries to give the question their best thinking, since "something must be done."

With or without the earnest thoughts of his two subordinates, however, Lincoln was bent on moving ahead. A little over a week later, on Tuesday, July 22, 1862, at a meeting of his Cabinet, Lincoln announced that he had drafted a proclamation declaring free the slaves in those states still in rebellion as of January 1, 1863. Lincoln's bold proposal took the Cabinet members, except for the forewarned Seward and Welles, by surprise. Giving them time to collect themselves, and hence more out of politeness than anything else, Lincoln invited any comments they might have.

Regaining their composure, the Secretaries had their say. One of them expressed the fear that the proclamation might lead to slave insurrections, and another was afraid that it would have a bad effect on Republican party fortunes in the coming fall elections. But Lincoln had previously weighed these considerations. Seward, however, brought up a point that Lincoln had completely overlooked—the question of timing. Seward pointed out that, in view of the recent military reverses before Richmond, the public might regard an emancipation proclamation as an act of desperation—"the last measure of an exhausted Government, a cry for help; the Government stretching forth its hand to Ethiopia, instead of Ethiopia stretching forth her hands to the Government." The soundness of Seward's point was obvious. The President reluctantly laid aside his proclamation until his military commanders could give him a victory on the battlefield.

Sixty-two days were to elapse before Lincoln could issue the proclamation. During this period he had to keep his intentions secret. Worse still, he had to endure the jibes of the abolitionists and the more restrained, but equally pointed criticisms of other reformist groups. Lincoln had to listen to the vehement antislavery views of his friend Cassius Clay, returned from his post in Russia. He had to receive religious groups who urged immediate emancipation, such as the large delegation of Chicago clergymen who spent an hour in "earnest and frank discussion" at the White House on September 13. "What good would a proclamation of emancipation from me do?" he asked the clergymen. "I do not want to issue a document that the whole world will see must necessarily be inoperative, like the Pope's bull against the comet!"

The most influential of the Lincoln critics during the two months while the proclamation lay in the darkness of a desk drawer was the energetic Horace Greeley, editor of the widely read *New York Tribune*. Greeley hit upon the idea of writing an open letter. Dated August 19, and printed on the editorial page of the next day's *Tribune*, was a piece from Mr. Greeley's own pen, bearing an impressive title, "The Prayer of Twenty Millions." Addressed to Lincoln, the editorial complained of the "seeming subserviency of your policy to the slave-holding, slavery-upholding interest." Loyal Americans, wrote Greeley, demanded that Lincoln enforce the second confiscation act liberating the slaves of rebels. "On the face of this wide earth, Mr. President, there is not one disinterested, determined, intelligent champion of the Union cause who does not feel that all attempts to put down the Rebellion and at the same time uphold its inciting cause are preposterous and futile."

Greeley's public letter was welcomed by Lincoln. It gave him a chance to do two things: restate his own position, and prepare the public mind for an emancipation proclamation issued upon military necessity. On August 22, in one of his most important state papers, Lincoln released his reply to the press.

His opening lines were even-toned and conciliatory. If, said he, Greeley's letter was impatient and dictatorial in tone, he overlooked it in deference to a long friendship. He did not mean, Lincoln continued, to leave anyone in doubt as to the policy "I 'seem to be pursuing' as you say."

My paramount object in this struggle is to save the Union ... If I could save the Union without freeing any slave I would do it, and if I could save it by freeing all the slaves I would do it; and if I

could save it by freeing some and leaving others alone I would also
do that. What I do about slavery, and the colored race, I do because I believe it helps to save the Union. . . .

These, added Lincoln, in a final, short paragraph, were his *official*
views, and were not intended as any change in his repeatedly expressed *personal* wishes that all men everywhere could be free.

Lincoln's reply was so well put that Greeley subsequently expressed the belief that it had been prepared long before Lincoln
ever saw "The Prayer." Greeley also pointed out that Lincoln,
although seeming to do so, had not really answered his letter, since
Greeley had called for the enforcement of an existing law, whereas
Lincoln's reply confined itself to the abolition of slavery generally.
But the shrewd Mr. Lincoln knew what he was doing; he may well
have suspected that Greeley had been tipped off about the forth-
coming proclamation and had written "The Prayer" in the hope of
forcing his (Lincoln's) hand.

Lincoln's reply to Greeley, however well reasoned, was a severe
disappointment to Negroes and to the champions of emancipation.
Their state of shock was short-lived, however. The month of September was barely half over when Lincoln got the military victory
he had been waiting for. The Battle of Antietam, fought on September 17, 1862, was actually less of a victory than a bloody stand-
off, but it did force the Confederates to retreat across the Potomac.
Hence Antietam was sufficient for Lincoln's purpose; as he confided to George S. Boutwell, "When Lee came over the river, I
made a resolution that when McClellan drove him back, I would
send the proclamation after him."

By Saturday, September 20, Lincoln was assured of the with-
drawal of the Confederate forces. On the next day he went to the
Soldiers' Home and wrote out his second draft of the preliminary
proclamation and then read it aloud to Vice-President Hannibal
Hamlin. With the document much as he wanted it, Lincoln was
now ready for the historic day of its promulgation—September 22,
1862.

On noon of that Monday, Lincoln met with his Cabinet in

special session, with everyone present. It was evident that this was an important occasion. Lincoln sought to reduce the tension by reading a passage from humorist Artemus Ward. Then, abandoning his light tone, Lincoln informed his solemn-faced and attentive associates that he had vowed he would issue an emancipation proclamation as soon as the rebels were driven out of Maryland. That time had now come.

He had brought them together, explained Lincoln, to hear what he had written. He did not solicit their advice on the wisdom of the step—he had determined that for himself—but he would listen to any comments on style or wording. Lincoln then read the document through, "making remarks," wrote Chase, "on several points as he went along." This preliminary emancipation proclamation was somewhat lengthy and touched on compensated emancipation, Negro colonization, the act of March 13, 1862, forbidding officers to return runaways, and the second Confiscation Act of July 17, 1862. But the heart of the proclamation was the opening phrases of the third paragraph:

> That, on the first day of January in the year of our Lord, one thousand eight hundred and sixty-three, all persons held as slaves within any state, or designated part of a state, the people whereof shall then be in rebellion against the United States shall be then, thenceforward, and forever free.

After he had finished, Lincoln waited for comments. Chase and Montgomery Blair made brief statements. Seward suggested two modifications, to which Lincoln had no objections. Then the Cabinet was dismissed.

Later that afternoon Lincoln and Seward signed the proclamation. This was done in plenty of time for it to be carried in the newspapers the following morning. "The great event of the day here," said the *New York Times* of September 23, "is the proclamation of the President." Another metropolitan daily of the same date viewed the proclamation as the turning of the tide: "The President has done a good deed, at a good time," stated the *Philadelphia Press*. "The rebellion is at an end!"

As NEGROES and their well-wishers read over the preliminary emancipation proclamation, they could not fail to note the complete absence of any abolitionist fervor or pro-Negro sentiment. Plainly Lincoln had not followed the abolitionist-Negro line that the favor of the Almighty was to be gained not by force of arms but by the panoply of righteousness. Indeed, this document of September 22, 1862, sounded like a cross between a military directive and a lawyer's brief. Its opening sentence set its tone: in it Lincoln called attention to his authority as Commander in Chief of the army and navy, and he stated that the aim of the war was the restoration of the Union. Moreover, in the edict Lincoln stated that efforts at Negro deportation would be continued. And, of course, slavery was to be abolished only in those places in rebellion, not in places where the Stars and Stripes actually flew.

To abolitionists the proclamation had another drawback: It gave the rebellious states the opportunity of keeping their slaves if they would lay down their arms by January 1. But nobody, the abolitionists included, made much of this alternative inasmuch as nobody, high or low, North or South, believed that the people of the Confederacy would listen to Lincoln's terms.

Despite the proclamation's limitations Negroes hailed it with much joy. The war, wrote Frederick Douglass, was now "invested with sanctity." A few celebrations were held; the largest was one of New York City Negroes at Shiloh Church on September 29. The man who called this meeting and organized it was Henry Highland Garnet, who simply could not wait until January 1, as he had already been waiting for nearly two decades. "I do pray," Garnet had written on September 3, 1844, from Troy, New York, to G.A. Thatcher, "that you and I may see that Great Day— I mean the 'Emancipation Day.' O that the Lord may hasten it on." At the enthusiastic and crowded meeting at Shiloh Church, Garnet presided, was one of the main speakers, and delivered the benediction.

Most Negroes were too prudent to follow Garnet's example, preferring instead to wait until January 1, when the final proclamation was due. For Negroes, while ever hopeful, were also ever realistic. They knew that Lincoln's preliminary edict was little more than the declaration of an intention; they knew that there was nothing in custom or in law that could compel him to follow it up.

Would the President issue the final proclamation? This was the momentous question before the Negroes during those fourteen weeks from September 22 to January 1—those fateful one hundred days of the countdown. During this period the Negro listened intently for telltale sounds from the White House, but Lincoln's words and actions seemed to take on all the ambiguity of a Delphic oracle.

There were some bad signs. Lincoln was not pleased with the North's initial response to the proclamation. "It is six days old," he wrote to Vice-President Hamlin in a letter marked strictly private, and "the stocks have declined, and troops come forward more slowly than ever."

Another bad omen was the results of the congressional elections held in the fall of 1862, which went heavily against the administration. In New York, New Jersey, Pennsylvania, Ohio, and Illinois the party of Lincoln suffered a series of setbacks. These reverses resulted in the main from war weariness. But Lincoln preferred another reason: his opponents won at the polls because they "were left in a majority by our friends going to the war." The foes of the emancipation edict advanced still another reason: the election results were a clear warning to the President that he should retrace his steps and revoke it.

Another factor that Negroes feared would dampen Lincoln's enthusiasm for the final proclamation was the slow progress of his colonization plans, for it was during the hundred-day period that Lincoln was forced to abandon his Chiriqui project. But, although Negroes did not know it at the time, Lincoln had turned to Bernard Kock and Cow Island. Happily perhaps for the Negro, Lincoln could not foresee the ultimate fate of his deportation schemes. "I have sometimes doubted," wrote Secretary Welles, "whether he would not have hesitated longer in issuing the decree of emancipation had he been aware that colonization would not be accepted as an accompaniment."

Lincoln's lengthy message to Congress of December 1, 1862, did nothing to ease the apprehension of Negroes. Nearly two-fifths of its 9167 words were devoted to compensated emancipation and colonization, and it was only in connection with these that passing mention was made of the Emancipation Proclamation. Lincoln pointed out that his mere recommendations of compensated emancipation and colonization would not end the war nor stay the proclamation of September 22. But, he added, there was no doubt in his mind that the adoption of such recommendations would end the war and stay the proclamation. This passage indicated that Lincoln had not forgotten the proclamation, but it was hardly reassuring to Negroes and abolitionists.

Reformers, however, were hopers for the best. As a means of keeping up their spirits, they often professed to foresee good things. Frederick Douglass, rubbing his crystal ball, was sure that the President would not back down on the proclamation. Lincoln might be slow, and he might desire peace even at the price of leaving slavery untouched, but he was not the kind of man "to reconsider, retract and contradict words and purposes solemnly proclaimed over his official signature." Chaplain Mansfield French, up from the Sea Islands of South Carolina, was also hopeful, having gone to the White House to assure Lincoln that the preliminary proclamation "had gone to the bone" of the rebels. Lydia Maria Child took hope from the sheer amount of discussion about the darker brother. "The manner in which poor Sambo's cause gets argued and listened to in all quarters now is the most encouraging feature of the times," she wrote to Lucy Searle four days before the Christmas of 1862.

No reformer was more certain of Lincoln's intentions than Charles Sumner. Late in December the Massachusetts senator sent reassuring missives to his constituents: "The President says he would not stop the Pro. if he could," he wrote to George Livermore, "and he could not if he would." Sumner shared some of his

inside information with his most widely known reformer correspondent, Harriet Beecher Stowe: "The Presdt. has repeatedly
assured me of his purpose to stand by his Proclamation. He says
that it is hard to move him from a position once he has taken it."

Mrs. Stowe was anxious to be convinced. Accompanied by Henry
Wilson, junior senator from the Bay State, she had gone to the
Executive Mansion in late November to see if she could get something definite. Lincoln knew Mrs. Stowe by reputation, if not by
her works (early that year someone at the White House had with-
drawn from the Library of Congress *The Key to Uncle Tom's
Cabin*, keeping it from June 16 to July 29, 1862). Almost without
waiting for Senator Wilson to complete his introduction of the
world-famed novelist, Lincoln had seized her hand and exclaimed,
"So this is the little lady who made this big war." Lincoln's cordiality and his praise did not divert the crusading Mrs. Stowe from
her mission, but she had to come away from the White House
with no direct answer to her direct question: Did Mr. Lincoln
intend to issue the proclamation?

IF OTHERS were uncertain of his intentions, Lincoln himself was
not. He never wavered in his determination to issue the final edict.
On November 21, 1862, he told a Kentucky delegation that "he
would rather die than take back a word of the Proclamation of
Freedom." This firm and definite decision stemmed from one
factor that many of his contemporaries overlooked: Lincoln had
studied the step inside out. He had issued the ultimatum to the
Confederate states only, as he himself said at the time, "after very
full deliberation."

Entering into Lincoln's deliberation and fixing his determination about issuing an emancipation proclamation were considerations of a varied nature—military, political, and diplomatic. To
Lincoln the first of these was pre-eminent: military necessity required that the enemy be deprived of his slaves. Lincoln knew that
the black population of the South was one of its greatest assets.
The Confederacy had not actually put a gun in the hands of the

colored man, but tens of thousands of its slaves saw front-line service, being employed as orderlies, teamsters, and military laborers. Slaves who remained on the home front supplied the skills for the factories and the brawn for working the mines. And it was the labor of the plantation slave that produced the cotton the South hoped to sell in England. To weaken this black arm of the Confederacy had become the first order of military business, a blunt fact from which Lincoln could not flinch.

In the late summer of 1863 (on September 2), Lincoln told Secretary Chase that the Emancipation Proclamation had been issued solely as a military necessity and not because it was politically expedient or morally right. Nonetheless, political considerations had influenced the issuing of the edict. Himself a Republican, Lincoln was obliged to make concessions to the point of view of his party, including its Radical wing. As the war went on with no end in sight, these Radicals became more insistent than ever that the abolition of slavery become an officially avowed goal of the war. The support of these Radicals was important to the Lincoln administration, and this support could be jeopardized without an edict of emancipation.

By the late summer of 1862 there were signs, as the politically astute Lincoln could see, that the Radical point of view on slavery was gaining strength. John W. Forney's *Philadelphia Press* carried a pointed editorial in its issue of July 30, 1862:

A million able-bodied men await but our word to ally themselves with us bodily, as they are with us in heart. A magnificent black blister as a counter irritant! A guerrilla power such as the world has never seen.

Such a point of view Lincoln might take in stride if uttered by an abolitionist or even by a Republican congressman. But the *Philadelphia Press* was such a defender of the Lincoln administration as to be considered an organ of the White House. When influential Lincoln men like Forney joined the emancipation chorus, no soothsayer of political behavior need be summoned to tell of tomorrow.

The extent to which political considerations shaped the issuing of the emancipation edict becomes evident in Lincoln's dealings with the Altoona Conference governors. Andrew G. Curtin of Pennsylvania and John A. Andrew of Massachusetts had called a meeting of loyal governors to be held at Altoona, Pennsylvania, during the last week of September 1862. As announced in the call, the chief aim of the conference was to press for action against slavery. Lincoln was not asleep. By a shrewd stroke he proceeded to undercut the scheduled conference. He summoned governors Curtin and Andrew to the White House and told them of the emancipation proclamation lying in his desk awaiting a battlefield victory. Curtin and Andrew realized that they had been outflanked; they had also been won over.

Fortunately for Lincoln, the victory at Antietam enabled him to issue his proclamation before the Altoona meeting. After their conference the governors came to Washington in a group and called at the White House on September 26. They congratulated Lincoln on the issuing of the proclamation, and Lincoln, with a straightfaced solemnity matching theirs, told them that their approval of the measure assured him, more than anything else, that he had done the right thing.

A third important factor in bringing about and supporting the proclamation was European, particularly English, opinion. In England the governing and aristocratic classes were anti-North and would have been glad to extend diplomatic recognition to the Confederacy. But the masses and the middle class in the British Isles were Union sympathizers and disliked the South as slavery's strongest bastion in the Western world.

In large measure the groundwork for this British antislavery sentiment had been laid by American Negroes who for a quarter of a century had been touring England, Ireland, and Scotland. Many of these Negroes were escaped slaves, like William Wells Brown, who in five years abroad made over a thousand addresses. William and Ellen Craft moved British audiences to tears with the story of their dramatic escape from Macon, Georgia, with Ellen disguised as a young slavemaster.

The procession of Negroes did not abate with the war. American Negroes like J. Sella Martin acted almost as if they were ministers without portfolio in furthering the Union cause. Far from her Salem, Massachusetts, home, the young, eloquent, and earnest Sarah P. Remond, always effective on the platform, exhorted her listeners to stand firm:

> Let no diplomacy of statesmen, no intimidation of slaveholders, no scarcity of cotton, no fear of slave insurrections, prevent the people of Great Britain from maintaining their position as the friend of the oppressed Negro.

The greatest drawing card among the American Negroes during the autumn of 1862 was William Andrew Davis, the escaped ex-coachman of Confederate President Jefferson Davis. These Negroes, like their counterparts before the war, did much to intensify the antislavery sentiment of the British masses.

Lincoln knew that reformist groups and workingmen's associations in England would hail an edict of emancipation. He was aware, too, that such a proclamation would be a heavy blow to the foreign policy of the Confederacy, striking "King Cotton diplomacy" in a most vulnerable spot. After the Emancipation Proclamation was issued, the Confederate agents stationed in European capitals were no longer able to play down the slavery issue by asserting that the North had no intention of changing the status of the black man.

"I did not know," wrote Lincoln's friend, Pennsylvania politician Alexander K. McClure, "and few were permitted to know, the importance of an Emancipation policy in restraining the recognition of the Confederacy by France and England." Equally emphatic on this point was one who did happen to be in the know—the Secretary of State. It was not alone the clamor at home, said Seward on January 22, 1863, that induced Lincoln to issue the proclamation. He had been influenced also "by the wishes of foreign Nations," who "were urging that the slaves should be declared free."

Lincoln did not underestimate the role the proclamation would play across the Atlantic. It enabled abolitionist groups like the London Emancipation Society to cry out that "the South is fighting for slavery, whilst the North is fully committed to the destruction of slavery." Like other antislavery organizations abroad, the London group was given a fresh impetus by Lincoln's edict, enlarging its program and personnel. Beginning in December 1862 and running through the following March, more than fifty well-attended public meetings in support of Lincoln's proclamation were held in the major cities of Great Britain and Ireland.

At each of these gatherings the chief order of business was the drafting of a resolution or an address to Lincoln, to be sent to him through the offices of the American ambassador to the Court of St. James. During the first weeks of 1863 Charles Francis Adams was kept busy receiving these resolutions, arranging them in batches, and forwarding them to Seward. Diplomatic pouches containing such resolutions of approval were mailed by Adams on January 22, February 5, February 12, and February 19. In the letter accompanying the February 19 mailing, Adams informed Seward that "the current of popular sentiment flows with little abatement of strength." The ambassador made bold to add that he was sure that Lincoln was unprepared "for the multiplication of addresses, from various quarters, which has ensued."

Seward asked Adams, in a letter of February 25, to find some way "of communicating the President's grateful responses" to those who had "generously addressed him concerning our affairs." Seward knew that Lincoln could never personally answer more than a handful of these impressive sets of resolutions, which sometimes bore hundreds of signatures, but he also knew that Lincoln did not wish to have his British supporters go unthanked.

Member of Parliament and reformer Richard Cobden, who was interested in free men as well as in free trade, was sure that Lincoln's edict turned the tide of public opinion in the British

Isles. "You know," he wrote to Charles Sumner from London's Athenaeum Club on February 13, 1863, "how much alarmed I was from the first lest our government should interpose in your affairs ... This state of feeling existed up to the announcement of the President's emancipation Policy. From that moment our old anti-slavery feeling began to arouse itself, and it has been gathering strength ever since."

HAVING PREVIOUSLY WEIGHED the major factors for issuing the preliminary proclamation, Lincoln was not likely to withhold the final edict. In setting the date for January 1, 1863, he had shown a good sense of the propitious moment. From the beginning he had been his own preacher, knowing that there was a time to wait, a time to warn, and a time to consummate. And now with the war about to enter its third calendar year, the North was ready to accept the Lincoln point of view that it was necessary to declare the rebel slaves free if the Union was to be saved. "In reference to the Proclamation of Old Abe's," wrote Illinois infantryman Michael Gapen to his sister from his campsite on Yacona Creek, Mississippi, on December 17, 1862, "I did not like it at first myself, but I have now come to the conclusion that it is the best thing that can possibly be done." Two days earlier the House of Representatives, reflecting grassroots sentiment, voted 78 to 52 in favor of a resolution supporting the Lincoln proclamation as a measure warranted to hasten the restoration of peace.

Lincoln never had any intention of withholding the final proclamation. True, the policy of emancipation may have originally been thrust upon him; but by the time he announced it to the world, it had become an integral part of his own thinking. Spiritualists might claim that Lincoln issued the edict upon the advice of mediums, and reformist and political groups might lay claim to having stiffened his backbone. Lincoln would not have bothered to dispute these claims, for he was secure in the knowledge that the decision had become his own.

THE FINAL emancipation proclamation was signed on the scheduled date. Considering the widespread discussion of it during the preceding one hundred days, the signing ceremonies were quiet and undramatic, indeed almost offhand. On the afternoon of January 1, the document was ready for the President's signature, after he had spent nearly half a week, on and off, working it over. He had held Cabinet meetings on each of the last three days of the year, on December 29 reading the proclamation to the heads of departments, on the next day furnishing them with copies for their criticisms, and on the last morning of the year reconvening them for final revisions.

The afternoon of that December 31 Lincoln spent in reviewing the notes and memoranda submitted by the Cabinet members, and in framing his language. He then began the rewriting of the entire document, making sure that his penmanship was Spencerian in clarity, if not in slant. Up early the next morning, and clear-headed after a New Year's Eve without revels, Lincoln completed his writing and sent the finished product to the State Department to be engrossed. Shortly before eleven o'clock the document was returned to the White House. Lincoln was on the point of signing it when he noticed an error in the attestation, as a clerk had used the phraseology common to a treaty, rather than to a proclamation. Staying his signature, the Chief Executive rushed off to the Blue Room to undergo a three-hour ritual of handshaking.

The reception at the White House on New Year's Day was a long established custom. Lincoln and his wife stood in the short receiving line to be wished a happy 1863. The first hour was reserved for officialdom—diplomats, high army brass, navy officers, congressmen, and federal judges. Then for two hours came the general public. Perhaps some of these visitors, thinking of the proclamation, looked inquiringly into the President's eyes. But readers of Lincoln's face had just about as much success as readers of his mind.

By midafternoon the reception was over, and Lincoln could return to the executive office. Waiting for him was the properly engrossed proclamation, spread out on the desk by Secretary Seward. Not more than a dozen, informally gathered witnesses were present as Lincoln reached for his steel-tipped pen, its ink-splattered wooden handle rough from gnawing. Lincoln feared that his signature would be tremulous and uneven—"three hours of hand shaking," he explained to Schuyler Colfax that evening, "is not calculated to improve a man's chirography." But if his arm was limp and his hand was unsteady, his will was firm. To himself, but loud enough so that it could be heard by Frederick Seward, the Secretary of State's son, he remarked, "Anyway, it is going to be done!" Carefully and slowly he traced "Abraham Lincoln," not abbreviating his first name as he so often did.

Seward reached for the document to take it to the State Department for the great seal. Lincoln let nobody take the pen; he had promised to save it for George Livermore of Boston, a friend of Charles Sumner. For several weeks Sumner had plagued Lincoln about the pen. Sumner had been bedeviled in turn by Livermore: "I do so much desire to have that freeing instrument come to Massachusetts," he wrote on Christmas Day, "that I would do almost anything to get it."

Sumner hardly needed vigorous prodding. He remembered, as he informed Livermore two days later, that shortly after the District of Columbia Emancipation Act had been signed, he had gone to the White House and asked for the pen Lincoln had used. Lincoln had reached to his desk and taken up a handful of pens, saying, "It was one of these. Which will you take? You are welcome to all."

This time Sumner was not to be denied. Lincoln signed the proclamation on a Thursday afternoon; that Saturday's newspapers announced that Sumner had the pen. Two days later, on Monday, January 5, Livermore received it in the mails. Wrote he to Sumner before the sun had set: "No trophy from a battlefield, no sword red with blood, no service of plate with an inscription . . . would ever have been to me half as acceptable as this instrument." In North Carolina the editor of the *Wilmington Journal* might sneer that Barnum ought to have the pen "which was employed to affix the name of Gorilla to the most infamous document that ever emanated from any civilized government." But nothing could dim the joy of the pen's possessor.

LIVERMORE'S FEELING about the Emancipation Proclamation was shared by another familiar figure in Boston reformist circles, Lydia Maria Child. "Hurrah! Hosanna! Hallelujah! Laudamus! Nunc dimittis! Jubilate! Amen!" she wrote to Quaker abolitionist Abby Hopper Gibbons.

Matching Mrs. Child's fervor, if not her Latin, was Henry M. Turner, pastor of Israel Bethel Church in Washington. "It was indeed a time of times," wrote he, "nothing like it will ever be seen again in this life. Our entrance into Heaven itself will only form a counterpart." On that January 1 evening, Turner went out to get a *Washington Star* and finally succeeding in grabbing a half-torn one which carried the proclamation. Turner ran for dear life down Pennsylvania Avenue to reach his church, nearly a mile away. He entered and hurried to the platform waving the newspaper. Ordinarily Turner would have had no difficulty in commanding the attention of a congregation—as might be expected from one who was known as the "black Spurgeon," and whose powerful preaching attracted white visitors every Sunday—but he could not compete with the news from the White House. As he stood in the pulpit, he noted, as he wrote later, that men were squealing, women were fainting, dogs were barking, and white and colored people were shaking hands.

At the hour Turner's congregation was expressing itself, another celebration in Washington was going on at the contraband camp, half a mile north of famed Willard's Hotel. The camp's six hundred freedmen had attended a watch meeting the preceding night —singing, praying, and parading around the campgrounds until daybreak. The activities of that tintinnabulary night had a tonic effect on these former slaves, and they felt no weariness as they gathered in front of the office of the superintendent, Dr. B.D.

Nichols. The well-liked Nichols read the proclamation and then carefully explained what portions of Virginia were affected by its provisions. Many of the listeners recognized their native counties, exclaiming, "I'm free," and "Dat means dis chile." After the edict had been read through, the exercises took on a camp-meeting quality, with spontaneous moving about, punctuated by improvised songs, loud prayers, and sudden shouts. The evening ended on a common note, however, with everyone joining in the song "There's a better day a coming."

Boston, as befitted a city housing the Cradle of Liberty, had two mammoth celebrations on January 1. At the Music Hall that afternoon the meeting was graced by one of the greatest rosters of American literary lights ever assembled under one roof—Henry Wadsworth Longfellow, Oliver Wendell Holmes, Charles Eliot Norton, John Greenleaf Whittier, Edward Everett Hale, Francis Parkman, and Ralph Waldo Emerson. The last-named opened the meeting with a reading of a "Boston Hymn" which he had completed that morning; its tone of elation is suggested by a typical stanza:

> I break your bonds and masterships,
> And I unchain the slave:
> Free be his heart and hand henceforth
> As wind and wandering wave.

Emerson was followed by music, all of it in a stirring mood and highlighted by Beethoven's Fifth Symphony, with Carl Zerrahn conducting the Philharmonic Orchestra. Just as the lengthy and impressive exercises were about to end, someone started a rhythmic call for Harriet Beecher Stowe. Deeply moved, Mrs. Stowe went down to the rail of the balcony where she had been inconspicuously seated. Looking into the hundreds of upturned faces, the author of *Uncle Tom's Cabin* could only dab her eyes and bow. "It was a day & an occasion never to be forgotten," wrote Elisa S. Quincy on January 2 to the lady of the White House. "I wish you & the President could have enjoyed it with us here."

The intense enthusiasm at the Music Hall had its counterpart at Tremont Temple that evening. This meeting was sponsored by the Union Progressive Association, a predominantly Negro group, but the jam-packed audience, numbering more than three thousand, was mixed, as were the speakers. "We were not all colored," wrote Frederick Douglass, "but we all seemed to be about of one color that day."

Missing were two of the high priests of abolitionism. Charles Sumner's letter of invitation had not reached him in time, "owing to the wretched condition of the mails between New York and Washington," as he explained in a letter of 1 January to the association's officers. Wendell Phillips could not be present because he had to be at the Medford home of George L. Stearns to unveil a marble bust of John Brown, in the company of Ralph Waldo Emerson, Julia Ward Howe, A. Bronson Alcott, and Moncure D. Conway. But the absence of Sumner and Phillips was made less acute by the other well-known reformers who had consented to appear.

The first Negro speaker of the evening, Boston attorney John S. Rock, pointed out that this was a great moment for his country and for his race. "As the old maid said, on the eve of her marriage—

> 'This is the day I long have sought,
> And mourned because I found it not.' "

To the dead-serious audience this was a somewhat ambiguous note, and Rock hastened on to an analysis of Lincoln. He could not bring himself to criticize the President, said Rock. When he remembered "what we said of him when he was elected, we must acknowledge that he has exceeded our most sanguine expectations." Three cheers went up for Abraham Lincoln, and the spectators rose, applauding.

Clearly the audience was attuned to Lincoln and to nobody else. Rock and the several speakers who followed him were little more than time-fillers, a circumstance that may have been a bit disconcerting to such professional spellbinders as Frederick Douglass and the beautiful and talented Anna E. Dickinson, both of whom were accustomed to the undivided attention of their audiences. But at Tremont Temple that evening no Demosthenes could have competed with the words expected from Abraham Lincoln.

As speaker followed speaker, the applause became more and more perfunctory, and the restlessness of the audience became more evident. But just as a let-down feeling began to grip the Temple, a messenger dashed into the hall shouting at the top of his voice, "It is coming! It is on the wires!" This was the moment sublime. Hats and bonnets went up in the air; three cheers were given for Lincoln. "I never saw enthusiasm before," wrote one participant, "I never saw joy before." The din was terrific; even proper Bostonians abandoned their reserve for once. Everyone was on his feet, each in his own way giving vent to his pent-up feelings—some by cheering, some by clapping, some by waving their hats, and some by just letting their eyes rove from scene to scene, as if to drink all of it in.

After things had calmed down, the audience sang hymns of deliverance. First came "Blow Ye the Trumpet, Blow," with Douglass serving as lead voice. This was followed by another paean:

> Sound the loud timbrel o'er Egypt's dark sea,
> Jehovah hath triumphed, his people are free.

After two hours the enthusiasm was still running full-tide. But Tremont Temple had been rented only until midnight. By acclamation the audience decided to transfer the meeting to the Twelfth Baptist Church on near-by Southac Street. Here they were welcomed by the pastor, "Father" Leonard Grimes, well known in abolitionist circles for the number of runaways he had assisted. After an opening prayer the transplanted celebrators resumed their singing. Bursting against the walls of the two-storied building went the strains of "Glory, Hallelujah," "Old John Brown," "Marching On," and "Blow Ye the Trumpet, Blow." Buoyed by refreshments, the happy company of proclamation welcomers continued their rejoicing until both they and the night were far spent. "No words can depict the enthusiasm of the occasion," wrote a *Liberator* reporter.

Following the example set in Boston, Negroes from the Atlantic to the Great Lakes celebrated the proclamation. New York Negroes held meetings at Bridge Street Church in Brooklyn and at Abyssinian Baptist Church. Biggest of the New York meetings, if not the biggest in the nation, was the one held at Cooper Union, which was filled to suffocation. "The meeting was attended by a large number of the leading merchants, ministers and lawyers of this city," wrote the *Tribune* reporter, "who were scattered all over the audience, many of them glad to enjoy even a place to stand." Public observances of the proclamation were held in such cities as Rochester, Columbus, and Chicago, to name a few.

Typical of most of the celebrations in the small towns was the one held on January 1 by the Negroes of Leesburg, Highland County, Ohio. Held in the schoolhouse, the meeting opened with a hymn and a prayer. Then, "after some remarks by the different gentlemen present," a series of resolutions was adopted. One of these bore a tribute to Lincoln, whose name "will ever be gratefully remembered by the colored race of America." These formal proceedings were followed by a "sumptuous" dinner, the last order of business being the return of a vote of thanks to the ladies who had prepared it.

In the South the only areas in which the proclamation could be publicly celebrated were those to which it did not apply—those under the federal flag. But even though the proclamation did not apply to them, the Negroes in the Union-held regions of the South celebrated anyway. In Norfolk on the first day of the year, some 2000 former slaves paraded along the principal streets, carrying banners and flags and accompanied by bands and a detachment of troops. The parade was cheered by the more than 10,000 Negroes who stationed themselves along the line of march. Among these was a former slave carpenter who could not help but mark the contrast between the present and the past New Year's:

In Norfolk on that day there was always begun a new list of heart-breakings and sorrows to end only with life. But this time, in place of the ring of the auctioneer's hammer and the suspicious nestling of the baby in its mother's arms, was this same property marching along the streets, and under the stars and stripes to the tune of "Hallelujah."

Of the exercises in the South, the most impressive were those held at Port Royal in the Sea Islands. Here on January 1, whites and Negroes assembled near the camp of the First South Carolina Volunteers, at a grove framed by live oaks. Shortly before noon the exercises began. The preliminary emancipation was read by a South Carolinian, Dr. W. H. Brisbane, who long before the war had freed his thirty slaves. The next scheduled event was the presentation of two flags to the regiment. But as Colonel Thomas W. Higginson reached for the flags, a voice was heard singing the opening phrases of "America":

> My country, 'tis of thee,
> Sweet land of liberty.

Other Negroes quickly joined in. "I never saw anything so electric," wrote Higginson; "it seemed the choked voice of a race at last unloosed." Another eyewitness was similarly moved: "Nothing could have been more unexpected or more inspiring," wrote army surgeon Seth Rogers.

As the music died away, Higginson was reluctant to go through with his short speech, sensing that "the life of the whole day was in those unknown people's song." But the beloved "Cunnel" spoke his piece and then delivered the flags to the color guards. Other speakers included Mrs. Frances D. Gage and General Rufus Saxton. The formal portion of the program then gave way to a dress parade. By the time the blue-coated men had gone through their paces, everyone was ready for the grand barbecue. Twelve oxen had been roasted over great pits containing live coals, and now were laid out on a long wooden table, flanked by plates of bread. Nobody was bashful as they dug into the beef. The celebrators did not forget Lincoln but paused to drink a toast to him in water and molasses.

Sent to the President that evening from Beaufort was a more formal expression of appreciation. The Baptist Church in Christ drew up a resolution giving thanks to God and to him:

> We have gathered together two or three times a week for the last five months to pray that the Lord might help you and your soldiers. We never expect to meet you face to face on earth, but may we meet in a better world than this: this is our humble prayer.

The general attitude of Negroes toward the proclamation was expressed by one of the slaves of Colonel John Montgomery Ashley of Kentucky. Located in a border state, these slaves were not legally affected by the Lincoln edict. But Ashley had assembled them in the grand hall which ran the length of the big house to tell them of it and to give them the choice of remaining with him or of branching out on their own. All of the slaves listened as their patriarch, Uncle Dan, expressed his opinion: "Freedom are a unbroke filly and mighty skittish, but I ar' gwine to mount her just the same—rheumatiz, cane, an' all. Marse Jack, yo' bin a good marster to dis people, but dar's nothin' like freedom—'cepting freedom."

NEGROES could give themselves fully to glorifying the Emancipation Proclamation because they did not view it in the round. They had their own authorized version of the Lincoln Testament, and it could be summed up in the scriptural phrase "Out of the house of bondage." Focusing their thoughts on the proclamation's anti-slavery side, most Negroes ignored its other aspects. Had these Negroes read the document, they would have known that it was only a declaration, and that it applied only to those areas in rebellion, excluding Tennessee. Readers of the proclamation would have noted that Lincoln, ever highly fearful of slave insurrections, had urged Negroes to abstain from violence except in self-defense. On the more positive side, the proclamation expressed Lincoln's intention to enlist former slaves into the armed services.

Lincoln
showing Sojourner Truth
the Bible he received
from the Negroes of Baltimore
Courtesy of
the Library of Congress

Frederick Douglass

Martin R. Delaney

The Lincoln Memorial
Courtesy of Washington Star

The tone of the proclamation did not disturb Negroes any more than did its content. They overlooked its dry, matter-of-fact style and its lack of any exalted sentiment, as if Lincoln's heart were not in it. To Negroes it was enough that the Emancipation Proclamation contained the words "henceforward shall be free." They did not bother themselves with the proclamation's other language, its "whereas's" and "to wit's." It was natural that the Negro's reading of the edict should be selective. In a document proclaiming liberty, the unfree never bother to read the fine print.

The printed proclamation could be used with telling effect among the Negroes. It was a widely circulated document; nearly fifty issues of various sizes and quantities rolled off the presses during the war, including a printing by the War Department on January 6, 1863, and one by the Navy Department eight days later. But no group responded to the proclamation the way the Negroes did. John Andrew of Massachusetts had 100,000 copies printed for them. "Governor Andrew means to let the darkies know they are free," wrote the Ogdensburg, New York, *True Advance*. "He has caused the proclamation to be bound up in tiny book form, and has had packages of them franked to the Massachusetts regiments, requesting the various officers to see that they are distributed." A large quantity of Andrew's shipment went to Colonel Thomas W. Higginson in Sea Island, South Carolina. Higginson reported that he seldom found Negroes who could read the proclamation, but "they all seemed to feel more secure when they held it in their hands."

The number of Negroes who saw the proclamation in print was small compared to those who got the news by word of mouth. In the big house no backstairs information was ever more widely whispered. Along slave row, no tidings ever went as quickly from cabin to cabin. From one plantation to another the good news winged its way; the black grapevine was activated as never before. More than one white Southerner first learned about the Emancipation Proclamation from his own slaves.

Of course there were thousands of slaves, particularly in the

Confederate heartland, who were late in getting the word. In the spring of 1863 Laura S. Haviland talked with a contraband at Camp Bethel, some forty miles from Memphis. "You know," said she, "that President Lincoln has proclaimed all slaves free." "Is dat so?" replied the old man. But there were many instances in which the ignorance was feigned. James Freeman Clarke asked a contraband whether the slaves she had left behind in Virginia were aware of the Lincoln edict. "Oh yes, massa!" she answered. "We all knows about it, only we darsn't let on." Slaves who let on that they had dangerous information were placed under closer surveillance and were faced with tightened patrol laws.

The esteem that Negroes had for the Emancipation Proclamation helped to make it one of the most far-reaching pronouncements ever issued in the United States. Negroes were instrumental in creating the image of the proclamation that was to become the historic image. For in its own day Lincoln's edict was destined to reflect the luster and take on the evocative power reserved only for the half-dozen great charter expressions of human liberty in the entire Western tradition. The proclamation soon assumed the role that Negroes had given it at the outset, and became to millions a fresh expression of one of man's loftiest aspirations—the quest for freedom. The Emancipation Proclamation did not have to await the verdict of posterity: within six months after it was issued, the mass of Americans had come to regard it as a milestone in the long struggle for human rights.

True enough, Lincoln had originally conceived of the proclamation as a measure for the self-preservation, rather than for the regeneration, of America. But the proclamation, almost in spite of its creator, changed the whole tone and character of the war. Negroes sensed this more quickly than did Lincoln. Long before he had ever dreamed of issuing an edict of freedom, Negroes had been hoping and praying for such a measure. Just as they were in advance of Lincoln in the time set for the proclamation, so they were in advance of him in a realization of the proclamation's broad implications for freedom in America.

But in accurately gauging the temper of the people on great public issues, nobody could stay too far ahead of the perceptive Chief Executive. Lincoln was not slow in sensing the new dimensions his proclamation had taken on. The more abiding meaning of his edict became ever clearer to him. That the Emancipation Proclamation brought to Lincoln a grasp of the deeper significance of the Civil War is illustrated by his celebrated Gettysburg Address of November 19, 1863.

The battlefield at Gettysburg was to be dedicated as a cemetery for the soldiers who fell there. Lincoln had not been selected as the orator of the day, but he had been asked to make a few remarks. The statement he prepared was a short one, running to three paragraphs and totaling fewer than three hundred words. Slowly rising when his name was called at the ceremonial gathering, Lincoln drew a manuscript from his pocket and began to read in a treble voice: "Fourscore and seven years ago . . ." What happened at that distant date, intoned the speaker, was the creation of a nation conceived in liberty, a haven where all men were created equal. The President's opening words were inspiring, but his closing phrases were just as memorable. We should, said he, dedicate ourselves to the task of giving to America "a new birth of freedom."

Thus did Lincoln reveal that he had fully grasped the great truth that the war had become not a war to restore the Union as it was, but a war to reconstitute the Union on a broadened base of human liberty. As nothing else had, the Emancipation Proclamation had brought home to Lincoln that a democracy cannot live on its past achievements, but that it has to be on the move.

Lincoln's mature opinion of the proclamation is revealed by a remark he made to portrait painter Francis B. Carpenter in February 1865: "As affairs have turned, it is the central act of my administration, and the greatest event of the nineteenth century." Lincoln came to believe that his chief claim to fame would rest upon the proclamation. It was the one thing that would make people remember that he had lived—so he confided to Joshua F. Speed in a rare moment of self-revelation.

THE EMANCIPATION PROCLAMATION did more than lift the war to the level of a crusade for human freedom. It brought some very substantial practical results, for it gave the go-ahead signal to the recruiting of Negro soldiers. By midsummer of 1863 Lincoln could report that "the emancipation policy, and the use of colored troops, constitute the heaviest blow yet dealt to the rebellion."

But Lincoln and the Negro soldier is a story in itself.

7

LINCOLN AND THE BLACKS IN BLUE

To H. FORD DOUGLAS, a runaway slave who had become an abolitionist orator, the Civil War was two things. It was the deliverance of a people; Douglas himself had enlisted in a white unit, Company G of the Ninety-fifth Illinois Volunteers, so that he might "play my part in the great drama of the Negro's redemption." To Ford the war was also a schoolmaster to Abraham Lincoln; it would, wrote Ford on January 8, 1863, from the company camp at Colliersville, Tennessee, educate the President out of his "pro-slavery" ideas about employing Negroes as soldiers.

War is a rapid educator. By the time Ford put these thoughts on paper, Lincoln had already shown himself a learner. In a letter of January 14, 1863, Lincoln asked General John A. Dix, commanding at Fort Monroe, whether it would not be feasible to garrison Yorktown and Fort Monroe with Negroes; the white soldiers stationed there would be sent elsewhere. Lincoln explained to Dix that inasmuch as the Emancipation Proclamation had been issued, the Union should take some benefit from it.

The exact day or week that Lincoln decided to support the recruiting of Negroes is not easily pinpointed. His last positive refusal to arm the Negro was in early August 1862. A deputation from Indiana visited the White House on August 4, and offered two regiments of colored soldiers. Lincoln told them that he was not prepared to enlist Negroes, although he would employ all he could get as laborers. Lincoln put up his familiar argument: to arm the colored man "would turn 50,000 bayonets from the loyal Border States against us that were for us." Two days later, on August 6, the assistant adjutant general, C.P. Buckingham, informed Governor Edward Salomon of Wisconsin that Lincoln declined to receive Negroes or Indians as troops.

But more and more Lincoln was being won over to having Negro soldiers. With the Union ranks thinning and with white enlistments falling off, the opposition to arming the Negro began to slacken. Lincoln was not slow in noting the unmistakable change in public opinion as reflected in the popular song "Sambo's Right to be Kilt." It became increasingly hard to ignore the question raised by the *Pine and Palm:* "How long will white Americans submit to be drafted solely because their colored fellow-countrymen are rejected?"

The changing mood of the country was reflected in a letter to the White House on July 30, 1862, signed by Governor Nathaniel S. Berry of New Hampshire and his Executive Council:

> We beg leave to say that our reading, intelligent, patriotic young men are inquiring into the propriety of wasting their strength and energy in daily and nightly watching of rebel states and other property, or building corduroy roads and bridges in Chickahominy Swamps—digging trenches, piling fortifications and the like, while strong and willing hands await only to be invited to do this laborious service, that they may show their appreciation of the glorious boon of freedom.

As the year 1862 drew to a close, it became evident to Lincoln that the manpower necessities of the North had made for a weakening of long-held fears about the Negro as soldier—fears that he lacked the qualities of a fighting man, fears that arming the Negro might be construed as an admission that white soldiers had not been equal to the job, fears that to put a gun in the hands of the Negro might lead to slave insurrections, and the deep, although unspoken, fear that to make the Negro a soldier would bring about a change in his status in American life.

Never the one to leap before looking, Lincoln had waited until he felt that the people of the North had been brought up to the proper pitch on Negro levies. And possibly, too, by January 1, 1863, Lincoln himself may have modified his opinion about the Negro as a fighting man. On November 8, 1862, Senator Sumner had sent to the White House a copy of George Livermore's *An Historical Research: Opinions of the Founders of the Republic on Negroes as Slaves, as Citizens, and as Soldiers.* This was a lengthy pamphlet, whose contents Livermore had read before the Massachusetts Historical Society on August 14, and which the society had offered to bring out at its own expense. Destined to be republished several times, Livermore's carefully documented pamphlet showed that large numbers of Negroes, slave and free, had borne arms in the Revolutionary War.

Livermore's study "interested President Lincoln much," asserted Charles Sumner, adding that Lincoln consulted it while working on the Emancipation Proclamation. On Christmas Eve the President told Sumner that he had mislaid the pamphlet and wanted to read it again. "I told him," wrote Sumner to Livermore on December 25, 1862, "that he should have my copy, and I accordingly sent it to him this Xmas morning." On that same day Sumner wrote about Lincoln to another of his blue-blood constituents, John Murray Forbes: "He let me know last evening of his plan to employ African troops to hold the Mississippi River, and other posts in the warm climates."

Finally the reasons for enlisting Negroes in the Union forces became so compelling as to convince a man of Lincoln's caution. On January 1, 1863, twenty months after the outbreak of the war, he authorized the enrollment of freed slaves in the army and navy. Even then his approach was indirect. His announcement about arming the Negro was tagged on to the Emancipation Proclamation, almost like an afterthought.

THE SANCTION of Negro levies by the Commander in Chief of the Union's armed forces marked the beginning of the large-scale tapping of this great reservoir of manpower. Prior to January 1,

1863, a handful of colored regiments had been organized, notably the First Regiment Kansas Colored Volunteers, the First Regiment Louisiana Native Guards, and the First South Carolina Volunteers. These regiments, however, were considered trial balloons and were intended primarily for local service.

Lincoln's go-ahead signal found a ready response in Northern state capitals. Many governors, desperately anxious to fill their quotas, now saw a solution to their problem. The lead was taken by John A. Andrew, the able wartime governor of Massachusetts. On January 26, 1863, at his own request, Andrew received authorization from Secretary of War Stanton to recruit "persons of African descent, organized into separate corps."

Boston's young Charles R. Lowell was not hopeful about Andrew's efforts to raise a colored regiment. "The blacks here are too comfortable to do anything more than talk about freedom," wrote he to his mother on February 4, 1863. But within a few weeks the first recruits of the Massachusetts Fifty-fourth Regiment were drilling at Readville. The example set by the Bay State was soon followed by several of her sister commonwealths, including Connecticut, Rhode Island, Pennsylvania, Ohio, Illinois, Indiana, Michigan, Iowa, and Kansas.

In New York the enlistment of Negro troops was handled by the Union League Club, whose five hundred members were well heeled and influential. When the governor of the state, Horatio Seymour, refused to take any action on enlisting Negroes, a delegation of prominent New Yorkers journeyed to the White House on May 30, 1863. Lincoln was sympathetic, but he told the visitors that the War Department was not inclined to act unless the governor of the state refused to do so. Such was precisely what happened: Seymour stated that he would not authorize Negro troops, whereupon Secretary Stanton granted such authorization to the Union League Club. Quickly uniting with the Association for Promoting Colored Volunteering, the Union League Club established a camp at Rikers Island, and in less than two months a regiment of 1000 Negroes, the Twentieth United States Colored Troops, had been organized.

In New York the efforts of prominent whites were seconded by Negroes. In the middle of March 1863 a delegation from Pough-keepsie succeeded in getting an audience with Lincoln, their pur-pose being to offer him the services of 10,000 "sable sons, called the Frémont Legion." The visiting Negroes hailed Lincoln as a de-liverer and a lamp by which their feet were guided. They informed him that their fathers had fought and died at New Orleans, Horse-shoe Bend, Pensacola, and Red Bank and on Lake Erie, Lake Champlain, and the Mediterranean.

When this short recitation was over, Lincoln replied that he recognized that the Negro was both patriotic and liberty-loving. Moreover, the government certainly wanted to obtain colored troops. But, explained the Chief Executive, there was one difficulty in giving a command to John C. Frémont: a second-ranking officer in the army, Frémont was entitled to a department, but at the moment there was no such vacancy.

The idea of a Frémont legion was pressed by Charles Sumner. Lincoln, in a letter of June 1 to the Massachusetts senator, repeated that he would be pleased to put 10,000 Negroes in the field under Frémont, but that he could not give the commander a department right then. A week later Frémont took himself out of the picture, writing to Sumner that the project never had his approval inasmuch as he was opposed to sending colored troops in the field in scattered and weak detachments.

Despite such all-out efforts as were made in New York, the recruiting of Negroes in the states above the Mason and Dixon Line encountered a major handicap—the relatively sparse Negro population. Many potential Negro soldiers were available, however, in those portions of the South that had come under the Union flag. Congress came to the aid of the states by passing a conscription act (July 4, 1864) which authorized Northern governors to send agents into the rebel states to enlist Negroes, who would be credited to the state's quota. Recruiting agents for the Northern states found the pickings quite meager, enlisting fewer than 6000 former slaves.

The number of state recruits in the South would have been larger if some Union generals had not been openly hostile. Commanders in the field wanted no tampering with their black military laborers. William T. Sherman in particular had an aversion to recruiting agents, and he took out on them his dislike of the prevailing policy whereby a drafted man could avoid military service by furnishing a substitute. In a telegram to General Halleck on July 14, 1864, Sherman gave vent to his feelings about recruiters: "I will not have a set of fellows hanging around on such pretenses." Halleck turned the message over to the White House.

Lincoln had a tender spot for a battle-winning officer. On July 18 he sent a telegram asking Sherman's co-operation and explaining the reasons for using recruiting agents: "Many of the States were very anxious for it, and I hoped that, with their State bounties, and active exertions, they would get out substantial additions to our colored forces, which, unlike white recruits, help us where they come from, as well as where they go to."

The chief reason for the small catch in the South by state recruiting agents was the formidable rivalry of the national government itself. Shortly after Lincoln had given his blessing to the recruiting of Negroes, the War Department launched its own program to raise an army of blacks. On March 25, 1863, Secretary Stanton dispatched Lorenzo Thomas, adjutant general of the army, to the Mississippi Valley, to organize Negro brigades and to appoint field and company officers for them. Stanton made it clear that Lincoln stood clearly behind the order:

> The President desires that you should confer freely with Major General Grant, and the officers with whom you may have communication, and explain to them the importance attached by the Government to the use of the colored population emancipated by the President's Proclamation, and particularly for the organization of their labor and military strength.

With Thomas assigned to the Mississippi Valley region, Lincoln quickly turned his attention to the lower areas bisected by the river.

On March 23, 1863, he wrote to commanding officer Nathaniel P. Banks, with headquarters at Opelousas, Louisiana, informing him that General Daniel Ullman and some two or three hundred subordinates were being sent to the Department of the Gulf to raise a Negro brigade. "To avail ourselves of this element of force," explained Lincoln, "is very important, if not indispensable." Lincoln requested that Banks support this Negro soldier effort, especially since his own ranks were soon to be greatly reduced by the expiration of terms of enlistment.

Always needing more men, Banks gave full support to the order from the White House. On May 1, 1863, he ordered a whole army corps to be raised. This "Corps d'Afrique," as Banks designated it, was to consist of eighteen regiments of 500 men each, representing all arms—infantry, artillery, and cavalry. No abolitionist, Banks made it clear that this unit was not to be organized upon any racial theories of equality but as a practical matter of business. The government should use Negroes just as it "makes use of mules, horses, uneducated and educated white men, in the defense of its institutions."

The orders from Washington to Thomas and Banks pointed the way for the major step of systematizing Negro recruitment. On May 22, 1863, the War Department established the Bureau of Colored Troops, under the adjutant general's office, with authority to supervise the organizing of Negro units and to examine candidates seeking commissions in them. "With the publication of this order," writes Dudley T. Cornish, "the whole movement to arm the Negro moved off its original amateurish, haphazard, and volunteer basis to a new footing of professional, organized, regularized activity under central control from Washington."

The work of the Bureau of Colored Troops had the full support of the White House. On July 21, 1863, Lincoln requested Stanton to make a renewed and vigorous effort to raise black troops along the Mississippi Valley. The Chief Magistrate added that he thought that General Thomas was the best man for the job. Lincoln's tribute to Thomas was deserved: in less than three months he had raised twenty regiments.

Lincoln spoke of Thomas' services in a letter to General Grant on August 9, 1863. Thomas had returned to the Mississippi Valley to raise colored troops, Lincoln wrote, adding that he was sure that Grant was doing all he could in that respect. "I believe it is a resource which, if vigorously applied now, will soon close the contest." The opening of the Mississippi, said Lincoln, in oblique reference to Grant's great victory at Vicksburg, made it practicable to recruit at least 100,000 Negroes along the river's shores.

Negro recruitment along the Atlantic, as along the Mississippi, found a strong supporter in Lincoln. He knew of the efforts to raise black troops in Florida, where colored units were to see much action in the numerous raiding expeditions along the coast. "I am glad to see the accounts of your colored force at Jacksonville, Florida," he wrote to General Hunter on April 1, 1863. "I see the enemy are driving at them fiercely, as is to be expected. It is important to the enemy that such a force shall *not* take shape, and grow, and thrive, in the South; and in precisely the same proportion, it is important to us that it *shall*."

ALTHOUGH LINCOLN wanted to induce the former slaves to join the army, he was reluctant to make use of Negroes as recruiters. Reflecting the President's wishes, the War Office pointedly ignored the suggestion repeatedly made by Major George L. Stearns, a Boston merchant who had befriended John Brown, that Negroes be employed in the recruiting service. The military authorities at Washington turned down requests from Negro applicants. Martin R. Delany, whose face "shone like black Italian marble," and self-made John Jones, a Chicago tailor worth $30,000, wrote a joint letter to Stanton on December 15, 1863, offering to raise "a regiment or brigade in a shorter time than could otherwise be effected." Delany had behind him nearly a year of successful recruiting for Massachusetts, Rhode Island, and Connecticut. But from Stanton came no reply.

Lincoln's coolness toward the use of Negroes as recruiters stemmed from his ever-present concern about the border states. "It seems to me we could send white men to recruit better than to send Negroes," wrote he on October 22, 1863, to a commanding officer at Baltimore.

But although he disliked to ruffle the touchy border states, Negro recruitment had become too vitally important to exempt them from it. With the program going on apace in the North and in the Union-held portions of the Confederacy, Lincoln and the War Department were ready to give attention to the last remaining untapped source of black manpower under the Stars and Stripes.

In the border region the national government had to take the initiative, as state officials had no stomach for Negro soldiers. Governors in these states reflected the fears of their constituents, who sensed that the recruiting of Negroes would undermine slavery and drastically reduce their labor supply. Border state masters knew that the slaves taken by the military authorities would be "prime stock," the cream of the crop. Moreover, the great majority of whites in these loyal slaveholding states wanted no gun-bearing Negroes stationed in their midst.

Lincoln did not propose to ignore the vast black potential in these states, but he was hopeful that Negro recruitment therein could be conducted without too much of an outcry and without issuing a general order. But the administration's hand was forced by events in Maryland. On June 30, 1863, General Robert C. Schenck, from his headquarters at Baltimore, wired the White House requesting permission to organize a regiment of sappers and miners from among the 4000 able-bodied Negroes at work on the fortifications. Four days later Schenck wired that his request must be answered quickly because he would be discharging these military laborers in a day or two. Moreover, added Schenck, some 200 Negroes from Cambridge on the Eastern Shore had come in that very day offering to shoulder a gun. Lincoln replied that night, promising an answer within twenty-four hours, and on July 6, Stanton notified Schenck that the Bureau of Colored Troops would issue an order authorizing him to raise a Negro regiment in his department.

The enlistment of blacks in Maryland did not proceed quietly. Recruiting officers found it hard to keep their hands off the slaves of loyal Marylanders. Colonel William Birney, the muster officer at Baltimore and son of the abolitionist politician James G. Birney, did not bother to check carefully on his subordinates. Birney's men would go into a neighborhood, establish themselves at a centrally located warehouse or barn, and then fan out in parties into the surrounding country, visiting each plantation and taking its black workers. A slave would be induced to throw down his hoe and join up on the spot, his owner standing by, helpless and infuriated.

Getting no satisfaction from Birney, Maryland masters took their appeal to Annapolis. Governor Augustus W. Bradford responded by drawing up a letter to Lincoln, protesting the enlistment of the slaves of loyal citizens. Not bothering with mail delivery, Bradford entrusted his letter to former Governor Thomas H. Hicks and Senator Reverdy Johnson, who brought it to Washington. Bradford's messengers found Lincoln quite sympathetic, and they left the White House with the presidential promise that Negro recruitment in Maryland would be suspended for ninety days.

As good as his word, Lincoln ordered the Union commander at Baltimore to stop recruiting Negroes until further notice. A copy of this order was to go to Colonel Birney, added Lincoln in a postscript line. Two days later, on October 3, 1863, Lincoln sent Birney a direct message, asking him to state the number of slaves he enlisted in Maryland. From Birney came an immediate reply that the figure ranged between 1250 and 1300. Lincoln's terse note had not ordered Birney to suspend black recruitments, but the young officer, catching the hint, proceeded to obey the unwritten directive.

Birney never lost his bad name with Marylanders, however, and perhaps with some cause. On January 10, 1864, the state Senate voted to appoint a committee to confer with President Lincoln about Birney's misdeeds in sending 150 Negro soldiers into two counties—Charles and St. Mary's—with orders to recruit slaves who were able-bodied and to free those who were not. The measure, however, was lost in the lower house, 26 for and 27 against.

The clash between Birney and the slaveowners impelled the administration to formulate a clear-cut policy. On October 3, 1863, the War Department ordered the establishment of Negro recruiting offices in Maryland, Missouri, and Tennessee. These stations were authorized to enroll three categories of colored men: free Negroes, slaves of disloyal masters, and slaves of loyal masters who had given their permission. These loyal masters were to receive $300 for each slave; in turn, the master must sign a deed of manumission. The order also addressed itself to the possibility that not enough Negroes might be secured from the three categories. If such were the case, recruiting officers were authorized to enlist slaves of loyal masters without the consent of the masters. In each state a special board would be appointed to pass on the validity of claims made by owners.

The last border state to become a recruiting ground for Negroes was Kentucky. The delay in getting around to her sprang from a reluctance to stir up a hornet's nest. It was always Lincoln's wish that the enlistment of Negroes should be conducted "with as little collateral provocation" as possible, as he wrote to General William S. Rosecrans on April 4, 1864. But in Kentucky a recruiter of Negroes was by his very existence the source and the object of considerable provocation.

Kentucky had shown its temper in the summer of 1863 when recruiting officers proposed to consider the state's free Negroes as subject to the comprehensive draft measure passed by Congress on March 3, 1863. Kentucky's violent reaction to having her free Negroes included in the draft brought telegrams to the White House in late June 1863 from commanding officers Jeremiah T. Boyle and Ambrose E. Burnside, asking that the War Department abandon any such intention. In exchange for the small number of men that might be obtained, cautioned Burnside, "we will lose a much larger number of good white volunteers & give the secret enemies of the Government a weapon to use against it." On June 28 Lincoln sent Burnside's telegram to Stanton, penning on it the notation: "I really think the within is worth considering."

Kentucky's hostility to Negro recruitment succeeded only in delaying the step for a few months; by the end of the year the national government was no longer disposed to yield to local sentiment. In January 1864 the War Department extended its operations into Kentucky by authorizing a Negro recruiting post at Paducah.

Governor Bramlette immediately got off a long letter of protest to Lincoln, dated February 1, 1864. Kentucky was a loyal state, he lectured, with power over its militia. The national government had no legal right to recruit in the state. The employment of Negro troops was unnecessary, added Bramlette; moreover, a recruiting officer faced a jail term of from two to twenty years if he enlisted the slave of a loyal master or prevented a master from recovering his runaway. Bramlette concluded by requesting that Negro recruitment in Kentucky be stopped at once.

What Lincoln did was to turn the letter over to the War Department. Equal to the task, Stanton took up Bramlette's points one by one, answering them in, for him, an unusually courteous tone, but yielded not an inch. In his opinion, added Stanton, recruiting in Kentucky did not impugn the loyalty of the state or disrespect for its governor. Hence, in view of all considerations, he hoped that Bramlette would concur in the action of the military authorities.

The Kentucky governor was not won over, however, and soon sought an opportunity to lay his views before Lincoln in person. On March 26, 1864, in company with former Senator Archibald Dixon and newspaper editor Albert G. Hodges, Bramlette called at the White House to protest against Negro levies. To the three fellow Kentuckians, Lincoln expressed himself at length, discoursing on slavery, emancipation, and the will of God. (At Hodges's subsequent request Lincoln sent him a letter, dated April 4, 1864, spelling out the thoughts he had expressed at this meeting—a letter

noteworthy for revealing his long-held views on slavery and emancipation.) Coming to the matter at hand, Lincoln promised that
no Negro would be enlisted in any Kentucky county that furnished
its quota of white men, and that any Negroes who were recruited
would be sent out of the state for their training. Two days later
Lincoln informed Stanton of the visit of the Bramlette trio, adding
that the recruitment or the drafting of Kentucky Negroes should
be conducted as far as possible without disorder or provocations.

Lincoln had promised Kentucky that she could avoid Negro
troops if she furnished enough whites. But after three months of
grace the counties still had not met their draft quotas. Hence, on
June 13, 1864 the War Department decreed that Kentucky slaves
should be recruited regardless of the wishes of their masters.
"Union men will cheerfully bring forth their slaves," ran the
order, "and if others do not, it makes no difference, as all who
present themselves for enlistment will be received." This order also
charged Augustus L. Chetlain with the organization of colored
regiments, subject to General Thomas' instructions, with headquarters at Louisville.

Negro recruitment was more bitterly resented in Kentucky than
anywhere else. To some degree this resentment was brought on by
overzealous officers who recruited by force, seizing Negroes against
their will. Lincoln was firmly against such strong-arm methods; on
June 13, 1864, he wired General Thomas at Louisville that complaints had reached the White House that military men in the
vicinity of Henderson, Kentucky, were carrying Negroes off without
their consent. Replying at once, Thomas assured the President that
he would take immediate steps to put an end to such practices.

But the abuse lingered on. In a letter to Stanton in early February 1865, Lincoln ordered him to look into the allegations that
recruiting officers around Maryville, Kentucky, were using violence
to get Negroes to join the army. Lincoln had in mind the charges
against Colonel John Glenn, of the One Hundred Twentieth
Colored Infantry, to whom he sent a stern wire on February 7:

Complaint is made to me that you are forcing Negroes into the Military service, and even torturing them—riding them on rails and the like—to extort their consent. I hope this may be a mistake. The like must not be done by you, or any under you. You must not force Negroes any more than white men. Answer me on this.

To Kentuckians these attempts by Lincoln to correct abuses in Negro recruitment were like putting perfume on a skunk. Negro troops, however carefully recruited, simply were not wanted. In 1864, when the colored regiments stationed at Louisville got ready to attend a Fourth of July picnic arranged for them by local Negroes, General Chetlain ordered each man to carry ten rounds of ammunition for his own protection. But despite the widespread hostility of the white population, the recruitment of Negroes in Lincoln's native state appreciably swelled the Union ranks. Of the 186,017 blacks who wore the blue, 23,703 came from Kentucky, which was second only to Louisiana with 24,052.

Kentucky illustrated a general truth: the Negro tended to respond willingly to invitations to join the army. In part this response was a tribute to the skill of recruiting agents, who were well schooled in the types of appeal that went over best. Negroes in the North were told that they should enlist because they were citizens with a citizen's responsibilities. Slaves in the border states were told that as soon as they signed up for military service, they would be freed on the spot. Former slaves in the Confederate states were told that by becoming soldiers they would learn the use of arms and thus be prepared to defend their newly won liberty.

Not the least among the techniques of persuasion used by recruiting agents was the magic name of Lincoln. In northern Alabama James T. Ayres, an ex-clergyman of salty temper who was "geathering up Sambo," made effective use of a large recruiting poster bearing the legend: "ALL SLAVES WERE MADE FREEMEN BY ABRAHAM LINCOLN, PRESIDENT OF THE UNITED STATES. Come, then, able-bodied COLORED

MEN, to the nearest United States Camp, and fight for the STARS AND STRIPES!"

ONCE IN THE ARMY, the Negro soldier found himself discriminated against in promotion practices, in pay, and in service assignments. Moreover, he faced special dangers: the medical care he received was far below that of his white counterpart; he was given far more than his share of inferior and obsolete weapons; and in battle engagements he was far more likely than a white soldier to be slain rather than captured. And, finally, if he fell into the hands of the enemy, he faced the prospect of being treated as a slave in rebellion rather than as a prisoner of war.

President Lincoln found it convenient to remain in official ignorance—that protective cloak of the busy executive—of some of the discriminations and dangers faced by the colored soldier, but on some others he was obliged to express an opinion or take a stand. An example of his response to discriminations against the Negro soldier may be described first.

One of the complaints of the Negro volunteer was that he had little chance of rising to the rank of commissioned officer. The Lincoln administration was reluctant to grant a commission to a Negro, even though colored troops were organized into segregated units. Out of a total of 7122 commissioned officers in Negro regiments, fewer than 100 were colored men, and nearly three-quarters of these were in one department—the Department of the Gulf.

The attitude of the Lincoln administration toward making officers of Negroes was illustrated by the experience of Stephen A. Swails, a first sergeant in Company F of the Massachusetts Fifty-fourth. For his soldierly qualities and for his bravery at Olustee, Florida, on February 20, 1864, the battle-wounded Swails was recommended for a commission by his colonel, E.N. Hallowell. Governor Andrew was, of course, pleased to comply. But there was one hitch: before Swails could receive a lieutenancy, he first had to be discharged as a sergeant. And the War Department simply refused to grant Swails a discharge. To Secretary Stanton came protests from the regiment, from the commanding officer in the Department of the South, and from John Andrew. Bitterly did the Massachusetts governor complain of the behavior of the War Department: "I wonder *Scipio Africanus* is not struck out of the list of Roman Heroes, on account of his cognomen." Finally, on January 17, 1865, after a wait of ten months, Swails was commissioned a second lieutenant.

A Negro less fortunate than Swails was Frederick Douglass who, during the spring and early summer of 1863, had been busy signing up Negroes for the army. On August 10, 1863, Douglass, in company with Senator Pomeroy, called at the White House. Lincoln listened attentively as the orator-reformer proceeded to air the grievances of the colored soldier, among them the failure to be promoted. Responding point by point, Lincoln reached the item about officer promotion. This he handled in one sentence, stating that he would "sign any commission to colored soldiers whom his Secretary of War commended."

Taking the President at his word, Douglass hastened to the War Department, bent on obtaining a commission. He had not served in the ranks—he was then over forty-five years old—but he had proved himself to be an able recruiter. Ushered into Stanton's presence, Douglass told the Secretary that he was willing to accept a military commission. Taken off guard, Stanton found himself promising to make Douglass an assistant adjutant general on the staff of Lorenzo Thomas, then in the Mississippi Valley region. As he walked out of Stanton's office, Douglass was in high spirits. "Frederick intends to go forth and help the recruiting among his people," observed Lincoln's secretary, John Hay, in his diary on August 11, after commenting on the Negro leader's visit to the White House.

Douglass took the first train to his home in Rochester, New York, to bring out the last issue of his monthly magazine and to wind up his affairs as a civilian. Within a day after his arrival, he received a letter from the adjutant general's office instructing him to report to General Thomas at Vicksburg. But the envelope contained no commission. Douglass wrote to the War Office, asking clarification of his official status or position. Back came a reply from the adjutant general's office, stating that he would be paid by Major George L. Stearns, but making no mention of a commission. A week later Stearns wrote, telling him that his salary would be $100 a month, plus subsistence. This was not a bad rate of pay, but for the third time no commission was mentioned.

The commission never came; Douglass never wore the Union blue. The administration—Lincoln or Stanton or both—had doubtless come to the conclusion that such a step was a little too radical just then. Although civilians, Lincoln and Stanton did not need to be told that the way to make good soldiers was to inspire them to become officers. But the President and his War Secretary also knew that concessions must be made to public opinion.

Another administration concession to popular prejudice was in pay: there was a differential of $6 a month between white and Negro soldiers. The former received $13 a month plus clothing, whereas the latter received $10 a month, $3 of which could be clothing. The Negro soldier was paid in accordance with the rate established for military laborers in the act of July 17, 1862. This measure did not have soldiers in mind, but the solicitor of the War Department, William Whiting, in a ruling on June 4, 1863, held that it must apply to Negro troops until Congress took appropriate action.

The men of the Fifty-fourth, anxious to let Lincoln know their sentiments, sent him a letter on 23 September 1863, which had been drafted by Corporal James Henry Gooding, who was destined to be mortally wounded at Olustee within five months. Gooding's letter first took up the question: Were they soldiers, or were they laborers?

> Let their dusky forms rise up, out of the mires of James Island, and give the answer. Let the rich mould around Wagner's parapets be upturned, and there will be found an eloquent answer. Obedient and patient and solid as a wall are they.

The Negro had done a soldier's duty, avowed Gooding, and he was entitled to a soldier's pay; all he lacked was "a paler hue and a better acquaintance with the alphabet." Spokesman Gooding wanted Lincoln to know that the free Negro of the North did not care to be measured by the slave in the South, and that the Fifty-fourth was not enlisted under any act relating to contrabands; its members were free by birth.

Leaving the lofty heights for a moment, Gooding struck a practical note. Black men were poor, and $3 a month would supply their needy wives and little ones with fuel. Let the government give the Negro equal pay, concluded the corporal, and his patriotism and his enthusiasm would be fired anew.

Particularly upset about the lower pay to Negro troops was Governor John A. Andrew, who had promised the men of the Fifty-fourth and the Fifty-fifth that they would receive the same treatment as the white regiments. With the state's good name at stake, Andrew requested the General Assembly to appropriate funds to make up the difference in pay. The lawmakers did so on November 16. But the Fifty-fourth, a proud regiment which had made a name for itself in the storming of Battery Wagner in Charleston Harbor, would not permit Andrew to make up for Abraham. "What false friend has been misrepresenting us to the Governor," wrote one of the men, "to make him think our necessities outweigh our self-respect?"

At their camp on Folly Island the soldiers were called together on December 14, 1863, by Major Russell Sturgis, who told them that it would be quite honorable to accept the money offered by Massachusetts. A Negro sergeant, James M. Trotter, stepped forward and explained the point of view of the men. Sturgis confessed that he agreed with them. Whereupon the regiment dispersed after giving three cheers for Andrew and Sturgis. The next day "the government pay master came with his large iron chest with as much as his horse could draw," wrote Private Western H. Moore to his parents on December 16, "but with a few exceptions had to drive on to the next camp."

Governor Andrew was a bit nettled by the action of the colored soldiers in refusing his offer. But he was also proud of them and more determined than ever to work on their behalf. Deciding to carry his appeal direct to the White House, he selected as a test case the chaplain of the Massachusetts Fifty-fourth, Samuel Harrison, whose application for a chaplain's salary of $100 a month had been turned down by the paymaster at Hilton Head, South Carolina, on the familiar grounds that colored people came under the act of July 17, 1862, and hence were entitled to $10 a month, and no more. Andrew drew up a letter, dated March 24, 1864, about the Harrison case and asked Charles Sumner to deliver it to the White House in person.

Lincoln had no love for any letter bearing the signature of the forceful and hard-driving governor of Massachusetts, and this one in particular he found vexatious. The equal-pay matter was then before Congress, in whose hands Lincoln was quite willing to dump the whole matter. A presidential campaign was coming up, and Lincoln was not anxious to lose political support by pressing for a measure that was unpopular in conservative circles. But Andrew and Sumner were men that even a President could not shrug off. Hence, Lincoln sent the Andrew letter to Edward Bates, accompanied by two questions: "Attorney-General please give me your legal opinion whether the Pay-Master should have paid as demanded, and if yea, is it the duty of the President to order him to pay?"

Bates soon had a reply on Lincoln's desk. It was his opinion, wrote the Attorney General, that Harrison should receive full pay as a chaplain. Moreover, it was the President's constitutional duty to direct the War Department to have its paymasters act in accordance with this "view of the law."

Lincoln sat on the Bates opinion for seven days and would have apparently kept sitting on it had not the Senate got behind him. Doubtless many congressmen knew of the nature of the reply from the Attorney General. At any rate, on April 30 the Senate asked the President to furnish a legal opinion on the equal-pay question.

A week later Lincoln transmitted to the Senate a copy of the Bates opinion.

But Lincoln found himself still pursued by Governor Andrew. In a long letter of May 13, Andrew described the heroism and the privations of the Negro regiments from Massachusetts, and he asked that Lincoln "interpose" his authority as Chief Executive to wipe out pay discrimination. Following through, Andrew sent George S. Hale of Boston, an original sponsor of the Fifty-fourth, to voice a personal appeal. Except for a courteous reception at the White House, Hale got little. He sent word to Andrew that Lincoln told him he wanted to see the colored troops get equal pay, but that he did not act "upon grounds of moral right without regard to his Constitutional powers."

Lincoln did not have much longer to endure the equal-pay advocates. An act of Congress on June 15, 1864, provided that, retroactively as of January 1 of that year, Negro soldiers were to receive the same pay as other troops. Moreover, those Negroes who had been free on April 19, 1861, would be paid the salary difference from the date of their enlistment until January 1, 1864. This latter provision still left out thousands of slave soldiers, and it was not until March 1865, a month before the end of the war, that Congress equalized the pay of all Negroes who had served in the Union armies.

ANOTHER DISCRIMINATION faced by the Negro soldier was the type of duty assigned him. Negro regiments performed an unusual amount of post and fatigue duty. The garrisoning of forts and arsenals, month after month, tended to become dull and demoralizing. Building bridges and throwing up entrenchments and never seeing field service tended to give the black soldier the feeling that he was only a common laborer, despite his uniform. This widespread practice of concentrating noncombatant services in Negro regiments was not halted until the summer of 1864. In mid-June the War Department ordered that Negro troops no longer be required to perform the bulk of the labor on fortifications or to do the bulk of the fatigue duties of the permanent camps and stations. Instead, Negro soldiers should be made ready "for the higher duties of conflict with the enemy." In line with this order, the Negro was to see his share of action before the combat flags were furled; Negro regiments took part in 449 battles, thirty-nine of which were major engagements.

Field service had its special hazards for the Negro soldier. As a rule, the firearms furnished to the colored units were not up to par, being either obsolete or faultily constructed. To Negro regiments went the rifles that had been lying in government storage since the war with Mexico. To Negro regiments went the antique flintlocks muskets which had been condemned by army inspectors.

Inferior weapons increased the risk of a Negro's being captured, and falling into the hands of the enemy was the greatest of all the special dangers the Negro faced. Fear of what might happen to him in Confederate hands must have haunted the dreams of many a black volunteer; for the military and the civilian authorities in the Confederacy were agreed that a captured Negro would be considered not a prisoner of war, but a slave in arms, and as such his punishment would be death.

The Confederacy had not masked its intentions. On August 21, 1862, the War Department at Richmond ordered that Union commanding officers David Hunter and John W. Phelps be treated as outlaws for their efforts to recruit Negroes. If Hunter or Phelps were captured, they were to be held in close confinement for execution as felons. On November 30, 1862, Confederate Secretary of War James A. Seddon, after a conference with Jefferson Davis, ordered the death penalty for four Negroes taken as prisoners. Five months later to the day, the Confederate Congress, in line with previous recommendations made by President Davis, passed a law decreeing that Negroes taken in arms should be dealt with according to the laws of the state in which they were seized. This was the equivalent of a death sentence, since the law in every Confederate state would have branded such Negroes as insurrectionists.

Prior to the assault on Battery Wagner in South Carolina waters on July 18, 1863, there was some doubt in the minds of Northerners that the Confederacy would carry out these threats. Fort Wagner, holding the key to the sea approaches to the important city of Charleston, had been stormed by Union troops led by the Massachusetts Fifty-fourth. The assault had been repulsed; the colonel of the Negro regiment, Robert Gould Shaw, had lost his life, two of the regiment's captains were missing, and many of the colored soldiers had been taken. The fate of the captured officers and men of the Fifty-fourth aroused much apprehension in the North, especially when it was learned that the young and gallant Colonel Shaw had been buried in a ditch "with his niggers," apparently as an intentional ignominy.

The people of the North could close their eyes to many of the discriminations against the Negro soldier, but they could not let the Confederacy treat him as a slave in arms. Newspaper editors and congressmen, reflecting public opinion, cried out for repayment in kind.

Lincoln, too, was greatly concerned. He had foreseen the problem of the fate of the captured Negro soldier. The Emancipation Proclamation had stipulated that the former slaves who were received into the army should be assigned to garrison duty. One of Lincoln's reasons for this was to protect the Negro soldier by putting him in out-of-the-way spots where he would not be likely to fall into enemy hands. As early as January 10, 1863, Lincoln had summoned to the White House the Secretaries of the Army and the Navy and instructed them to try to confine their use of Negroes to locales where, as Welles puts it in his diary, "they would not be liable to be captured." To Stanton the President suggested two such places: Memphis and Columbus. The Chief Executive had addressed most of his remarks to the Secretary of War, turning to the Secretary of the Navy only long enough to say that he thought that the Negroes on board the Union vessels "were well cared for."

Fort Wagner seemed to confirm Lincoln's long-held fears. With Northern public opinion aroused by the Confederacy's announced policies about Negroes taken in arms—policies that were apparently to be carried out—Lincoln knew that some action by the White House was necessary. One week after Fort Wagner, he sent for General Halleck and told him to prepare an order for the protection of Negro prisoners. The draft submitted by the War Department reflected Lincoln's views, ordering that, for every Union soldier killed in violation of the laws of war, a rebel soldier would be put to death, and that, for every Union soldier sold into slavery, a rebel soldier would be put at hard labor on the public works.

Signed on July 30, this retaliatory order, strong as it was, did not wholly please Charles Russell Lowell, colonel in a Massachusetts cavalry regiment. It was, he wrote to Robert Gould Shaw's sister, "one immediate good out of Rob's death and out of the splendid conduct of his regiment." But at Port Hudson the Negro troops had been treated "just as barbarously," and the administration had not lifted a finger. Moreover, continued young Lowell to his fiancée, "I wish the President had said a rebel soldier shall die for every Negro soldier sold into slavery. He ought to have said so."

If Lincoln's retaliatory order did not wholly please the extreme apostles of an-eye-for-an-eye, it had a marked effect in protecting the great majority of captured Negro soldiers. True enough, there would be isolated instances of Negroes not being treated as prisoners of war—instances of captured Negro soldiers being put to labor or sold into slavery—but, in general, after Lincoln's order of retaliation, the Confederate authorities treated them much the same as they treated white prisoners.

On one point, however, the Confederate military command would not budge: they refused to exchange captured former slaves. The Richmond government could not bring itself to return to the Union armies a Negro who was some Southerner's property. Moreover, to exchange a black man for a white man was to be a party to racial equality.

The uncompromising stand of the Confederacy on this point was matched by that of the Lincoln administration. Unless all prisoners, regardless of color, were exchanged on an even footing, Secretary Stanton favored a policy of exchanging none at all.

"Stanton is entirely right on the black-prisoner question," wrote Charles Russell Lowell to John Murray Forbes on September 17, 1863, "and I think he will yet keep the President straight." The beardless colonel had a comment to make on the cast of the President's mind: "I believe Mr. Lincoln has a way of stating to himself and to others as strongly as may be, the arguments *against* the course he really has in mind to adopt—many women are made so."

The unbending position taken by both the Confederate and the Union authorities on the exchange of Negroes led to a general suspension of exchange in the summer of 1863. During that entire calendar year not a single Negro soldier or an officer in Negro troops was exchanged. However, by the spring of 1864 the hard-pressed Confederacy, feeling the pinch of a growing manpower shortage, decided to back up a bit. The Richmond government instructed its commissioner of exchange to propose that free-born Negroes might be considered as prisoners of war and hence eligible for trading. The Davis administration hoped that this concession would be the opening wedge to a general cartel of exchange.

But the Northern military authorities, now headed by Ulysses S. Grant, wanted no exchange of prisoners of any kind, for by the spring of 1864 the North's superiority in manpower had begun to turn the tide. Grant did not need the Union prisoners held by rebels nearly as much as Lee needed the Confederate prisoners held by the North. But Grant knew that if he had come right out and said that he was against exchange, he would have been loudly denounced in the North, especially with so many stories being circulated about the horrors of the notorious rebel prison pens of Libby and Andersonville. Hence, the unyielding attitude of the South toward exchanging ex-slave soldiers played right into Grant's hands, giving him a plausible excuse for withholding his consent to any proposal of exchange. "A great clamor was raised on this specious pretext in order to reconcile the soldiers and the people of the North to the discontinuance of the exchange, and blind their eyes to the real reason," wrote Confederate commander Jubal A. Early somewhat bitterly.

A final peculiar danger faced by the Negro soldier was that the enemy might prefer to kill him rather than to take him prisoner. A Confederate general like E. Kirby Smith advocated a policy of giving no quarter to armed Negroes and their officers. A bloody incident that seemed to bear out this "no quarter" policy was the so-called "massacre" at Fort Pillow, an earthwork along the Mississippi, not far from Memphis. Here on April 12, 1864, a garrison of 560 Union soldiers, half of them colored, was surprised by a Confederate force led by Nathan B. Forrest. As ruthless as he was able, Forrest held that "war means fighting, and fighting means killing." At Fort Pillow there was much needless slaughtering; many Negroes were put to death while holding their hands above their heads in token of surrender. The losses among colored troops were exceptionally heavy, and Forrest later boasted that the river along the fort was dyed with blood for 200 yards.

Fort Pillow horrified the North. Killing Negro soldiers in cold blood seemed to be an example of racial antagonism at its worst. But regardless of the race angle, the North could not ignore its responsibility to its soldiers. The War Department ordered William T. Sherman at Nashville to have a thorough investigation made on the spot by a competent officer. Congress ordered the Committee on the Conduct of the War to get at the bottom of the incident at once.

Satisfied that the military authorities and Congress were doing all they could about Fort Pillow, the country wanted to know the President's reaction. Lincoln was scheduled to speak at a soldier's relief rally in Baltimore on April 18, six days after Fort Pillow, and he took the occasion to express his views. He noted that there seemed to be some public concern about whether the government was doing its duty to the colored troops. He shared this concern, for it was he who had made the Negro a soldier: "I am responsible for it to the American people, to the Christian world, to history, and on my final account to God." The administration did not propose to dodge its responsibility: "Having determined to use the

Negro as a soldier, there is no way but to give him all the protection given to any other soldier." The Fort Pillow incident was under investigation, said Lincoln, and if a massacre was proved to have taken place, retribution must come, although in what form he could not say just then.

Days after the Baltimore address, the War Department received a preliminary report about the Fort Pillow affair, a report that supported the massacre and atrocity allegations. By early May the Committee on the Conduct of the War had piled up a formidable body of data against General Forrest and his troops. Lincoln thereupon sent a circular letter to his Cabinet, asking each member to let him have in writing an opinion about what measures of retribution the administration should take.

On May 6 a meeting was held at which each member presented his views. On only one point was the entire Cabinet agreed: the Richmond government should be requested to avow or disavow the massacre. Four members favored confining Confederate prisoners as hostages, as assurances there would be no more Fort Pillows, a proposal that perhaps came the nearest to winning Lincoln's own approval. Three Cabinet officers were opposed to any retaliatory measures except against the actual culprits—Forrest and his men. Particularly, added one Secretary, would retaliatory action be inexpedient at the moment, as the Union was about to launch a major thrust on the battlefield. The meeting was adjourned with no decisive steps taken.

There the matter ended. For in the thunder and smoke of the Battle of the Wilderness, Fort Pillow receded from Lincoln's thoughts and from the public mind. In the rush of events in the spring of 1864, Lincoln was occupied with many matters. To a petition from a group of Congregational clergymen of Chicago proposing a day of national fasting and prayer for Fort Pillow, Lincoln had to wait six weeks before he could get around to sending a reply. And then he had time, he informed the clergymen, only to acknowledge their letter and to thank them for it.

LINCOLN had reason to feel satisfied with the reports of the performance of the colored troops. For, despite the discriminations and dangers he encountered, the Negro soldier as a rule made a special effort to do his best. "I have given the subject of arming the Negro my hearty support," wrote General Grant on August 23, 1863, from Cairo, Illinois. "This, with the emancipation . . . is the heavyest [sic] blow yet given the Confederacy." A few days after receiving this letter, Lincoln read it to Secretary Chase, along with a similar one from General Banks praising the combat efficiency of the Corps d'Afrique. "These letters," wrote Chase in his diary on August 29, "gave much satisfaction to the President."

From the Secretary of War came a glowing appraisal of Negro troops, expressed in a long letter justifying the recruitment of Negroes in the border states. Wrote Stanton to his superior on February 8, 1864, "At Milliken's Bend, at Port Hudson, Morris Island and other battlefields, they have proved themselves among the bravest of the brave, performing deeds of daring and shedding their blood with a heroism unsurpassed by soldiers of any other race."

Such reports left their impress on Lincoln. Writing to James C. Conkling on August 26, 1863, he said: "Some of the commanders in the field who have given us our most important successes believe the emancipation policy, and the use of colored troops, constitute the heaviest blow yet dealt to the rebellion; and that at least one of those important successes could not have been achieved when it was, but for the aid of the black soldiers." In this appraisal of the role of the Negro, Lincoln was, of course, borrowing the exact language of the letter he had received from Grant.

In his annual message of December 8, 1863, the Chief Magistrate had a restrained word of approval for the blacks in military service: "So far as tested, it is difficult to say they are not as good soldiers as any." Four months later he was able to present a more rounded evaluation. Writing to a Kentucky editor on April 4, 1864, Lincoln pointed out that the use of colored troops had brought with it no "loss" in foreign relations, in home populai sentiment, or in "our white military force." On the contrary, he added, the step had gained for the Union cause 130,000 soldiers, seamen, and laborers. Later in the year Lincoln reaffirmed this opinion of the role of the black man. The North could not spare the Negroes now serving it, wrote Lincoln on September 12, in replying to a letter of invitation to a political rally in Buffalo. Making use of the Negro was not a question of sentiment or taste, he added, but of physical force: "Keep it and you save the Union. Throw it away, and the Union goes with it."

IN LINCOLN'S THINKING, the colored man was every bit as important to the South as to the Union. Lincoln's view of the role of the Negro in the Confederacy was revealed in his comments about the enactment by the Richmond government of a slave-soldier bill. In the winter of 1864-65 the dying Confederacy, in the final throes of desperation, debated anew the issue of making soldiers of its Negroes. Having left his mark in Georgia, Union commander William T. Sherman was marching through the Carolinas, and something had to be done. But to make the Negro a soldier was a most painful step to the Confederate authorities, as it was in essence a repudiation of the traditions of the South. The advocates of a Negro-soldier bill might have lost but for the stand taken by General in Chief Robert E. Lee, the most revered figure in the South. In a letter to a Confederate congressman on February 18, 1865, Lee made his position clear. "In my opinion, the Negroes, under proper circumstances, will make efficient soldiers. I think we could at least do as well with them as the enemy, and he attaches great importance to their assistance." On March 13, 1865, President Davis signed the Negro-soldier law.

This move disturbed Lincoln not in the least. Four days later, speaking to an Indiana regiment that had come to serenade him, Lincoln pointed out one hard fact. The Negro could not do two things at once: he could not fight in the Confederate armies and at the same time "stay at home and make bread for them." That being true, it mattered little whether or not the slaves of the enemy became soldiers. But he tended to favor the measure, added Lincoln in a mellow mood, and would, if he could, "have loaned them a vote to carry it."

LINCOLN'S OPINION that the Negro soldier was "as good as any" seems to have been essentially sound. Of course, colored regiments had their quota of those who would have preferred to hire a substitute. Five days after the conscription law of 3 March 1863, Jason B. Moore, writing to his brother from Clermont County, Ohio, confessed a coolness to military service. "I have no inclination to go to war," said he. "I had as soon pay three hundred dollars if I had it." Moreover, Negro regiments had their deserters: nearly 15,000 colored men took informal leave of the service during the course of the war. A heavy preponderance of Negroes, however, served out their periods of enlistment. "The number of desertions have been few," wrote General Lorenzo Thomas on December 24, 1863, concerning the 20,830 Negroes he had recruited up to that time.

The typical colored volunteer made a dependable and resolute soldier. He was fighting for the Union, as were all Northerners. But the Negro soldier was also fighting for a country in which freedom would no longer be a dream deferred. He was fighting for a new dignity and self-respect, for an America in which his children would have greater liberties and greater responsibilities. To dress in military uniform was to the Negro the ultimate accolade; it was to put on the whole armor of freedom. "With these troops," wrote a *New York Tribune* reporter on December 14, 1863, after watching a review of the thirty regiments of the Corps d'Afrique, "we have an army that will fight forever rather than have Government fail."

The morale of the Negro soldier was good, because he felt that the army had something to offer him. It was a step upward in the social scale. It offered him a chance to learn to read and write, to do something about his longing for an education. To the ex-slave the army offered the opportunity of making something of himself. The army would help to prepare him for the responsibilities that would await him when the guns were stacked. To the Negro, military service was less of a Glory Road than it was a pathway to citizenship.

Moreover, the Negro soldier in the main found army life exhilarating—with its din and bustle, its marching and countermarching to the music of bugle, fife, and drum, with flags and colors waving. To wear their soldier suits—the dark blue, brass-buttoned blouse, light blue trousers, and rounded cap—was, literally and figuratively, to be dressed to kill.

A final contributing factor to the morale of the Negro volunteer was his attitude toward Lincoln. The President's great popularity among soldiers was fully shared by the Negro units. At Port Hudson on Christmas of 1863 the men of the Seventh Regiment of the Corps d'Afrique began the day with amusements—the greased pole, the sack race, and the greased pig. But as noon neared, they gathered at the schoolhouse, their purpose—as defined by a tall orderly—"to afford de soldiers of de Seventh an opportunity for expressin' dere feelings for dis first free Christmas." These feelings were set forth in a formal resolution, unanimously approved by the regiment: "We cannot express in words our love for the President of the United States, as language is too weak to convey that estimation in which we hold him."

In other theaters of war the sentiment was the same. In the late afternoon of June 21, 1864, when Lincoln was making a return ride after visiting General Grant's headquarters at City Point, his party met a brigade of Negro troops. When the men recognized Lincoln, they rushed forward yelling, "Hurrah for the Liberator, Hurrah for the President." It was, wrote Sylvanus Cadwaller, a spontaneous outburst of love and affection for Lincoln, who took off his hat as he rode through the ranks, bowing from one side to the other.

THE GOOD WILL that Lincoln and the Negro volunteer felt for one another was not unlike the feeling between the President and the Negro on the home front in the months following the Emancipation Proclamation. Yet this mutual relationship had its own manifestations and its own importance, and to these we now turn.

8

A STAKE IN AMERICA

FORMER SLAVE Don Carlos Butler had a problem he wished to share with President Abraham Lincoln. Don Carlos wanted to buy the land on which he lived at Frogmore on St. Helena's in the Sea Islands. He had already planted cotton, and the potatoes and corn were "coming along very pretty." What he wanted to find out from Mr. Lincoln was whether the land would be put up for sale and, if so, how much it would cost. In his letter, dated May 29, 1864, Don Carlos admitted he was getting along in years, "for I waited upon Mrs. Alston that was Theodosia Burr, daughter of Aaron Burr, and I remember well when she was taken by the pirates." But he was sure, added Don Carlos, that he could support himself and his family, and he would rather do his own farming than work for someone else, "for if I could sell my cotton for only 30 cts. a pound, it would pay me." The ex-slave ended his petition to Lincoln on a note of complete trust: "Whatever you say I am willing to do." Schoolteacher Laura M. Towne, to whom Don Carlos had dictated his letter, added a postscript: "He with others of the Freedmen often expresses a wish to be able to speak to Massa Linkum feeling that *he* will listen to their plea for land and do what is best for them."

This belief among former slaves that Lincoln was interested in their welfare had some foundation. The fate of the tens of thousands of former slaves who had left, or been left by, their former masters was a problem to which the President gave considerable thought. On July 31, 1863, he had a lengthy talk with John Hay about the freedmen. Hay did not report just what Lincoln said, but the young secretary left the office with the feeling that Lincoln considered the fate of the former slaves "the greatest question ever presented to practical statesmanship." "While the rest," added Hay, "are grinding their little private organs for their own glorification, the old man is working with the strength of a giant and the purity of an angel in this great work." If Hay was overly generous in describing Lincoln's efforts on behalf of the freedmen, he was sound as to Lincoln's interest in them. "How to better the condition of the colored race has long been a study which has attracted my serious and careful attention," wrote Lincoln to James S. Wadsworth in January 1864.

Chaplain John Eaton, who in the summer of 1864 had 113,640 freedmen under his supervision in the Mississippi Valley, confessed himself much surprised by Lincoln's keen interest in them. In two visits to the White House, in July 1863 and thirteen months later, Lincoln questioned Eaton closely about his charges, seeking information as to their reasons for coming into the Union lines, their understanding of "the changes that were coming to them," and their efforts on their own behalf. Eaton noted that in both interviews the President showed an interest not only in the typical freedman, but in the personal traits of those who had demonstrated unusual diligence or ability.

Lincoln's most explicit statement of his interest in the former slave was expressed in a letter of February 15, 1864, to General Daniel E. Sickles. Lincoln asked Sickles to make a trip from Cairo down to New Orleans and then along the Gulf and up to the Atlantic, his mission to gather information he deemed important for the administration to have. Sickles was given full discretion as to what kind of information he would compile, but Lincoln specifically requested that he include the Negro:

> Learn what you can as to the colored people—how they get along as soldiers, as laborers in our service, on leased plantations, and as hired laborers with their old masters, if there be such cases. Also learn what you can about the colored people within the rebel lines.

Lincoln's interest in the freedmen perhaps outran his accomplishments on their behalf. With his own time and energies at a premium, the President could not do everything he might have wished to do for the former slaves. That he was not indifferent to their welfare, however, is shown by his recommendations concerning them and by his observations, spoken and written, about their welfare.

One of the President's earliest recommendations about freedmen resulted from an inquiry made by Ben Butler at New Orleans. In late May 1862, within a few weeks after the Crescent City had fallen into Admiral David G. Farragut's hands, General Butler begged the War Department to advise him what to do about the thousands of Negroes who were flooding into the lines. Stanton's reply, as he made clear to Butler, was a transmittal of the President's recommendations. These former slaves, wrote Stanton, were to be fed and clothed by the commissary and quartermaster departments. Those who were well and healthy should be given jobs at reasonable wages. Stanton's letter emphasized that Lincoln did not mean to establish any general policy by these recommendations; he was simply making provision for that particular case.

Lincoln's reluctance to issue a policy statement on freedmen certainly permitted him the flexibility of meeting each case as it arose. But it did little to solve a problem that became more acute with each passing week. In the fall of 1863 a *Philadelphia Press* reporter stationed in Nashville took note of the great influx of Negroes into the region. These freedmen, he wrote on October 11, 1862, came in from all quarters, entering towns "singly, in pairs, and in settlements."

As of January 1, 1863, Lincoln himself had a hand in this flight of the freedmen. The Emancipation Proclamation actually was little more than an official sanction of a movement that had already gotten under way. The proclamation was an accessory after the fact: Negroes had been making themselves free since the beginning of the war. But the proclamation did tend to increase the readiness of the slave to take flight, emboldening and assuring them once they learned about it.

Lincoln's general attitude toward the freedmen was clear: he held that they should be put to work and that they should be treated fairly. In the Emancipation Proclamation he had recommended to them that they "labor faithfully for reasonable wages." A believer in the principle that government should not do anything for a person that he could do for himself, Lincoln advocated a policy of direct negotiation between the man who needed a laborer and the laborer who needed a job. Hence, Lincoln favored having the freedmen find employment and make salary arrangements on their own initiative, wherever possible.

For freedmen who could find no jobs, Lincoln supported the lessee system. Under this system, more common in the Mississippi Valley than elsewhere, military commanders assigned certain officers to act as superintendents of camps for the unemployed. These superintendents were empowered to hire out such freedmen as could not be profitably employed by the army or on public works. The hiring party was generally a white civilian of unquestioned Union loyalty who had leased the plantations abandoned by, or seized from, the rebels. Such a lessee would put his freedmen employees to work producing cotton, corn, or potatoes, and agreed to feed and clothe them and to pay them a stated sum—generally seven dollars a month for an able-bodied man, with clothing to be deducted.

As to the wage scale, Lincoln favored "fair contracts of hire," as he informed Alpheus Lewis, a cotton merchant operating along the lower Mississippi, who had been put in touch with the White House by influential Kentucky friends. Five weeks later, in a letter to General Thomas of March 1, 1864, Lincoln asked that he assist Lewis in whatever way he could, but that nothing be done that would contravene "fairness to the laborers." Late in July 1863, when Lincoln learned from A.J. Hardee that the freedmen who had been hired to repair the roads around Washington had not been paid "for some time past," he referred the matter to the Secretary of War, pointing out that it "deserves attention."

The lessee system did not work out to the advantage of the freedmen. Many of the lessees were get-rich-quick operators who simply ignored their obligations to their employed hands. This could hardly be blamed on Lincoln: lessees should be men of character, he had written to General Stephen A. Hurlburt at Memphis in August 1863. But, in the absence of a careful screening process, Lincoln's words were little more than an exercise in wishful thinking.

In the Sea Island regions the former slaves wished to become their own employers, a step that called for land ownership. Indeed, the South Carolina lowland Negro had a deep desire, unmatched by his brethren elsewhere, to obtain a small farm of his own. Lincoln, in sympathy with this ambition, ordered that the abandoned lands be sold at $1.25 an acre, with first choice going to those already occupying the lot. But again the President's wishes were thwarted. On a technicality his order was set aside by the local tax commissioners, who then proceeded to sell the land in large parcels rather than in small lots. This was good for investors and speculators, but it froze out the former slave who counted his savings in nickels and dimes.

In ADDITION to charging the freedmen to make an honest living, Lincoln besought them to do one other thing: to abstain from violence, except in self-defense. Lincoln's longtime friend, Joshua Speed, had told him, in a letter of September 1, 1861, that "all who live in the slave states have great fear of insurrection." Lincoln needed no such admonition. From the day the war began, his greatest apprehension concerning the slaves had been that they might attempt to stage mass uprisings, smiting and slaying.

Lincoln would consider no scheme that might lead the bondmen to take the law in their own hands. To a proposal brought to him by James R. Gilmore that the Negroes around Murfreesboro, Tennessee, be given military assistance in staging a general insurrection, Lincoln turned thumbs down. A somewhat similar proposal made at the same time, in August 1863, by General Hunter shared a like fate. Hunter asked permission to land a force of 10,000 men at Brunswick and march through Georgia, Alabama, and Mississippi to New Orleans. He would carry arms and ammunition for one hundred thousand slaves, who would join him on the way. His army would subsist on the country, with the abundant corn crop a guarantee against hunger. This movement, said Hunter, would make for a general rebellion among the slaves. Stanton's reply was conclusive, if somewhat less than candid: he said that both he and the President approved the plan, but that they could not spare the men for it.

THE SCHOOLING of the former slaves did not call for any worry by Lincoln. The work of teaching the three "R's," as has been noted, had been taken over by the various freedmen's aid societies. These organizations, numbering some twenty by the middle of 1864, had established schools and hired teachers. But their funds had a limit, and apparently the number of freedmen was without limit, as each week brought in additional thousands. Before the war was over, the relief societies had succeeded in raising one million dollars, but long before then they had come to the conclusion that the federal government alone had the resources to handle the problem.

Early in December 1863, delegates from the large associations brought to the White House a petition that the government establish a bureau of emancipation. The magnitude of the work, stated the petition, was beyond the reach of the freedmen's organizations, being such as to require "government authority, government resources and government ubiquity." An agency was needed that would be both an expression and an organ of the national power. The delegates asked Lincoln to use his influence with Congress to help create such a bureau.

In response Lincoln said that he favored such a step and that he would send Congress a message to that effect. But what he sent to Congress was the petition the delegates had presented to him. However, his covering letter urged the legislators to give the matter their imperative attention.

The need for a federal agency was supported by the American Freedmen's Inquiry Commission, a three-man group appointed in March 1863 by Secretary Stanton to report upon the condition of the former slaves. "For a time we need a freedmen's bureau, but not because these people are Negroes," ran the commission's final report, issued on May 15, 1864, "only because they are men who have been, for generations, despoiled of their rights." The proposal had its opponents on Capitol Hill, and it was not until March 3, 1865, that Congress passed a bill establishing the Bureau of Refugees, Freedmen, and Abandoned Lands. Lincoln signed the measure that very day.

ADVOCATES of a freedmen's bureau could point to one inescapable fact: the Negro problem was not going to be solved by emigration. By the summer of 1864 Negro emigration schemes had received a death blow. The finishing stroke had been the colonization experiment at Cow Island, Haiti, an ill-starred venture in which Lincoln had a hand.

In the late months of 1862, as noted in an earlier chapter, Lincoln had shown a keen interest in Cow Island as a colonization spot and had been a party to a contract with promoter Bernard Kock to have Negroes transported there. But Secretary Seward had held up the contract. In the middle of April 1864, more than three months after the Kock contract had been drafted, Lincoln issued a proclamation canceling it. In the meantime the wily Kock had sold his Cow Island lease to Paul S. Forbes and Charles K. Tuckerman, New York financiers.

These partners, learning of the administration's aboutface on the Kock contract, hastened to Washington to lay their case before the President. Still a believer in Negro colonization, Lincoln permitted himself to be persuaded into making an agreement similar to the one he had made with Kock. For $50 per person, Forbes and

Tuckerman were to transport 500 Negroes to Cow Island and to guarantee them certain personal rights and job opportunities. But there was one reservation the Lincoln administration insisted upon: the contract would be valid only when its terms had received the approval of the Haitian government.

Forbes and Tuckerman chose the Fortress Monroe region as recruiting ground, and they enlisted the services of William J. Watkins, Negro proponent of colonization. Within a few days Watkins succeeded in rounding up 453 Negroes, ranging in age from two to eighty-three, and including five who had never been slaves. This group, accompanied by Watkins and with the ubiquitous Kock in charge, sailed out of Fortress Monroe in mid-April 1863 on the *Ocean Ranger*.

Everything went wrong with the experiment. On board ship a smallpox outbreak took thirty lives. On arriving at Cow Island, the emigrants found that no housing had been prepared for them. Before they could get used to the tropical climate and the poisonous insects, they had to cope with a siege of malarial fevers. Worst of all, the soil turned out to be poor. As if to cap everything, the venture never secured the proper legal underpinning, for Haiti refused to give a written pledge validating the Forbes-Tuckerman contract with the administration.

News of the plight of the Cow Island Negroes reached Washington, and the Interior Department sent down a special agent to investigate. He arrived on December 15, 1863, but by that time the last act was being played. The emigrants had had enough; their only wish was to be carried back to Virginia. On February 3, 1864, Lincoln ordered that a transport be sent to bring back the hapless blacks. The ship chosen for this service, the *Marcia C. Day*, reached Cow Island on the last day of February 1864 and embarked shortly after. On March 20 she docked in the Potomac, discharging 368 Negroes, 85 fewer than had set out in such high spirits eleven months earlier.

The misfortunes of the Cow Island colonizers had saddened Lincoln. John Eaton, a White House visitor in July 1863, relates that Lincoln told him about the Negro emigrants, mentioning particularly that they were suffering from a "pest of jiggers," from which there seemed to be no escape. The keenness of Lincoln's distress made Eaton marvel: "The spectacle of the President of the United States, conducting the affairs of the Nation in the midst of civil war, and genuinely affected by an insect no bigger than a pinhead, was a spectacle that has stayed by me all my life."

Just as the Cow Island experiment was fizzling out, Lincoln received discouraging reports about the attitude of the Negroes toward colonization. Late in 1863 a handful of Negroes had shown an interest in emigration, among them J. Willis Menard, who wrote to Lincoln on September 6, 1863, asking permission to send him some pamphlets describing his visits to British Honduras. A week later the managers of the African Civilization Society asked Commissioner of Emigration Mitchell to furnish them with $5000, and to bring to the attention of Lincoln "the fact of our existence and the object of our organization."

But such evidences of interest were few indeed. On November 23, 1863, Commissioner Mitchell sadly informed Lincoln that the colonization movement still lacked "a proper body of discreet colored men." Mitchell's point of view was echoed by the Secretary of the Interior. "But little disposition," wrote J.P. Usher to Lincoln on March 11, 1864, "has yet been manifested by the freedmen of the United States to leave the land of their nativity."

Perhaps the Cow Island fiasco cured Lincoln of colonization. The *Independent* for March 31, 1864, asserted that he had at last learned his lesson and would "never renew the folly." John Hay, writing on July 1, 1864, expressed himself as being happy "that the President has sloughed off the idea of colonization." But Congress took no chances on Lincoln's recovery from the colonization bug. A week before the *Marcia C. Day* arrived with its cargo of disillusioned Negroes, a bill was introduced in the Senate to repeal all acts that made funds available for colonization. Congress passed the measure on July 2, 1864, thus freezing permanently the unexpended monies for the deporting of Negroes.

Of the $600,000 originally made available to the President for the colonization of colored Americans, he had spent only $38,329.93. Of this, nearly two-thirds ($25,000) had gone to Senator Pomeroy, promoter of Chiriqui; the remainder was spent on such miscellaneous items as Commissioner Mitchell's salary and the rescue expedition to Cow Island.

The colonization movement did not succumb without one final gasp. Late in 1864 and early in 1865 proposals were introduced into Congress to set apart certain portions of the lower Mississippi for exclusive occupancy by Negroes. But Lincoln was no longer a party to colonization schemes. Interest he may have had, but his principal had been taken away.

IN HIS person-to-person relationships with Negroes, Lincoln was characteristically kind and considerate. He did favors for Negroes, favors that could bring him no political advantage or private gain. On one occasion a newspaper reporter visiting the White House found him counting greenbacks and putting them in an envelope. It turned out that the money belonged to a porter in the Treasury Department, who was hospitalized with the smallpox. Unable to sign for his pay, the stricken Negro had gotten word to Lincoln, who had gone to some trouble to get the money.

This Negro in whom Lincoln took a personal interest was undoubtedly William Johnson, who in February 1861 had accompanied the President-elect on his journey from Springfield to Washington. On this circuitous train trip of nearly two weeks, William served as Lincoln's attendant and valet, taking care of his tall silk hats, Scotch-weave gray shawl, broadcloth overcoat and suits, satin vest, and thick winter boots. William won the commendation of Henry Villard, who was making the trip as a newspaper reporter. William, "although not exactly the most prominent, is yet the most useful member of the party," wrote Villard in the *New York Herald* of February 20, 1861. "The untiring vigilance with which he took care of the Presidential party is entitled to high credit."

Lincoln had planned to use William at the White House as his attendant and private messenger, but the President reckoned without the incumbent domestics. These old hands at the White House opposed William in part because he was a newcomer; this Lincoln could understand, being familiar with the seniority system. But he was astonished to learn that much of the opposition to William stemmed from his color. For a long time the White House had been staffed by light-skinned Negroes, to whom a richly pigmented person like William was simply beyond the pale. Bowing to the wishes of the White House colored, Lincoln gave up his plan to make William his valet.

Lincoln was bent on getting William placed somewhere. On March 7, 1861, he wrote a to-whom-it-may-concern letter, attesting to William's honesty, faithfulness, sobriety, and industry. A little more than a week later, he asked Secretary Welles to give William a job, explaining that he had been forced to let him go because of "the difference of color between him and the other servants." When neither of these letters brought anything, Lincoln spoke to Secretary Chase. On November 29, 1861, Lincoln put his request to Chase in writing, and on the following day William was informed that he had been named for a laborer's job in the Treasury Department at $600 a year. Thereupon, William left the furnace room of the White House, where he had been working as a fireman while Lincoln had been looking around on his behalf.

Getting William placed in a steady job did not mark the end of Lincoln's contacts with the Negro he had brought from Springfield. Now and then Lincoln asked the Treasury Department to give William a leave of absence for a day or two. These were occasions, doubtless, when the regular valet had time off. For these temporary services Lincoln paid William out of his own pocket, sometimes in cash and sometimes by check.

Upon William's death in January 1864, Lincoln requested that his job be given to Solomon James Johnson. No relative of William's, this Johnson had been one of the four colored men serving in the Seventh Independent Company of Ohio Volunteer Cavalry, a unit that acted as bodyguard and mounted escort for Lincoln in his daily trips from Soldiers' Home to the White House and back. The twenty-two-year-old Solomon had also done some barbering at the White House. Lincoln's request that he be given William's job was quickly honored: Solomon's letter of appointment came within four days.

Solomon was more ambitious than his predecessor. He apparently was not satisfied to remain in the job Lincoln had secured for him, for thirteen months after he had been hired, Solomon again came to the attention of the Secretary of the Treasury. And again it was through a note from the President. "I would be glad," wrote Lincoln on March 15, 1865, "if S. James Johnson, the bearer, could get a little promotion." Eventually Johnson held responsible white-collar jobs in the government.

Another Negro recipient of Lincoln's favor was a beggar on crutches who stopped him on the sidewalk one day as he was returning to the White House from the War Department. When the beggar hobbled away, he bore with him a check destined to become the best known of all the 234 checks written by the President. In the amount of five dollars and dated August 11, 1863, this instrument was made payable to "Colored man, with one leg."

On behalf of another Negro unknown to him personally, Lincoln offered to go into his pocket to the extent of five hundred dollars. In this instance Lincoln proposed to buy the freedom of a slave belonging to Judge George Robertson of Lexington, Kentucky. In November 1862 this slave ran away and took refuge in the camp of the Twenty-second Wisconsin Volunteers, then stationed at Nicholasville. Robertson, a man used to having his own way, got busy. Driving up to the regimental headquarters in an elegant carriage, he informed Colonel William L. Utley that he was a friend of Lincoln's and that he had come looking for his slave—a smallish, yellow-skinned boy named Adam. Robertson then flashed an order from Quincy A. Gillmore, commanding the Army of Kentucky, granting him permission to make the search for his slave.

Colonel Utley listened stonily; antislavery himself, his command was often called "the Wisconsin abolitionist regiment." Coolly ignoring the order from General Gillmore, Utley told Robertson that he could not permit his camp to be searched. But he promised that he would see if Adam could be found, and would give him up if he would consent to go.

Within a few hours Robertson drove back to the camp, asking as he alighted from his carriage, "Have you found the boy?" Robertson quickly learned that Adam was indeed within the lines, but that he had not consented to leave. The young slave had been definite: he wanted nothing to do with his former master. As Utley explained it to Lincoln: "The boy refused to go with him and claimed protection from the power of one whose cruel treatment, as he asserted, had already made him a dwarf instead of a man."

Utley's support of the runaway slave meant that Robertson would have to go away empty-handed. Angrily the aged judge left the camp, vowing aloud that this would not be the end of the matter. But back at his office in Lexington, Robertson had one thing he must do before preparing legal papers against Utley. This was to send a wire to the White House, protesting against army officers detaining the slaves of loyal Kentuckians.

Lincoln could not treat lightly a man who had been his legal counsel, representing him in 1849 in the case *Todd's heirs v. Robert Wickliffe*, and who had been an important public figure: he had been a member of the Sixteenth Congress, which in 1820 had enacted the Missouri Compromise, and had sat as chief justice of the Kentucky Court of Appeals, where he had acquired his reputation as the most learned jurist in the state. But if Lincoln could not ignore Robertson's wire, he could neatly sidestep the legal and constitutional issues it raised. This Lincoln did by offering, in a letter of November 26, 1862, to pay the judge any sum up to $500 if he would free Adam.

Robertson, fighting for a principle and still full of wrath, turned down the offer, informing Lincoln that he had "misconceived the motive of my dispatch." Robertson never recovered Adam, but he did win a court judgment against Colonel Utley, which Congress eventually paid.

Lincoln extended courtesies to Negroes in his public capacity as President, no less than in his private and unofficial actions. On July 4, 1864, Lincoln took the unprecedented step of permitting Negroes to use the White House grounds for a Sunday-school picnic. Three colored Catholics, headed by Gabriel Coakley, had called on Lincoln in late June, asking permission to hold a lawn party on the space surrounding the Executive Mansion. They told him that they were trying to raise money to build a Catholic church for Negroes, there being none in the District. Lincoln told them to go ahead, but advised them first to clear the request with the Commissioner of Public Buildings, Benjamin B. French. On June 27 Coakley wrote to French, telling him of the visit to the President and asking for a written permit to use the White House grounds, "in order to avoid difficulty with those who might question our right to be there." Three days later French wrote back, informing Coakley that the permission would be granted provided that Lincoln's assent was given. Coakley went at once to the White House and told Lincoln that his signature was required. The President reached for the note from French and jotted on it: "I assent. A. Lincoln."

The picnic went off as scheduled, with the children of the Catholic and the Protestant Sunday schools dividing the White House grounds between them. Apparently everyone had a good time. The artist Francis B. Carpenter took a day off from working on his painting of Lincoln reading to his cabinet the first draft of the Emancipation Proclamation, and spent much of the afternoon looking out of a White House window at the colored children as they sat under the trees or strolled along the shaded paths. "No celebration of the day," he wrote, "presented a greater appearance of enjoyment and success."

A month later Lincoln gave the Negroes of the city special permission to use the White House grounds in observance of the national day of prayer that Congress had recommended. The day-long celebration on the President's lawn was highlighted by preaching at eleven and three o'clock and by an oration at four. But sermons and speeches were not hard to take while one sat on a roomy, sun-streaked bench or under the shade of a tree, with a lemonade stand not far away.

IN HIS informal encounters with colored people, the President was the soul of friendly courtesy. Typical of Lincoln was his behavior on a visit to Columbia College Hospital, a military hospital on the outskirts of Washington. Lincoln had consented to make the visit upon the urging of Rebecca R. Pomroy of Chelsea, Massachusetts, who had nursed Lincoln's wife and their son Tad in the early spring of 1862. Mrs. Pomroy had been recommended to the Lincolns by Dorothea Dix, superintendent of women nurses.

At the hospital Lincoln was escorted through the building and over the tent-filled grounds by Nurse Pomroy. At the tour's end Mrs. Pomroy introduced Lincoln to the surgeons and to her staff of nurses. Then, to the astonishment of everyone present except herself and the President, Mrs. Pomroy asked one of the nurses to go downstairs and send the kitchen help up.

Soon three Negroes were standing before Lincoln, a woman and two men. Told that Lucy was the woman's name, Lincoln extended his hand, saying, "How do you do, Lucy." Mrs. Pomroy introduced the men, Garner and Brown, who, said she, were serving their country by cooking the "low diet" required for the sickest soldiers. Lincoln gave each a hearty grip, accompanied by a "How do you do, Garner," and "How do you do, Brown." The three former slaves backed out of the room, their faces aglow.

Lincoln showed a like spirit in his treatment of the White House domestics. Each one of them felt his friendliness, be it Cordelia Mitchell, the cook; Peter Brown, the butler; or William P. Brown, the coachman. Aunt Rosetta Wells, who did the plain sewing at the White House, told interviewer John E. Washington that Lincoln treated the servants like "people." He was not indifferent to their comfort, on one occasion sending a wire to Mrs. Lincoln in Boston: "Mrs. Cuthbert & Aunt Mary want to move to the White House, because it has grown so cold at Soldiers Home. Shall they?" Housekeeper Mary Ann Cuthbert was not colored, but Nurse ("Aunt Mary") Dines was a runaway slave from Maryland.

The White House domestic whom Lincoln came to know best was middle-aged William Slade, a combination of steward, butler, and valet. Light-skinned, as was his wife, Slade had straight hair and wore a little goatee. An ideal personal attendant, Slade was cheerful and even-tempered. He was also a tight-lipped man, telling almost nothing of his experiences at the White House or of his journeys to Gettysburg and elsewhere with the presidential party. Outliving Lincoln, Slade was destined to remain as presidential butler-valet until his death in March 1868. His funeral was attended by Andrew Johnson, Lincoln's successor, and by Washington's mayor, Richard Wallach.

But Slade was not the most influential Negro at the White House during the Lincoln years. This distinction went to Elizabeth Keckley, dressmaker to the President's wife. In her late thirties, Mrs. Keckley was a stately mulatto with a classic head—thin lips, aquiline nose, and high cheekbones—crowned by a mass of straight black hair parted in the middle with a neat bun in back. Mrs. Keckley carried herself like a woman of station, her bearing made more impressive by her clothes, which were of the best fabrics and fashioned in quiet style. Members of the congregation of the First Presbyterian Church, comprising the Negro élite of the city, hastened to Sunday morning services so as not to miss Mrs. Keckley as she made her entrance and moved down the aisle to her pew.

Elizabeth Keckley met Mrs. Lincoln for the first time on March 5, 1861, the day after the inauguration. At eight in the morning Mrs. Keckley arrived at the White House by appointment, having been recommended by a customer. Ushered upstairs into Mrs. Lincoln's presence, Mrs. Keckley was asked about her references and about her competence. Satisfied on these points, Mrs. Lincoln turned her attention to prices. "We are just from the West, and are poor," said she. "If you do not charge too much, I shall be able to give you all my work." Mrs. Keckley assured the First Lady that her prices were reasonable. Taking Mrs. Lincoln's measurements, Mrs. Keckley left the White House carrying the materials for a dress, which she promised to finish in time for a reception scheduled for the following week.

On the night of the affair Mrs. Keckley was very much in evidence, brushing Mrs. Lincoln's hair and adorning it with red roses, helping her to get into the "rose-colored moire-antique" dress, and fastening her pearl necklace and earrings. The dress won a word of admiration from Mary Lincoln's husband. As she took his arm to go downstairs, her face was serene and smiling.

As of that mid-March evening, Mrs. Keckley became Mrs. Lincoln's modiste, a job that she held all during the White House years. To a newspaper reporter of a later day, Smith D. Fry of the Minneapolis *Register*, Mrs. Keckley described her work:

> I dressed Mrs. Lincoln for every levée. I made every stitch of clothing that she wore. I dressed her hair. I put on her skirts and dresses. I fixed her bouquets, saw that her gloves were right, and remained with her each evening until Mr. Lincoln came for her.

Although not a woman easy to please, Mrs. Lincoln found no fault with Mrs. Keckley's work. The mulatto modiste knew just how to fashion Mrs. Lincoln's gowns so as to reveal her shapely neck and arms and to give her more height. One of these Keckley creations drew a comment from the President. Himself indifferent to matters of dress, Lincoln's attention on this occasion was attracted by the swish and rustle of his wife's gown, a white satin affair trimmed with black lace. "Whew!" said he, "our cat has a long tail tonight." Emboldened when she held her tongue, Lincoln ventured a suggestion: "Mother, it is my opinion, if some of that tail was nearer the head, it would be in better style."

In her first six months in the White House, Mrs. Lincoln had Mrs. Keckley make her fifteen dresses. But after Willie Lincoln's death on February 20, 1862, the dress orders fell off, as Mrs. Lincoln discontinued the White House receptions and went into heavy mourning. But if Willie's passing cut down on Mrs. Keckley's White House business, it brought her much closer to the bereaved First Lady. For Mrs. Lincoln never got over the death of her most beloved of sons. "Willie, darling Boy! was always the idolized child of the household," she wrote to Mrs. John Henry Shearer nearly three years after the blustery winter's day when he was laid away.

In her distress Mrs. Lincoln turned to Mrs. Keckley. She had been drawn to her mulatto dressmaker from the first months of their acquaintance. When Mrs. Keckley lost her only son on a Missouri battlefield in August 1861, Mrs. Lincoln was most sympathetic. "She is a very remarkable woman," wrote Mrs. Lincoln to her cousin, Elizabeth Todd Grimsley, on September 29, 1861, in a note telling her the news of young Keckley's death.

At Mrs. Lincoln's urging, Mrs. Keckley applied for a pension. It was granted, doubtless because of Mrs. Keckley's connections in high places, for her pension application contained one glaring inaccuracy. In it she stated that she had been married to her son's father, a white man named Alexander Kirkland. Actually when her son was born, she was a slave. ("I was compelled," said she later, "to become a mother without marriage.") She had made enough money by her needle to purchase her freedom and that of her son. Her only marriage had been to James Keckley, a ne'er-do-well from whom she had been separated several years before his dissipations carried him off.

Mrs. Lincoln was attracted to Mrs. Keckley as one bereaved mother to another. There was another reason for Mrs. Lincoln's turning to her mulatto modiste for solace and companionship. Mrs. Keckley was a soothing person—soft-spoken, cheerful, and always composed. Her influence on Mrs. Lincoln was not unlike that wielded some thirty-five years earlier by old Mammy Sally, a slave but an important member of the Todd household during Mary's motherless years at Lexington.

By the summer of 1862 Mrs. Keckley had become a combination confidante, companion, and personal maid to Mrs. Lincoln. It was to Mrs. Keckley that the First Lady confided her opinions (all of them unflattering) of some of the men around her husband—Secretaries Chase and Seward, Andrew Johnson, and Generals McClellan and Grant. On her trips to Boston and New York, Mrs. Lincoln took Mrs. Keckley along. In a letter to her husband, dated November 2, 1862, from New York, Mrs. Lincoln spoke of her traveling companion: "A day or two since, I had one of my severe attacks, if it had not been for Lizzie Keckley, I do not know what I should have done."

Mrs. Keckley may have had a hand in Mrs. Lincoln's year-long flirtation with spiritualists. According to Noah Brooks, Mrs. Keckley persuaded Mrs. Lincoln to enlist the services of a medium who went by the name of Lord Colchester. Once in the presence of Mrs. Lincoln, Colchester assured her that he could put her in touch with her lost Willie. For a time Colchester made periodic visits to the White House, and on such occasions a room would be darkened, and soon the air would be filled with sounds of uncertain origin—table tappings, bells ringing, drums beating, and banjos twanging. But the séances came to an end when Brooks, a friend of the Lincolns, told the producer of the sound effects that he would be thrown into the dreaded Capitol Prison if he did not leave the city in twenty-four hours.

One definite influence Mrs. Keckley had upon the First Lady was in enlarging her sympathies toward the Negro. As late as January 1, 1860 (in a letter to Mrs. John Henry Shearer), Mrs. Lincoln could refer to Negroes as "darkies." It is doubtful that she used that word after coming to know Mrs. Keckley. Under Mrs. Keckley's influence Mrs. Lincoln became a donor to Negro charities. Mrs. Keckley was the founder and first president of the Contraband Relief Association, made up of forty Negro women who wished to help the former slaves who had come into the District. Organized on August 9, 1862, the association raised $838.68 in its first year; its first donation was $200 from Mrs. Lincoln. In addition to her money gift, "Mrs. President Lincoln" contributed 15 boxes of clothing, 500 tin plates, 20 turkeys, and an unspecified quantity of apples and cranberries.

Mrs. Keckley's contacts with President Lincoln were formal but friendly. To Mrs. Lincoln she was "Lizzie," or "Lizabeth"; to Lincoln she was "Madame Keckley." But the mulatto dressmaker did not find the President condescending or ungracious. He was, as she related to newspaper reporter Smith D. Fry, as kind and considerate of her "as he was of any of the white people about the White House."

To NEGROES who visited the White House, Lincoln behaved much the same as with Mrs. Keckley; if he was not hail-fellow-well-met, neither was he unfriendly. He treated Negroes as they wanted to be treated—as human beings. As has been noted earlier, Lincoln was no solemn ass: he loved unsophisticated dialect stories, and in his day the central figure in many such stories was Sambo. But to the Lincoln of the White House years, the Negro was not only a butt for humor, he was also a person. A sensitive man, quick to penetrate the color curtain and discern the individual behind it, Lincoln knew that there were certain words like "nigger" and "Cuffee" that would not be relished by Negroes. He knew that plantation stories might not set well with former slaves. Hence, in the presence of Negro visitors to the White House, Lincoln abandoned his storytelling and became a virtual sobersides.

Negro visitors to the White House were treated without false heartiness, but without any sign of disdain. Never condescending, Lincoln did not talk down to Negroes, nor did he spell out his thoughts in the one-syllable language of the first reader. Actually Lincoln may have enjoyed the visits from Negroes. True, he could not tell his jokes, but he could relax. Negro visitors were not looking for appointments, or for government contracts, or for confidential information. With Negroes, Lincoln could let his guard down; he need not be as reticent and secretive as often was his wont.

How Lincoln's colored visitors affected him, we do not know. Possibly they caused him to revise his opinion somewhat about

Negroes. To two of them, on different occasions, he gave letters of introduction to Secretary Stanton, characterizing one of the bearers, L.H. Putnam of Brooklyn, as "a very intelligent colored man," and the other, well-known Martin R. Delany, as "this most extraordinary and intelligent black man."

But if we cannot be sure of Lincoln's impressions of his colored visitors, there can be no doubt as to their impressions of him. Bishop Payne, who visited the White House in the spring of 1862, was so graciously received that he could not help contrasting Lincoln with John Tyler, who had been stiff and distant when Payne came to the Executive Mansion to preach a sermon over a Tyler servant who had been killed by an explosion on a warship. Payne's opinion of Lincoln was shared by another Negro leader, Frederick Douglass. "Perhaps you would like to know how I, a Negro, was received at the White House by the President of the United States," said he to a packed Cooper Union audience on January 13, 1864, at a meeting sponsored by the Woman's Loyal League. "Why, precisely as one gentleman would be received by another. He extended to me a cordial hand, not too warm or too cold." The Negro orator-reformer told his listeners that Lincoln addressed him as "Mr. Douglass."

Of all Lincoln's host of visitors, white or black, none admired him like Sojourner Truth, the almost legendary abolitionist of indeterminate years (she would not tell her age because, she said with a twinkle, it would spoil her chances). It could have been Sojourner whose image was before Walt Whitman as he penned "Ethiopia Saluting the Colors":

> Who are you dusky woman, so ancient hardly human,
> With your woolly-white and turban'd head . . . ?

Sojourner's personality was as striking as her appearance: Harriet Beecher Stowe, using the jargon of the spiritualists, described her as "having a strong sphere."

Ushered into Lincoln's presence, Sojourner showered him with the most unabashed praise, assuring him in a deep-toned voice that he was the greatest President this country ever had, a man to be likened unto Daniel. Lincoln managed to get in some sentences of his own, behaving throughout as though it were perfectly natural to be conversing with a slave-born, unlettered old woman, dressed in Quaker gray, a bright turban on her head, and wearing heavy traveling shoes. As Sojourner got ready to leave, she reached into her spacious pockets for an autograph book she carried. Turning to a blank page, the President wrote:

For Aunty Sojourner Truth

October 29, 1864   A. Lincoln

Sojourner left the White House thanking God she had been a Lincoln supporter all along. A journalist, transcribing Sojourner's broken English but losing nothing of its sense, reported her as saying that she was "never treated with more kindness and cordiality than I was by that great and good man, Abraham Lincoln."

On one occasion the favorable impression Lincoln made on his Negro visitors was due in part to his granting their request. In August 1863 a delegation of colored clergymen, representing the American Baptist Missionary Convention, came to the White House seeking permission to go into the military lines to minister to the spiritual needs of the boys in blue. Lincoln gave several minutes to these earnest men who were bent on getting the soldiers to substitute a pocket Bible for a deck of cards. Lincoln also gave his visitors what they had come for—a statement, addressed to whomever it concerned, asking that Negro ministers be permitted to enter the lines to work with their brethren, except when such a step would impede military operations.

Some of the Negro visitors to the White House brought gifts, among them war nurse Caroline Johnson of Philadelphia, who gave Lincoln a collection of wax fruits, together with an ornamented stem table. Mrs. Johnson told Lincoln that God had hewn him out of a rock, to do great things. Thanking Mrs. Johnson for the gift, Lincoln murmured that God, not he, was to be praised for whatever good might result from the war.

At the White House a few months later, Lincoln was presented with a gift that pleased him more, according to Francis B. Carpenter, than any other he ever received as President. To the White House came a letter, dated August 26, 1864, and signed by James S. Tyson: "I am requested, on behalf of the colored men of Baltimore, to ask when it will be convenient for you to receive at their hands, a very elegantly bound edition of the Bible, which they have prepared as an evidence of their regard and gratitude."

Five delegates from the Baltimore Negroes came to the White House on a Wednesday afternoon in early September. After they had been introduced, their spokesman, the Reverend S.M. Chase, stepped forward for a short, rehearsed speech, ending on a personal note: "Towards you, sir, our hearts will be ever warm with gratitude. We came to present you with this copy of the Holy Scriptures as a token of respect for your active participation in furtherance of the cause of the emancipation of our race." As the speaker concluded, two delegates stepped forward and handed the gift to Lincoln.

Uttering "many expressions of admiration," the Chief Magistrate lifted the Bible from its silk-lined black walnut case. Costing $580.75, a sum contributed by 519 Negroes, of whom 272 were women, it was indeed an impressive piece. A pulpit-sized volume, with two heavy gold clasps, it was bound in royal purple velvet. The front cover bore an engraving representing Lincoln striking the shackles from the wrists of a slave. The back cover was ornamented by a gold plate, four inches by two, its inscription expressing the respect and admiration that the colored people of Baltimore bore Abraham Lincoln.

After the President had expressed his thanks, he sensed that the five Negroes expected him to say something. The occasion, said he, seemed to call for "a lengthy response," but he was not prepared to make one. He would promise to express his feelings in writing, he continued, but he knew from past experience that the pressure of business might intervene. But, he added, "I can only now say, as I have often before said, it has always been a sentiment with me that all mankind should be free."

Coming to the Bible itself, Lincoln said that everything the Lord gave to the world was "communicated" through it; without it, men would not know right from wrong. The Chief Magistrate closed with a word of appreciation: "To you I return my most sincere thanks for the very elegant copy of the great Book of God which you present." Then he moved from one member of the delegation to another, shaking hands with each in parting.

Like so many of his words, Lincoln's words at this presentation ceremony were destined to live on. In thanking the colored Baltimoreans, he referred to the Bible as "the best gift God has given to man." Ninety years later, in 1954, this expression would be chosen by the Layman's National Committee as the theme for National Bible Week.

LINCOLN'S POPULARITY among Negroes was greatly on the upswing during the last two years of the war. Noah Brooks relates that one spring day as the Lincolns were driving around the city, their carriage came upon a camp of contraband Negroes. Suddenly the presidential party was surrounded by the entire population of the camp, materialized "as if by magic." Young and old, the Negroes sent up a long cheer for "Massa Linkum." Turning to her husband, Mrs. Lincoln asked him to hazard a guess as to the number of "picaninnies" there who bore his name. "Let's see," he replied; "this is April, 1863. I should say that of all those babies under two years of age, perhaps two-thirds have been named for me."

Later that year the inhabitants of the Washington contraband camp asked Lincoln to address them at a Thanksgiving Day celebration. Lincoln could not come, but his third secretary, William O. Stoddard, was drafted at the eleventh hour. The reluctant Stoddard was told that the Negroes would be inconsolable if they did not have somebody from the White House. The young clerk was advised that there was one other thing he must do in order to lessen the disappointment of the Negroes: "You must look as much like Lincoln as you can."

This love and admiration for Lincoln was common among former bondmen. He was the man who signed the "Freedom Bill." The welcome given to Union troops by slaves was expressed in many ways—the waving of bonnets, hats, aprons, and handkerchiefs, singing, and dancing—but invariably the demonstrations were capped by loud cheers and hurrahs for Lincoln. Officers in the freedmen's relief organization used Lincoln's name to keep their charges in line, telling them that everything they did would be reported to him, particularly if they did not behave and were unwilling to work.

Lincoln had made his mark on the Negro long before that fateful night at Ford's Theatre. The Negroes of the war years viewed history not in terms of forces or movements, but in terms of a personal hero. To them, Lincoln admirably fitted into this role.

Lincoln furnished a father image to Negroes, an image lacking in the lives of the majority of the plantation dwellers of the Old South. In the days before the war, it was the Negro woman who was the dominant figure in the family life of the slaves, the father being elsewhere or unknown. To thousands of freed slaves, Lincoln became a symbol of the male parent they had never known. The rice people of the Sea Islands, wrote Elizabeth Botume, always spoke of the President as "Papa Linkum."

To many Negroes, Lincoln was a child of God. He bore an Old Testament name, Abraham. Although not a "technical Christian" (his wife's phrase), Lincoln was regarded by religiously minded Negroes as one who had been born again. To them he talked and behaved as if he were a church-going man.

Some Negroes thought of him as a Moses. When Betsey Canedy showed a plaster bust of Lincoln to a group of colored carpenters working on her schoolhouse at Norfolk, she heard one of them say, "He's brought us safe through the Red Sea." General Saxton, in a letter to Secretary Stanton on December 30, 1864, took note that, no matter what griefs and disappointments the Sea Island freedmen underwent, they never lost faith in Lincoln. They regarded him as their deliverer, one who would "at last bring them to the promised land."

To some Negroes, Lincoln was the word made flesh. Once at Beaufort, according to the preliminary report of the Freedmen's Inquiry Commission, a gang of colored workers in the quarter-master's corps were discussing the many good things that Lincoln had brought to pass. As they were speaking, a white-headed "praise man" interrupted them impatiently: "What do you know 'bout Massa Linkum?" asked he in solemn tones. "Massa Linkum be ebrewhere. He walk de earth like de Lord." According to the *New York Times* of April 19, 1865, when this incident was related to Lincoln by the member of the Freedmen's Inquiry Commission who had witnessed it, the President was visibly affected, turning away to the window to hide the moisture gathering in his eyes.

The attitude of the Negro toward Lincoln had varied roots, among them hero worship, father image, and messianic deliverer. But whatever its origins, this high opinion of Lincoln gave to the Negro one inestimable boon—the feeling that he had a stake in America. And as the war moved toward its close, the Negro's sense of identity with the land of his birth grew deeper, nourished anew by its source—Abraham Lincoln.

9

"GOOD NEWS, CHARIOT'S COMING"

ON THE FIRST DAY of 1864, a letter came to Lincoln's desk from an old Springfield acquaintance, William de Fleurville, Billy the Barber. Billy had no particular ax to grind; he had simply taken it into his head to write a friendly letter to a respected former customer. Billy opened by thanking the President for having previously sent him personal greetings by Dr. Anson Henry and Governor Richard Yates. Billy then expressed his condolences about Willie: "I thought him a smart boy for his age, so considerate and so manly." His own son, said Billy, was married and in business for himself. Billy informed Lincoln that the dog left behind by Tad was alive and kicking, and that the Lincoln house was being well taken care of, its tenant having no children to ruin things.

Sounding a broader note, Billy wrote that he hoped and trusted that Lincoln would run for a second term. No man, added he, was better fitted for the highest office in the land. If Lincoln succeeded himself at the White House, everything would come out all right, and then "the oppressed will shout the name of their deliverer, and generations to come will rise up and call you blessed (so mote it be)."

Billy's attitude toward a second term for Lincoln reflected the wishes of the overwhelming majority of Negroes. Four years earlier when Lincoln had been selected as the Republican standard-bearer, Negroes received the news with a shrug of the shoulders. But in 1864, when the Republicans nominated him at their convention held in Baltimore in June, Negroes were overjoyed. At the convention the Republicans had also taken a new name for the campaign, the National Union party, in an attempt to meet the criticism that they represented only one section of the country. Negroes cared little for such niceties; their eyes were on the man, not the party label.

During the election year the Negroes followed one edict as though it had been handed down from on high: Thou shalt have no other candidates before Lincoln. This commandment they kept, even though it meant turning away from such a favorite as John C. Frémont. In the spring of 1864 a Frémont movement was sponsored by Republicans who were unmindful of Lincoln's advice not to swap horses while crossing a stream. Numbered among the leaders of this third-party effort were some abolitionists of note, among them Wendell Phillips and Elizabeth Cady Stanton. Hopeful of forestalling Lincoln's nomination at Baltimore, this group of self-appointed delegates met at Cleveland in late May and selected a ticket with Frémont as head and General John Cochrane as his running mate.

It was expected that Negroes would support such a ticket. Frémont's had been a popular name in Negro circles ever since he had run for national office in 1856. Cochrane, Attorney General of New York, was not a reformer, and he certainly was no abolitionist, but he was the nephew of Gerrit Smith, who was by far the most generous financial contributor of his day to Negroes and to Negro causes. Hence, Cochrane was expected to win approval among Negroes, since he was (to borrow the Louis Napoleon tag) "the nephew of his uncle."

But in 1864 a "stop Lincoln" movement was doomed among Negroes, no matter who headed it. Not a single prominent Negro attended the convention of the Lincoln critics at Cleveland, and the rare Negro leader who did not hold the President in high esteem said as little as possible, taking cover lest he be run over by the black bandwagon. But most Negro leaders, taking their cue from the rank and file, were strong supporters of a second term for

Lincoln. John Mercer Langston, addressing a Toledo audience at White Hall two days before the Lincoln critics had met in Cleveland, said that if there was one thing for which he was grateful to his Heavenly Father, it was that this country had such a President. On the eve of the election Henry Highland Garnet said much the same thing at a standing-room-only political rally held at his Fifteenth Street Presbyterian Church in Washington. Had it not been for Lincoln, said Garnet in oblique reference to the curfew for slaves, many of those present would have been making long tracks about ten o'clock that evening.

The pro-Lincoln sentiment of the home-front Negro was duplicated by his brother on the battlefield. "We are all for Old Abe. I hope he will be elected," wrote James Ruffin from Folly Island, October 16, 1864, to his sister-in-law, Josephine Ruffin. "Let the colored men at home do their duty."

The Negro's attitude toward Lincoln must have puzzled the Radical Republicans. These men of Lincoln's own party repeatedly accused him of billing and cooing with slaveholding rebels. Lincoln, they said, talked as though he were against slavery, but he acted as though he favored it.

These charges that Lincoln was tender to slavery were lost on the Negro of 1864. Perhaps Negroes sensed that the Radicals were using any weapon at hand to strike at the President, that these proslavery charges against Lincoln were simply a phase of the power struggle going on within the Republican party. But Negroes may not have sensed these things, because their thoughts were elsewhere. To Negroes the issue in 1864 was not to be found in power politics; it was to be found in a personality: Lincoln, the man, had become the issue. All else could be told in dumb show.

In late August the Negro sentiment for Lincoln became practically total when the Democrats, meeting in Chicago, named General George B. McClellan as their standard-bearer. To Negroes, not only did McClellan symbolize anti-Lincolnism, but he was obnoxious in his own right, having returned fugitive slaves and having been cool about making the Negro a soldier. The race for the presidency became further simplified for colored Americans when Frémont withdrew his name late in September.

Knowing that the Negro-abolitionist vote was practically 100 per cent for Lincoln, the Democrats, with nothing to lose, decided to make the most of any anti-Negro sentiment. Playing upon color prejudice was standard operating procedure in American politics, and Lincoln was sure to come in for his share of campaign race-labeling. He was charged with openly avowing "the beastly doctrine of intermarriage" and with practicing social equality and racial togetherness at the White House; his Negro visitors were offered as proof. In one piece of campaign literature, a pamphlet entitled *The Lincoln Catechism*, he was portrayed as being a tool for the colored man: "What is a President?" ran a typical question. "A general agent for Negroes," was the ready answer.

Lincoln's opponents did not ignore the tar brush. This time there was no Hannibal Hamlin to charge with having Negro blood, as Andrew Johnson of Tennessee had replaced him as Lincoln's running mate. In the absence of Hamlin, the Democrats seized upon Lincoln himself. He was dubbed "Abraham Africanus I" and was shown in cartoons as having Negroid features.

These campaign tactics of Lincoln's opponents had some effect, but in the late summer of 1864 the supporters of the President were disturbed by the military situation above all else. Grant had not taken Richmond, nor had Sherman reached Atlanta. War weariness was on the rise, and the Democrats were making the most of peace-at-any-price sentiment. Many Republicans felt that their party was doomed at the polls.

Lincoln shared some of this feeling that he might turn out to be a one-term President. Fearing that he might have to bring the war to a close by a negotiated peace within a few months, Lincoln let his mind dwell upon the probable fate of the slaves within the Confederacy. What would happen to them, he wondered, if he were compelled to agree to talk peace with the Richmond government?

Wishing to think aloud about the problem, Lincoln sent for

Frederick Douglass. While waiting in the President's outer office, Douglass was the object of a close scrutiny by another White House caller, Joseph T. Mills, who reported his impressions to Lincoln, and then wrote them into his diary under the date of his visit, August 19, 1864:

> Mr. President I was in your reception room to day. It was dark. I suppose that clouds & darkness necessarily surround the secrets of state. There in a corner I saw a man quietly reading who possessed a remarkable physiognomy. I was rivetted to the spot. I stood & stared at him. He raised his flashing eyes & caught me in the act. I was compelled to speak. Said I, Are you the President? No replied the stranger, I am Frederick Douglass.

A few minutes after this encounter Douglass was ushered into Lincoln's presence. Saying nothing about the Negro orator's previous visit, Lincoln plunged into his proposal that the government establish an unofficial agency to urge slaves to escape as soon as possible. This federally sponsored "underground railroad" would be manned by a general agent and twenty-five assistants who would persuade the slaves to leave the plantations and would conduct them to the Union lines.

Douglass was not enthusiastic about the proposal, even though he would be the logical choice for the general agent's job. This proposal was disturbing to him, because it revealed that Lincoln considered the Emancipation Proclamation valid only as long as the war lasted, and that once peace came, the status of the slaves outside the Union lines would remain unchanged. Moreover, Lincoln's proposal struck a somber bell in Douglass's mind. At Chambersburg, Pennsylvania, five years earlier almost to the day, John Brown had asked Douglass's opinion of a somewhat similar proposal, and Douglass had had to express his coolness toward it.

The talk between Lincoln and his Negro guest was unhurried. "We were long together and there was much said," wrote the latter. But no conclusions were reached. Unable to warm up to the proposal, Douglass asked the President to let him sleep on it. Lincoln readily agreed; Douglass had already given him what he really wanted—a chance to think aloud.

The Douglass visit to the White House did Lincoln no harm in Negro circles. "Did you ever see such nonsense!" wrote Negro army surgeon John H. Rapier on August 19, 1864, in mock horror to a friend. "The President of the United States sending for a 'Nigger' to confer with him on the state of the country!" Negroes were impressed by Lincoln's choice of Douglass as the colored leader to be invited to the White House, a man who had no talent for putting prominent people at their ease. Never the one to bite his tongue, Douglass was wholly unlike the smiling and glad-handed type of spokesman who, in the presence of the powerful, was likely to wag his head up and down, agreeing to everything in advance.

Aside from helping to solidify Lincoln's hold on the Negro, nothing came of the Douglass visit. Three weeks after it had taken place, Douglass wrote a long letter to Lincoln, saying that he had discussed the proposal with several responsible Negroes, and that "some of them think it practicable." In this none too hopeful tone Douglass proceeded to outline a series of seven steps whereby slaves in the rebel states might be brought within "loyal" lines.

But Lincoln was not listening. By the time Douglass's letter reached Washington, Lincoln had received glorious news from the battlefronts. "Atlanta is ours, and fairly won," wired William Tecumseh Sherman on September 2. A few hours later Lincoln received additional news almost as joyous: Admiral David G. Farragut had forced his entrance into Mobile Bay, scoring a notable naval triumph. Making Lincoln's re-election virtually certain, these war-front successes removed his fears of having to make a premature peace which might leave slavery untouched in the Confederate states.

When the voters went to the polls on election day, November 8, 1864, the secret (or Australian) ballot was not known. But the Negro did not miss it; he wanted everybody to know where he stood. It was Lincoln all the way. At Nashville the Negroes of the

Fourth Ward held an election at Sumner's Livery Stable, which they turned into a polling place. These Negroes had bestowed the ballot upon themselves, and so their vote did not count in the official returns. But it did serve to indicate the Negro's preference, the results reading:

Lincoln and Johnson	3193
McClellan and Pendleton	1

The candidates of the Democratic party made a better showing elsewhere, but Lincoln won by a comfortable majority. Negroes were most happy. "Since the re-election of Mr. Lincoln, the Royal Blood of Africa—the *crème de la crème* of colored society—have been extremely jubilant," wrote political pamphleteer L. Seaman. "*Soirées d'Afrique* are being held throughout the country." Seaman's words were derisive, but they caught the mood of the colored American. "We are all glad to know that President Lincoln is re-elected," wrote infantryman Edgar Dismore to Carrie Drayton on December 25, 1864, from bleak and cheerless Morris Island. "It gives us renewed hope and makes us eager to meet the foe." At New Orleans a "Convention of Colored Men," meeting in January, affirmed its faith in the American people for having re-elected Abraham Lincoln.

Now THAT HE HAD WON a second term, Lincoln could press anew for the abolition of slavery by legal means. To young John Hay, writing several months before the election of 1864, all discussion of slavery was pointless, being nothing more than the "puerile babble over a ghost of an institution which is as odorously defunct as Lazarus." As the year 1864 drew to a close, all signs seemed to bear out Hay's conclusions. But Lincoln was not quite as positive as his secretary that slavery had breathed its last. In any case he wanted to give the corpse a decent, legal burial, with the tomb nailed down lest there be a raising of the dead.

Lincoln fully supported the two movements for the legal abolition of slavery—by the states, and by Congress through the enactment of a constitutional amendment. As to the states, Lincoln made a difference, of course, between those that were in rebellion and those that were loyal. States that were members of the Confederacy were told by Lincoln that they could not be readmitted until they abolished slavery.

In the loyal slave states, whose legal rights Lincoln respected, his approach was one of friendly persuasion and fatherly approval. "I have very earnestly urged the slave-states to adopt emancipation," he wrote on June 22, 1863 to General John M. Schofield, stationed at St. Louis. Six months later, in his annual message to Congress, he noted with pleasure the steps that had been taken: "The movements, by State action, for emancipation in several of the states, not included in the emancipation proclamation, are matters of profound gratulation."

One of the states to which Lincoln had reference was West Virginia. On the last day of 1862 he had signed a bill admitting West Virginia to statehood, provided that she emancipate her slaves. The admission of this new state would "turn that much slave soil to free," wrote Lincoln, and thus strike a blow against "the cause of the rebellion."

When West Virginia came into the Union in June 1863, her constitution provided for a system of gradual emancipation: children of slaves born after July 4, 1863, would be free. Gradual emancipation was Lincoln's preference over immediate emancipation. The former, he wrote to a supporter in Maryland, John A.J. Creswell, "would produce less confusion and destitution." When this point of view was presented to a group of Missourians, one of them, James Taussig, likened it to the "illustration of the dog whose tail was amputated by inches." But Lincoln made no attempt to foist his gradualist views on the people of the border states; on the contrary, he told them that he had no objection to immediate emancipation, if that was what they wanted.

Actually, by the autumn of 1864 when the border states other than West Virginia got around to freeing their bondmen, it mattered little what Lincoln or anyone else thought of the merits of gradualism. That matter had been decided by the border state slaves themselves. And as much as they loved and respected Lincoln, they did not subscribe to his gradualist views.

Possibly Lincoln was more pleased by Maryland's action in freeing her slaves than by that of any other state. Not only were Maryland's slaves numerous, totaling over 85,000 by the census of 1860, but she was located right at the gates of the national government. When Maryland became a free state on November 1, 1864, Lincoln characterized the event as "a big thing." Horror-stricken language purists charged the President with having uttered a vulgarism, but help came from an unexpected quarter, the *New York Herald*. The phrase "a big thing," said the *Herald*, could be found in Terence's *Phamio*, Act II, scene ii, line 18; hence Lincoln was a man who was versed in the Roman dramatists. True, Lincoln might be charged with plagiarism, said the *Herald*, but in "pitching into Terence," he had exhibited the purest classical taste.

Approval of Lincoln's sentiment, regardless of his language, came from a group of Negroes who assembled on the White House lawn on an evening in late October. Lincoln moved out to the portico, attracted by the brass band and the cheering. When the demonstrators quieted down for a moment, Lincoln asked them in a friendly tone why they were serenading him. One of them stepped forward and shouted, "The emancipator of Maryland, sah." Lincoln responded with a short speech expressing his pleasure that a state had abolished slavery of its own volition, and urging his listeners to improve themselves morally and intellectually. The Negroes then gave a rousing cheer before moving on.

In abolishing slavery, the people of Maryland hoped to receive payment from the national government. Indeed, the new state constitution paved the way for such a step by authorizing the General Assembly to accept money or securities from Congress, pledging that such donations would be used as specified by the donor. But the three loyal states that abolished slavery prior to Lincoln's second term—West Virginia, Maryland, and Missouri—

soon found that their hopes of receiving federal funds for their black bondmen were not to be realized.

Their disappointment was shared by Lincoln, who was even more reluctant to give up on compensated emancipation than he had been on Negro colonization. In the closing weeks of the war he went so far as to extend the idea of compensated emancipation to the defeated Southerners, startling his Cabinet on 5 February 1865 by outlining a plan to have Congress appropriate $400 million to pay rebel owners for the loss of their slaves. The Cabinet unanimously rejected the idea. They did not see the measure as a magnanimous act that might shorten the war by a few weeks; they saw it as an act of appeasement that might be misconstrued by the enemy.

With his own closest advisers dead set against the proposal, Lincoln dropped it. Perhaps it was well for him that it was never sent to Congress. On Capitol Hill there was a marked coolness toward compensating masters of any stripe—loyal or rebel. The District of Columbia Act of April 16, 1862, was destined to be the only instance in which Congress appropriated money for the freeing of slaves.

DURING THE CLOSING MONTHS of the war the real crusher to both gradual and compensated emancipation was the Thirteenth Amendment. No halfway measure, this amendment forthrightly prohibited slavery anywhere in the United States and its territories. It had taken over a year to get this measure through Congress. Introduced in December 1863, it had passed the Senate four months later, but it was rejected by the House in June 1864.

Few men were more concerned about the adoption of the measure than Lincoln. He needed no one to tell him of the limitations of the Emancipation Proclamation: that it did not apply to the border states, and that as a war measure, it would no longer be valid when peace came. Solicitor William Whiting, in *The War Powers of the President*, had made it clear to Lincoln that his proclamation had not done away with the institution of slavery even in the rebel states. There was a difference, said Whiting, between emancipating the slaves and abolishing the laws that sustained slavery:

> If all the horses now in Massachusetts were to be confiscated or appropriated by the government to public use, though the proceeding would change the legal title to these horses, it would not alter the laws of Massachusetts as to personal property; nor would it deprive our citizens of the legal right to purchase and use *other* horses.

The limitations of the Emancipation Proclamation became more displeasing to a Lincoln who seemed to grow in moral stature with each passing season. Hence, he welcomed the opportunity of supporting the effort to make the abolition of slavery a part of the supreme law of the land. His efforts were twofold: to place the Republican party on record as supporting an antislavery amendment, and to persuade Congress to pass such a measure.

It was Lincoln who proposed that the Republican party incorporate into its platform a plank calling for the abolition of slavery by constitutional amendment. A few days before the party convention was held at Baltimore in June, Lincoln sent for the chairman of the national committee, Senator Edwin D. Morgan of New York, and asked him to present an antislavery proposal in his address calling the delegates to order. Morgan followed this suggestion, and both he and Lincoln were gratified by the ovation the proposal drew. The delegates proceeded to write into the platform a recommendation that the "gigantic evil" of slavery be done away with by constitutional amendment.

On the day after the convention adjourned, a committee came to the White House to notify Lincoln of his renomination to the presidency. In his brief reply Lincoln singled out one plank of the party platform for his express approval. An amendment abolishing slavery, said he, was "a fitting and necessary conclusion to the final success of the Union cause." The country should adopt this measure "in the joint names of Liberty and Union." Lincoln's reply to the notifying committee was not written out, and hence he may not have carefully weighed his word order. But perhaps it is not without significance that he placed "Liberty" before "Union."

In November, Lincoln and his party were highly successful at the polls. This victory Lincoln construed as a mandate by the people that Congress pass the amendment abolishing slavery. The mood of the re-elected President was suggested by Henry Ward Beecher. "The Abraham Lincoln of today is an abolitionist, an emancipator," he wrote in *The Independent* of November 17, 1864. "If Congress is not expeditious in agreeing to a constitutional amendment, I look for a second proclamation, freeing every slave in the Union, upon military necessity."

In his annual message to Congress on December 6, 1864, Lincoln recommended the proposed amendment. Such a step was the will of the people, said he; hence, the sooner the legislators passed the measure, the better. If they refused to do so, they would succeed only in delaying the inevitable, admonished Lincoln, since the newly elected Thirty-ninth Congress would certainly uphold the mandate given at the polls. Lincoln did not mention it, but everyone knew that although the newly elected Congress was not scheduled to meet until December 1865, a year hence, the President could call a special session any time after he began his second term on March 4.

A practical politician, Lincoln knew that he could not depend upon exhortation alone to gain his ends. Foreseeing the need of every possible vote for the thirteenth amendment, he had strongly supported statehood for Nevada. He had authorized Charles A. Dana, Assistant Secretary of War, to approach three members of the House, offering them political plums in exchange for their support. Nevada had become a state in time to vote for Lincoln and to support the amendment. In January 1865, as the House prepared for its final vote on the amendment, Lincoln authorized Congressman James S. Ashley to sound out two or three on-the-fence Democrats, with a view to swapping favors.

Lincoln also employed personal persuasion. On a card he penciled a note to Congressman James A. Rollins of Missouri, asking him to call at the White House. "I have sent for you as an old Whig friend to come and see me, that I might make an appeal to you to vote for this amendment," said Lincoln after shutting the office door. "It is going to be very close, a few votes one way or the other will decide it." When Rollins said that he was going to support the amendment, Lincoln got up and grasped his hand, saying, "I am most delighted to hear that." Lincoln then asked Rollins if he would not sound out the other border state congressmen and report back to him. Rollins said he would do both.

On Tuesday, January 31, 1865, the final vote was taken in the House. That afternoon the chamber was packed as never before; among the spectators were numerous senators, five Supreme Court justices, and a host of well-dressed women who took over the reporters' gallery, doubtless preferring to see history made than to read about it. The Negro, too, was on hand, his presence chronicled by spectator Henry Highland Garnet: "Amongst them were many a black brother and sister. Yes, there was the ubiquitous Negro—the universal black man—amongst the whites. Oh, it was quite a pepper and salt mixture!"

White and colored grew still and tense as the clerk called the roll. When he had run down the alphabet, the clerk handed a piece of paper to the Speaker, Schuyler Colfax. With every eye upon him, Colfax announced the fateful vote: yeas, 119; nays, 56. The measure had been carried: Congress by a two-thirds majority in both houses had voted to send to the states a constitutional amendment abolishing slavery throughout the United States.

Schuyler's announcement of the yeas and nays was greeted by deafening cheers. The ladies waved their handkerchiefs; the men clapped and shook hands in turn. Some danced for joy, pulling others around with them. For ten minutes the demonstrations went on, with the chair making no effort to restore order. "The scene was grand and impressive beyond description," wrote the *New York Times* reporter. As the members left their seats, they could hear the salvos of artillery guns firing one hundred times in joyful salute. In elation the departing Republican leaders hastened to the White House to thank the President for his support.

Lincoln's joy was second to none. On the original copy of the amendment he wrote, "Approved, February 1. 1865. A. Lincoln," although his signature was not a legal requirement. That evening a jubilant procession marched to the White House, bent on a serenading mission. After the brass band had played several airs, Lincoln appeared at the central upper window of the portico. A great cheer went up. Then Lincoln made a short speech, striking a thoughtful, reflective note. Slavery had been the cause of the war, he told the torchlight crowd; hence it was necessary that it be rooted out. This he had attempted to do by the Emancipation Proclamation; however, the proclamation had its weaknesses. "But this amendment is a King's cure for all the evils. It winds the whole thing up." Lincoln closed on a note of congratulation—to the serenaders, to himself, to the United States, and to the whole world—for "this great moral victory."

Lincoln's words of congratulation were not expressed in a tone of gloating over the South or in praise of the righteousness of the North. Rather, they were an expression of deep thanksgiving, the realization of having taken a momentous step in human affairs, a step that made him feel exalted and humble at the same time—grateful to have had a hand in it, but aware that it was too vast for self-glorification. Lincoln would have agreed with the line appearing in a *New York Times* editorial of that morning: "The adoption of this amendment is the most important step ever taken by Congress."

NATURALLY Negroes were pleased by this turn of events. But by January 1865 they were no longer focusing attention on slavery; to them, as to John Hay, it was a body from which all life had departed. The issue that gripped the Negro of 1864 was the right to vote. Colored leaders and spokesmen held the opinion that freedom without suffrage was somewhat of a sham; it was freedom with a small "f." To Negroes political equality was the very basis upon which to build other equalities.

Black men had let Congress know of their wish to vote. In December 1862 two tailors from Hartford, Connecticut—T.P. Saunders and his brother, P.H.B. Saunders—sent a petition to the Senate stating that because they were Negroes, they were deprived of the "privilege of taking part whatever in matters of Government—both State and National." They prayed relief. Early in 1864 the Israel Lyceum, a group of Negroes of the District of Columbia, distributed a printed petition to the House and Senate, asking that colored male citizens be given the ballot. At the polls "a man confirms his manhood; and defends, supports and preserves his country." Negroes asked for this right "in the name of our blood, sweat, suffering and constancy to our country, the United States of America."

Two months later another group of Washington Negroes sent a similar petition to Congress. They called attention to their role as property holders, as taxpayers, as churchgoers, and as responsible parents, and they advised the legislators not to be alarmed by the prophets of gloom. The experience of the past, said the petition, showed that the fears arising from reforms founded on justice were almost never realized, the freeing of the slaves in the District being a case in point.

The greatest war time expression by Negroes of this desire for the ballot was a national convention held in Syracuse in early October 1864. Among the 144 delegates from eighteen states were several Negro notables: Frederick Douglass, Henry Highland Garnet, William Wells Brown, George T. Downing, and John M. Langston. Out of their four days of deliberation the delegates drew up an "Address to the People of the United States," a lengthy document which devoted most of its attention to the ballot. Claiming that Negro Americans had fully earned the elective franchise, the "Address" raised some pointed questions: "Are we citizens when the nation is in peril, and aliens when the nation is in safety? May we shed our blood under the starspangled banner on the battlefield, and yet be debarred from marching under it at the ballot-box?" To be without the vote in a republic is to be at the mercy of others in the exercise of all other rights. The Negro wanted the franchise "because we don't want to be mobbed from our work, or insulted with impunity at every corner. We are men, and want to be as free in our native country as other men."

Among the first to let Lincoln know of this desire for the ballot were the Negroes of New Orleans. At a meeting held at Economy Hall on November 5, 1863, they agreed to ask George F. Shepley, military governor of Louisiana, for permission to vote. "If we cannot succeed with the authorities here," ran one of their statements, "we will go to President Lincoln." When Shepley ignored their request, the Crescent City Negroes, operating through their Union Radical Association, decided to send a delegate, P. M. Tourné, to Washington to lay their case before the administration. But before Tourné departed, the Negroes received the news that an emissary from Lincoln was on his way to the city. This was James McKaye, favorably known to Negroes as a member of the Freedmen's Inquiry Commission, and now traveling on a roving assignment as Lincoln's eyes and ears concerning the Negro in the South.

At the meeting held at Lyceum Hall on February 8, 1864, McKaye told the Negroes that Lincoln had a great interest in them and was anxious to find out what their wishes were. The assembled Negroes gave McKaye the information he sought. They told him that they wanted public schools; they wanted to be treated like men; they wanted the black codes abolished; and, above all, they wanted the ballot. Then, in resolutions read in both English and French, the Negroes expressed their "unbounded and heartfelt thanks to the President of these United States." They prayed for his "long continuance in his present high and responsible position."

The mass meeting closed on a note of hope. But it was not long before New Orleans Negroes decided that they must go ahead with their original plan to send a delegation to Washington. Louisiana was scheduled to hold a constitutional convention in April 1864, and all signs pointed to the likelihood that the convention would make no provision for equal suffrage. Hence, the Negroes of New Orleans drew up a petition, bearing 1000 signatures and addressed to Lincoln and to Congress. The signers asked for the right to vote, basing their claim on three grounds, one of which was military service. They had borne arms for their state: many of them (twenty-seven in number) had served under Andrew Jackson in the Battle of New Orleans on January 8, 1815, and others had served in the present war under Generals Butler and Banks. Moreover, said their petition, every one of them was a man of property, most of it in real estate; and, finally, every one of them had been born free. The petitioners hastened to add that they did not have in mind their group or class only:

> Your memorialists pray that the right of suffrage may be extended not only to natives of Louisiana of African descent, born free, but also to all others, whether born slave or free, especially those who have vindicated their right to vote by bearing arms, subject only to such qualifications as shall equally affect the white and colored citizens.

To bring this document to Washington, the Negroes selected Jean Baptiste Roudanez and Arnold Bertonneau. The former had been an engineer on large sugar plantations. Bertonneau was a wine merchant who had become a captain in the first Negro regiment raised by Butler. In the spring of 1861 he had served as secretary of the group of New Orleans Negroes who had offered their services to the municipal authorities in case of enemy invasion.

The two light-skinned Negroes came to the White House on March 12, 1864. Lincoln received them with his customary courtesy, but he gave them little satisfaction. "I regret, gentlemen, that you are not able to secure all your rights," Colonel Forney quotes him as saying, "and that circumstances will not permit the government to confer them upon you." The best he could do, said Lincoln, was to refer them back to the constitutional convention soon to be held in their own state.

Roudanez and Bertonneau left the White House with their feathers down. Some days later their spirits picked up when the abolitionists of Boston gave them a complimentary dinner, with Governor Andrew as toastmaster, and attended by William Lloyd Garrison, Frederick Douglass, J. G. Palfrey, and James Freeman Clarke. The spirits of the two delegates would have soared a bit higher had they known that they and their petition had made an impression on Lincoln. On the day after their White House visit the President penned a private letter to Michael Hahn, the newly elected governor of Louisiana. Its contents were significant, marking a step forward in Lincoln's thinking:

> Now you are about to have a Convention which, among other things, will probably define the elective franchise. I barely suggest for your private consideration, whether some of the colored people may not be let in—as, for instance, the very intelligent, and especially those who have fought gallantly in our ranks. They would probably help, in some trying time to come, to keep the jewel of liberty within the family of freedom.

James G. Blaine, writing at a later day, commented that Lincoln's closing expression "may have been pleonastic." But, added Congressman Blaine in the same breath, "his meaning was one of deep and almost prophetic significance. It was perhaps the earliest proposition from any authentic source to endow the Negro with the right of suffrage."

Although Lincoln's letter was private, Governor Hahn undoubtedly showed it to General N.P. Banks, commanding in Louisiana. Hitherto doubtful about giving the Negro the vote, Banks on March 28, in a letter to James McKaye, expressed himself as favoring the franchise for Negroes of intelligence. Banks's conversion had some effect on the delegates to the constitutional convention, which held its first meeting on April 6. This body granted the franchise to white males only. But Banks, using all his influence, persuaded the delegates to grant authority to the legislature to extend voting privileges to such other persons as might merit it by military service, payment of taxes, and intellectual capacity. On the day the convention adjourned, July 25, Banks wrote happily to Lincoln that Negro suffrage was sure to come soon. Banks misread the times; the Louisiana legislature was not destined to use its power to extend the ballot to the Negro.

Two MONTHS after Roudanez and Bertonneau came to Washington, the President had another visit from Negroes who wanted the vote extended to black and white alike in their commonwealth. Early in May 1864 five Negroes from North Carolina called at the Executive Mansion and were shown in. Their spokesman, Abraham H. Galloway of Beaufort, informed Lincoln that in North Carolina colored men had voted until 1835 with no detriment to the public welfare. The Negroes of present-day North Carolina, continued Galloway, wanted the President to finish the noble work he had begun: "Grant unto your petitioners that greatest of privileges, when the State is reconstructed, to exercise the right of suffrage." The ballot would "extend our sphere of influence" and "redound to your honor."

The listening Lincoln apparently said little. But, according to the *Anglo-African* of May 14, 1864, he gave assurances "of his sympathy and earnest cooperation." The visiting Negroes left the White House feeling that they had a friend in Lincoln. Clinton D. Pearson, one of the two former slaves in the delegation, speaking at a meeting in his honor at New York's Mt. Zion Church, informed his audience that the President was very much interested in the struggle of the colored people.

Lincoln undoubtedly sympathized with the disfranchised. But as a rule he believed that the people of a state should themselves take the lead in matters affecting their welfare. On the suffrage, as in so many other things, Lincoln believed in federal noninterference. He wanted the states, as he told Governor Hahn, to confer the ballot on Negroes who had seen military service or who were highly intelligent. But if, as in the case of Louisiana, a state was unwilling to enfranchise the colored man, Lincoln was not willing to penalize her.

Of course Negroes and their supporters were dismayed that Lincoln would require qualifications from colored citizens that he would not ask of whites. And naturally they were displeased that he would readmit to the Union former rebel states, even if their constitutions were silent on Negro suffrage. Lincoln was ever a growing man, but he did not fully perceive the role of the ballot as a source of protection for the former slave. What he did sense was that the South was not ready for Negro suffrage.

He was almost equally sure that most of the people in the North had the same reluctance to give the ballot to the black man. Lincoln did not feel like compelling the South to do something that the North also had not got around to doing. This line of reasoning was vexing to equal-rights champion Charles Sumner. Seeking an outlet for his sense of frustration after two and a half hours spent in conversation with Lincoln one morning in early January 1865, the Senator from Massachusetts sent a letter to Zachariah Chandler relating something of what he had gone through:

PRESDT: "Mr. S. Do murders occur in Mass.?"
MR. S.: "Unhappily, yes, Mr. Presdt."
PRESDT: "Do people ever knock each other down in Boston?"
MR. S. : "Unhappily yes, Mr. Presdt., sometimes."
PRESDT: "Would you consent that Mass. be excluded from the Union on this account?"
MR. S. : "No, Mr. Presdt., surely not."

So GREAT was Lincoln's popularity among the Negro rank and file that it was hardly affected by his go-slow policy on equal suffrage. But if Negroes felt any sense of being let down by Lincoln, this feeling was made easier to bear by his appointment of a successor to Roger B. Taney as Chief Justice of the Supreme Court. For this highest judicial office, the President named Salmon P. Chase, a name more revered among Negroes than any others in public life except those of Lincoln and Senator Sumner.

Chase's friendship for Negroes had been demonstrated ever since his early years as a lawyer in Cincinnati, where he defended runaway slaves and took an active part in the antislavery movement. As Secretary of the Treasury in the Lincoln Cabinet, Chase ordered the dismissal of clerks who expressed anti-Negro sentiments. In one instance a clerk who refused to contribute to a fund to assist in the raising of a colored regiment found himself without a job. It was Chase who in September 1862 sparked a legal opinion that Edward W. Bates regarded as the most important decision he ever made as Attorney General. A schooner was being held at Perth Amboy because its captain was a Negro and hence presumably unable to meet the requirement of United States citizenship. Chase sent a letter to Bates, outlining the details of the case, stating that Negro captains were numerous in the coastwise trade, and requesting an official answer to the question: "Are colored men citizens of the United States, and therefore competent to command American vessels?"

After seven weeks of intensive study, including a reading of George Livermore's treatise on the role of the Negro in the Revolutionary War, Bates informed Chase that a free Negro who was born in the United States was a citizen, citizenship being a "natural-born right" under the Constitution. In his official opinion, running to twenty printed pages and delivered on November 29, 1862, Bates struck a roundabout blow at the Dred Scott decision by ruling that the "Constitution is silent about race as it is about color." The decision that the free Negro was a citizen was made by Bates, but the pleased colored people gave their thanks less to him than to Chase.

In naming Chase as Chief Justice, a step he took on December 6, 1864, Lincoln had some misgivings, feeling that Chase had been hopelessly bitten by the presidential bug and would never be satisfied with a lesser post. But Negroes had no reservations about their long-time supporter. A convention of colored men of Ohio, held at Xenia early in January 1865, passed a resolution hailing with joy the "installation" of Chase as Chief Justice. An editorial in the *Anglo-African* of December 17, 1864 professed to see in the appointment of Chase a proof of Lincoln's own antislavery principles.

The new Chief Justice did not lose his interest in the Negro. On the night of January 31, a few hours after witnessing the passage of the Thirteenth Amendment by the House, Chase came to Baltimore upon invitation to attend a Henry Ward Beecher lecture sponsored by the Baltimore Association for the Moral and Educational Improvement of the Colored People. The officers of the Negro-run organization had also sent a letter of invitation to the President, enclosing a ticket on which was written, "Admit Abraham Lincoln, President United States." At the lecture, delivered at the Maryland Institute, Beecher held forth for two solid hours. When he had finished, however, the presiding officer, Hugh L. Bond, asked Chase to say something. The Chief Justice obligingly "made a few remarks."

On the following morning Chase, back in Washington, performed an official duty that he found most agreeable. At eleven o'clock sharp he entered the court chamber at the head of the procession of gowned judges and took his seat. Thereupon Charles Sumner arose and said in quiet tones, "May it please the Court, I move that John S. Rock, a member of the Supreme Court of the State of Massachusetts, be admitted to practice as a member of this Court." If candidate Rock had any trace of "white blood," it was not visible; in skin color, texture of hair, shape of skull, formation of nose, and size of lip, he was "unqualifiedly, obtrusively, defiantly" Negro. As Sumner completed his short statement, Chase nodded his massive head in assent. A clerk came forward and administered the oath to Rock, thus making him the first Negro ever empowered to plead a case before the Supreme Court.

"Good news, chariot's coming," were words from an old spiritual, and hence familiar to Negroes. To them such events as the passage of the Thirteenth Amendment and the admission of Rock to the bar of the highest tribunal were evidences that freedom's chariot was rolling along in juggernaut fashion. Another evidence, more personal than political, was the manner in which the colored people were being received at public receptions held at the White House. Negroes wanted such marks of full citizenship as the right to vote, but they also wanted to be received and welcomed at public receptions and ceremonies as were other Americans. The Lincolns were the first couple to make the Negro feel that he might dare to put in an appearance at White House functions open to the public.

At the public reception held on January 1, 1864, from twelve noon until two o'clock, four Negroes stood in line, persons "of genteel exterior and the manners of gentlemen." When their turn came, they were presented to the President by Marshal Lamon and to the First Lady by Commissioner B.B. French. The Lincolns betrayed no distaste or surprise. Nobody seems to have been hurt, reported the *Washington Chronicle* of January 2, hastening to add a word lest its position be misconstrued: "We are neither amalgamationists nor the advocates for the levelling of all social distinctions; but we rejoice that we have a President who is a democrat in fact as well as by nature."

A year later at the annual New Year's reception in the Blue Room, a "throng" of Negroes, men and women, put in their appearance, some well dressed, others in patched clothes. They waited until the closing minutes when the reception lines had thinned, as if a rebuff would be easier to bear if not witnessed by too many. They soon found that they had nothing to fear. Lincoln's hand had grown weary, and his grasp was languid, but he seemed to take on fresh vigor at the sight of the dark faces. Heartily he shook hands with the Negroes, as they murmured, "God bless you," and "God bress, Massa Linkum." Some of the more excitable ones moved away laughing and weeping by turns.

Two months later, Negroes took part for the first time in an Inauguration Day parade. At noon on March 4, Lincoln was to be sworn in for his second term. In the line that marched from the White House to the Capitol were four companies of the Fifty-fourth Regiment of United States Colored Troops, forming part of the military escort. The Negro soldiers were cheered all along the route. Keeping step close behind them were three lodges of Negro Odd Fellows—Union, J. R. Brooks, and Friendship—dressed in full regalia and bearing a gold-laced silk and satin banner with a portrait "of some colored celebrity." One of the most unusual floats in the procession was the "Temple of Liberty," which was filled with youngsters, some of them colored, singing "Rally Round the Flag, Boys."

At the Capitol the Negroes, marchers and spectators, stood in ankle-deep mud to listen to Lincoln's brief but immortal second inaugural address. The President spoke of the cause of the war—slavery—and said that God might have visited the present troubles upon America as a punishment. Leaving vengeance to a Higher Power, Lincoln called upon his countrymen to bind the nation's wounds, pursuing this task with malice toward none and with charity for all. Finishing his speech, Lincoln waited for the applause to die down before turning to the Chief Justice for the oath of office.

On that Saturday evening, from eight to twelve, the customary inaugural reception was to be held. Frederick Douglass decided to attend, as sort of a climax to his experiences during the preceding twenty-four hours. That afternoon he had heard Lincoln's address and had witnessed the swearing-in ceremony. The preceding evening he had taken tea with Chief Justice Chase and had assisted Kate Chase Sprague in helping her father try on the new robe in which he was to administer the oath of office to the President.

It was in the mood of these experiences that Douglass went to the White House grounds and took his place in the inaugural reception line. When he reached the outer entrance, two policemen told him to turn around and go back. Douglass replied that he would not leave until he had seen the President. Spying a visitor that knew him, the Negro asked him to tell Lincoln that he was being detained at the door. Some minutes later the policemen got an order to let Frederick Douglass pass. Lincoln's cordiality did much to restore the Negro leader's peace of mind. Telling Douglass that he was glad to see him, the President asked him his opinion of the inaugural address. "Mr. Lincoln, that was a sacred effort." The President was pleased, saying that he was glad Douglass liked it.

Possibly Douglass' success in getting into the Blue Room became known that night to other Negroes, and they followed suit. According to the *Baltimore Sun* of March 6, 1865 and the Philadelphia *Press* of the same date, "many colored persons" were among the some 5000 visitors who came to pay their respects to the President and Mrs. Lincoln.

A MONTH after Inauguration Day, another large group of Negroes —those in Richmond—had the opportunity to greet the President face to face. On April 3, 1865, Richmond fell to the Union troops; the Confederate government officials fled the city a few hours before rebel commander Richard S. Ewell put it to the torch. The North was elated over the news, everyone sensing that the war must come to a close very soon. Sharing this mood of thanksgiving and celebration, Lincoln decided to give it free rein by paying a visit to the captured city. He scheduled his trip for the following day, April 4.

Late that morning, as the gunboat carrying Lincoln sailed up the James River, it ran aground just outside Richmond. Thereupon Lincoln and a small party—his son Tad, Admiral David D. Porter, three junior officers, and a dozen sailors—boarded a twelve-oared barge. Some minutes later the barge pulled up at Rockett's Landing, a point at the foot of the city. The arrival of the small party was unexpected; hence, there was no military escort or guard to meet them and conduct them to General Godfrey Weitzel's headquarters more than a mile away. But the Lincoln party soon found that there was no lack of welcomers, for Richmond numbered Negroes in its population.

The city's ten thousand blacks were in the right frame of mind to greet Lincoln. On the preceding day they had been overjoyed when the Union forces made their triumphant entry, their ranks swelled by a Negro cavalry regiment, the Fifth Massachusetts, along with the foot soldiers of the Ninth U.S. Colored Troops and the Twenty-ninth Colored Volunteers. When the imprisoned bondmen in Lumkin's Jail learned that black infantrymen were parading past the building, they raised their voices in "Slavery Chain Done Broke at Last," giving birth to a new song, one that caught the mood of the city's Negroes.

Doubtless some of Richmond's sable inhabitants knew of the incident that had taken place that morning involving a Negro war correspondent for a white daily. Thirty-year-old T. Morris Chester of Harrisburg, Pennsylvania, who wrote under the name "Rollin," had been seated in the Confederate House chamber writing his dispatch for the *Philadelphia Press*. At the sight of a colored person settled comfortably in the very chair of the Speaker of the House, a paroled rebel officer was unable to restrain himself. "Get out of there, you damned nigger," said he, moving toward Chester. There had been a tussle, and when it was over, the tall and muscular Chester had gone back to his seat to finish his dispatch.

After twenty-four hours of such miracles, perhaps Richmond Negroes were not wholly unprepared for the coming of Lincoln. As the President stepped ashore holding Tad by the hand, the only persons at the wharf were a group of Negro laborers. Almost at once they recognized him from his pictures. One of them, a man of sixty, straightened up and exclaimed, "Bless de Lord, dere is de great Messiah! I knowed him soon as I seed him. He's bin in my heart fo' long yeahs, and he's cum at las' to free his chillum from deir bondage! Glory, Hallelujah!" The old man fell on his knees, the other Negroes following suit. "You must kneel to God only," said the embarrassed Lincoln.

The Negroes arose and, joining hands in a circle, began to sing a hymn. As they sang and Lincoln listened, the crowd got larger and larger, coming "from over the hills and from the waterside." The alarmed Admiral Porter ordered the sailors to fix bayonets to their rifles to prevent the party from being crushed to death. The Negroes showed no sign of dispersing, behaving as though Lincoln had come expressly to greet them. Surrounded by admirers whose number was multiplying, the captive President realized that he must yield.

Holding up his hand for silence, he began to speak. Assuring his listeners that they were free, he told them that it was now up to them to prove themselves worthy of their freedom. This, said he, they could do by obeying the laws and keeping the commandments. The President's brief remarks were received with loud cheers and shouts, after which the satisfied Negroes fell back, opening a path.

Followed by an ever growing throng, Lincoln and his party left the waterfront and walked through streets, that had suddenly become alive with Negroes. Their eyes were riveted on the man in the long black duster and the high silk hat. Many of them could not contain themselves at the sight of him and gave expression to their feelings by shouts, screams, whoops, ejaculations, and body twistings. Many Negroes gave way to the urge to take something off, so that, according to spectator George A. Bruce, the streets through which the procession passed were "literally covered with abandoned hats and clothing."

Just before the President and his party reached their destination, they were met by a cavalry escort. Admiral Porter breathed easier. It was rash to have permitted Lincoln to enter Richmond as he did, without adequate military escort. Yet, surrounded by his Negro admirers, Lincoln was not without protection; it would have been a rash man who would have laid a finger on him.

At General Weitzel's headquarters, President Davis' former official residence, Lincoln sank into a chair and said that he was thirsty. A Negro manservant, considerately left behind by Mrs. Davis, got water for Lincoln and something stronger for the other notables. After resting awhile, Lincoln got into an open carriage to make a sightseeing tour of the city. His cavalry escort were colored, and it seemed to the whites in Richmond that they were the blackest of their race.

Lincoln's trip around the city was slowed not only by the fallen bricks which littered the streets of the badly burned city but also by the mass of Negroes who were bent on seeing him and, if possible, on touching him. On one occasion when the party had to make a stop, two colored urchins climbed on the top of Lincoln's carriage and took a downward peep into the President's eyes. All along the way the Negroes gave expression to their sentiments. "De kingdom's come, and de Lord is wid us," chanted one woman. "I'd rather see him than Jesus," exclaimed another, trying to get in front of the carriage so that she might get a full-face view of Lincoln.

That evening the weary President returned to the wharf to take leave of Richmond. Reporter T. Morris Chester, in a dispatch filed the following morning, related that as Lincoln prepared to step into the rowboat that would take him to the flagship *Malvern*, a "good old colored female shouted out, 'Don't drown, Massa Abe, for God's sake.'"

ABRAHAM LINCOLN did not drown, but he returned to Washington only to meet a fate more tragic—a fate, however, that would do much to enshrine his fame, fixing it in the image set by the Negro.

10

A SLEEP AND A REMEMBERING

On the day that Lincoln died, the weather in Washington was bad, a cold rain falling. "Were you there when the sun refused to shine," runs an old spiritual in describing the kind of day it was when "they crucified my Lord." To Negroes it was a totally sunless day when Abraham Lincoln's hour struck.

The blow was harder to bear for having come without warning. On the preceding night, April 14, Lincoln had gone to Ford's Theatre for a few hours of relaxation. He was watching the comedy unfold when the door of his box quietly opened, and John Wilkes Booth let himself in. A professional actor casting himself in the real-life role of avenger of the defeated Southland, Booth pointed a derringer at the President's head and pulled the trigger. Lincoln's eyes closed, never to open again; he died a few minutes before seven thirty the next morning.

The news of Booth's deed stunned the Negroes of the city. Overwhelmed with grief, many of them walked up and down in front of the dwelling on Tenth Street where the dying President lay in the plain wooden bed of a rented room. Other Negroes had gone to the Executive Mansion and pressed their faces against the wet iron fence. "The Negroes who idolize Lincoln here line the sidewalk in front of the White House," wrote paymaster's clerk Charles A. Sanford. "Oh! how terrible!" Secretary Welles, afoot early that fateful morning, said that although strong men wept without shame, nothing moved him more deeply than the unrelieved sorrow of the Negroes.

Not far from the White House grounds that morning, Jane Gray Swisshelm heard one Negro woman express puzzlement that Lincoln should have met with violence in Washington after being down to Richmond where the danger supposedly was. Giving up trying to fathom such a mystery, the woman stamped her foot and shouted, "My good President! I would rather have died myself! I would rather have given the babe from my bosom! Oh, Jesus! Oh, Jesus."

Another colored woman whose grief was just as intense but whose manner was more restrained was Mrs. Keckley. Sent for by the inconsolable Mrs. Lincoln, she had snatched up her bonnet and shawl and hurried to the White House. Once there, she relieved Mrs. Gideon Welles, who had attended Mrs. Lincoln throughout the night. With Mrs. Keckley bathing her head, the bereaved First Lady became a little less violent. When Mrs. Keckley felt that she could be spared for a few minutes, she asked permission to view the body of the President, which had been escorted to the Executive Mansion at 9:30 A.M.

As the distinguished-looking and stylish mulatto entered the guest room where the lifeless form lay in state, the Cabinet officers and military commanders broke their circle so that she could make her way forward. Looking down into Lincoln's face, Mrs. Keckley's composure left her for a few moments; her eyes filled with tears and her throat suddenly became dry and tight. She recalled that the last time she had seen Lincoln, he had spoken kindly to her. But her feelings of personal bereavement soon merged into a more inclusive sense of loss: "No common mortal had died. The Moses of my people had fallen in the hour of triumph." When her bittersweet reflections had been brought under outward control, Mrs. Keckley filed out of the room, her heart pounding and her footsteps not wholly steady.

In addition to the tens of thousands of personal lamentations by Negroes on that dread Saturday morning, there was one formal and official expression of sorrow, doubtless the first in the country. At Baltimore, the forty-eighth annual conference of the African Methodist Episcopal Church happened to be in session, having begun its deliberations on Thursday of that week. When the Saturday morning session was called to order, the presiding officer, Bishop Daniel A. Payne, "announced the death of Lincoln in a very feeling manner," as the *Baltimore Sun* reported it. Thereupon the delegates drew up a series of resolutions expressing their deep sorrow over the "cowardly assassination" of "the great and good Abraham Lincoln" and extending their profoundest condolences to his widow. Like most of the tens of thousands of resolutions, speeches, and sermons that would flood the country within the next few days, the resolutions bore a tone of outrage reaching the proportions of vengeance. Invoking the memory of John Brown (whose blood "was shed to inaugurate the meting out of justice to those who had long oppressed the Savior in the person of the bondmen"), the conference resolutions pledged to President Johnson two hundred thousand muskets to protect the flag.

As Washington prepared for the funeral exercises, the city's Negroes went into mourning. Many families went without a meal to buy a yard or two of black ribbon to hang above the door or window. By some means or other, most Negro women managed to procure mourning dresses, veils, and bonnets, while the Negro men faced a lesser problem of obtaining crepe bands for their hats. Such black-bedecked colored men and women were among the more than 25,000 visitors to the East Room on Tuesday, April 18, come to take a last solemn look as they filed past the President's bier.

On the following afternoon the impressive funeral services were held at the White House. Then came the procession to the Capitol, where the body was to lie in state. Forty thousand mourners were in the line of march following the long, black hearse and keeping a slow step to the dirges played by the regimental bands. Marching at the head of the line was a detachment of Negro soldiers, the Twenty-second U.S. Colored Infantry.

To have a Negro contingent lead the funeral procession had not been in the plans. It resulted, rather, from an accident of timing. Just up from Petersburg and hurrying down the avenue to be assigned to their proper place in the line of march, the Negro detachment reached the front of the procession just as it was about to move off, precisely at two o'clock. With the middle of the streets solidly filled with marchers, and with the sidewalks massed with onlookers, the three hundred soldiers could proceed no further. And since they could not be conjured away, the parade marshals, swallowing hard, decided to let them lead the way. Whereupon the black regiment wheeled about, reversed its arms, and "formed the advance of the whole."

If Negroes led the long parade, they also brought up the rear. Separated from the Negro regiment by over a mile in space, and by some two hours in time, were more than a dozen colored organizations and groups. Leading this contingent were the conference delegates of the A.M.E. Church, headed by Bishops Payne and W.A. Wayman, who had chartered a train and come over from Baltimore in a body that morning. A number of fraternal organizations were out in full strength, such as the Blue Lodge of Ancient York Masons and the Harmony Lodge of Odd Fellows. The clergymen of the various Protestant denominations, other than the A.M.E.'s, marched in one group; the Catholic Benevolent Association marched in another. Regardless of the organization to which they belonged, all the colored marchers bore one basic similarity: "their walk and their mien," wrote a *New York Times* reporter, "were the very impersonation of sorrow."

The same type of response came from the Negro spectators. With tearful eyes they watched the black hearse roll by. Grief-stricken to the bottom of their hearts, their lament for Lincoln was in part a sorrow for themselves. As they listened to the dirgeful sounds that were pealing from every church and firehouse, they felt that the bells were not tolling for Lincoln alone.

Taken to the Capitol rotunda, the body lay in state that night and the next day. At eight o'clock on Friday morning, six days after the death, the funeral cortege left Washington to make its journey to Springfield, Illinois—a trip of 1600 miles, lasting for twelve days. More than a million and a half mourners were to take a look at the rigid face of Lincoln, as the funeral procession paused at Baltimore, Harrisburg, Philadelphia, New York, Albany, Syracuse, Rochester, Buffalo, Cleveland, Columbus, Indianapolis, and Chicago.

In these cities the typical response of the Negroes may be illustrated by their behavior in Philadelphia. In the procession that escorted the body to Independence Hall were eleven lodges of Masons and eight lodges of Odd Fellows, all in black uniforms. Represented also were several other groups, including the Colored Union League Association, the Banneker Literary Institute, and the Delmonico Benevolent Association, all wearing black suits with white badges pinned on.

At Independence Hall the head of the coffin was placed near the Liberty Bell. Standing on a pedestal near both was a home-made wreath of fir, which had been brought to the building early that morning by an old Negro woman. As reported in the *Philadelphia Press*, she had presented it to a guard, saying that it was all she had to give.

The lines waiting to get into Independence Hall extended three miles and were "liberally sprinkled" with colored men and women. At the hall the scene was solemn, as the mourners filed in and out. At one time, however, the quiet was broken when a Negro woman, "sixty-five or seventy, thrilled the spectators with open expressions of grief." Crying and clasping her hands, she kept repeating that Lincoln was dead. According to the *National Intelligencer*, her deep devotion found a ready response in every listener's heart and seemed to intensify the general sorrow.

On May 3 the funeral cortege reached Springfield, where the body was brought to the Capitol to lie in state. Shortly before noon the thousands of mourners were directed to their proper positions for the two-mile trek to Oak Ridge Cemetery; the local committee on arrangements had divided them into twenty-one groupings, with "Colored Persons" numbered last. To Springfield Negroes their position in the procession was far less important than their desire to pay their respects to one whom they had designated as "the benefactor of our race" at a mass meeting at the Baptist Church a few days after his death. Lining up with the other Negroes was Billy the Barber, who qualified for a position more to the front, but who preferred to be among those whom he felt to be the truest mourners.

Bringing up the rear, the Negroes followed the coffin to the burial grounds. Here under a burning sun, there were prayers and hymns and a reading of the second inaugural address. The brief but impressive services were rounded out with the doxology and a benediction.

At Oak Ridge a Lincoln monument would be dedicated some nine years later. The men of the armed forces contributed $27,682 to the fund to build it. Of this sum, $8000, or more than one-quarter, came from the Negro regiments. Indeed, the Seventy-third U.S. Colored Troops gave $1437, the greatest single contribution except those of the states of Illinois and New York. And the donations made by white regiments might include a Negro giver; in one Illinois company the last name on the list read thus: "Anthony E. Carter—Captain's Cook, Colored Man—$10.00."

THE GRIEF of the Negro was nationwide, embracing the crowded haunts of the cities and the huts and cabins of the plantation regions. Perhaps no tears were more sincere than those of the former slaves. Some of them feared that Lincoln's death meant that they would be returned to bondage. At St. Helena a Negro asked schoolmistress Laura M. Towne if it were true that "Government was dead."

To the Negro in the South, Lincoln was the personification of the freedom for which they had watched and prayed. He had redeemed their manhood. If they had known of Julia Ward Howe's "Battle Hymn of the Republic," they would have restated one of its passages thus: Christ died to make them holy, and

Lincoln died to make them free. But their own idiom conveyed the same meaning: the Lord had saved them from sin, and Lincoln had saved them from "secesh." Among some Sea Islanders the manner of Lincoln's death strengthened their belief in his supernaturalism. One of them told Miss Towne that "Lincoln died for we, Christ died for we, and me believe him the same mans."

Typical of the Lincoln funeral exercises in the coastal regions was that held at Beaufort, South Carolina. In a schoolroom draped in black, the mourners assembled. Everyone wore some emblem of sorrow—a black headband or a black bow on a topknot. One man had turned his coat inside out in order to achieve the proper color; equally spectacular, and more resourceful, was a woman who sported a gown of black cambric basted with white cotton up and down in front and all around the bottom. Wearing their black "sacredly," and hence sensing nothing ludicrous in their appearance, the solemn-faced Negroes listened to prayers and chants, one leader calling Lincoln by every endearing name he could think of. Many gave way to low sobs and moans, which seemed to deepen the general fervor.

In the lower South the grief of the Negro was no less marked. At Mobile the Negro quarter—buildings and inhabitants—had taken on a somber appearance, with black cloth and clothing everywhere. The mood of the city's Negroes was so overwrought that many white people became alarmed. Going to Thomas W. Conway, the general superintendent of the freedmen in the Department of the Gulf, they urged him to use his influence to keep the colored people quiet.

New Orleans was the scene of the largest of the Negro observances of Lincoln's death. Pooling their resources, the city's one hundred benevolent organizations called a mass meeting for Saturday, April 22, one week after the assassination. Ten thousand Negroes paraded the main streets of the city—Rampart, Canal, St. Charles, Poydras, and Camp—to assemble at Congo Square, their favorite historic spot. Here they drew up resolutions pledging themselves to wear mourning bands on their left arms for thirty days, and expressing their indebtedness to Lincoln. Their general sentiment may be summed up in a line from the city's Negro journal, *Black Republican,* which came out that day: "In giving us our liberty, he has lost his own life."

In the North in the months following Lincoln's death, the meetings held by Negro organizations invariably passed resolutions saying that his name would be cherished forever. The Colored Men's Convention of Michigan, held in Detroit in early September, spoke of "the noble, patriotic, philanthropic and humane deeds of our much beloved and ever to be praised late Chief Magistrate." At the first annual meeting of the Equal Rights League, held in Cleveland in mid-October, the delegates expressed joy that heaven permitted "so good and great a man to live so long among us."

Many of these meetings, such as those just mentioned, were primarily efforts to obtain the ballot. Hence by speaking of Lincoln and Negro enfranchisement in the same series of resolutions, it became possible to run the two together, as though they were interchangeable, if not inseparable. Any gap between Lincoln and Negro suffrage was bridged by the Illinois State Convention of Colored Men, which met at Galesburg in October 1866 and issued an "Address to the American People":

> A voice from the tomb of the martyred Lincoln seems now to reach the national ear, saying, "The hour is come in which to enfranchise the colored people, that they may help you keep the jewel of liberty in the family of freedom."

Having identified Lincoln with the ballot, the Negroes found the next step much easier—that of linking him firmly to the Republican party. The chieftains of the G.O.P. soon found that the name of Lincoln cast a spell over the Negro voter, a charm that would lose its potency only after nearly three quarters of a century.

SOME NEGROES would keep Lincoln's memory alive by voting the straight Republican ticket; others would do so by keepsakes and mementos. As other Americans did, Negroes enjoyed owning articles identified with the martyred President. Remembering that her husband had often mentioned that he would like to present Douglass with some token of his regard, Mrs. Lincoln sent his favorite walking stick to the Negro orator. (Lincoln had several canes which had come to the White House as presents.) In his gracious letter of acknowledgment Douglass said that he regarded the gift not only as a mark of Lincoln's kind regard for him personally, "but as an indication of his humane interest in the welfare of my whole race." Douglass's thanks to Mrs. Lincoln were heartfelt; no gift from any other prominent person did he prize as highly, including a similar walking stick presented to him by Queen Victoria on his third visit to the British Isles in 1887. Another cane of Lincoln's was given to Henry Highland Garnet, who offered to assist Mrs. Lincoln in promoting the sale of some of her gowns and jewelry.

Negroes less renowned than Garnet and Douglass had to make themselves content with souvenirs less personal. One colored man proudly wore a ring made out of a few strands taken from the mane of one of Lincoln's horses; it had been the gift of his brother, James R. Davis, groom to the Bostonian who had purchased the President's stable.

The Negroes most likely to come into possession of Lincoln souvenirs would naturally be those who worked at the White House. The messenger-valet William Slade removed a lock of the dead President's hair (which may be seen at the Lincoln National Foundation at Fort Wayne, the gift of Negro dentist John E. Washington, author of *They Knew Lincoln* and collector of Lincolniana). To Slade went the President's heavy gray shawl, plus another of his walking sticks. Slade's wife was given the black silk dress worn by Mrs. Lincoln at Ford's Theatre, bearing the stains of the President's blood. Mrs. Slade subsequently gave this souvenir to Major Christian A. Fleetwood, Negro recipient of the Congressional Medal for heroic conduct on the field of battle.

The Negro who possessed by far the most Lincoln mementos was Elizabeth Keckley. Indeed, most of the articles given away by the generous Mrs. Lincoln had first to pass through Mrs. Keckley's hands. For the six weeks following the President's death, Mrs. Keckley was his widow's companion and attendant, her travel bills and other expenses being officially paid out of federal funds. A few weeks before Booth's bullet, Mrs. Keckley, at her request, had received the glove worn by the President at the public reception on the night of the Second Inaugural. Among other objects coming into her possession were the earrings, bonnet, and velvet cloak worn by the First Lady on the night of the assassination, plus Lincoln's comb, brush, and overshoes.

Mrs. Keckley sent three of her souvenirs to Daniel A. Payne, president of Wilberforce College, her son's alma mater. The main building of the college had been burned to the ground, the work of incendiaries, on the day Lincoln was shot. To assist Bishop Payne in raising money to erect a new building, Mrs. Keckley sent him, on January 1, 1868, the dress worn by Mrs. Lincoln on the day of the Second Inaugural, along with the cloak and bonnet she wore at Ford's Theatre. Signing herself "Your sister in Christ," Mrs. Keckley let Payne know that she had refused to sell these objects, despite many offers, but that she was willing to donate them "for the cause of educating the four millions of slaves liberated by our President, whose private character I revere."

A quarter of a century after she last entered the White House, Mrs. Keckley was still in possession of Lincoln souvenirs. A sampling of these she sent to Jesse W. Weik, the literary associate of Lincoln's law partner, William H. Herndon; she described them in an accompanying letter, dated 2 April 1889:

> I want to present you with a few strands of President Lincoln's hair, cut off by my own hands the day after he was assassinated, and a few strands of Willie's, cut off by my own hands after death. There is also a piece of the gown Mrs. Lincoln wore on the night Mr. Lincoln said our cat has a long [tail] tonight, and also a piece of the dress worn by Mrs. Lincoln at Mr. Lincoln's second inaugural ball. Both dresses were made by my own hands, at which time I was also Mrs. Lincoln's modist [sic].

LINCOLN would be kept alive less by wisps of hair and bits of cloth than by a constant retelling of his story. "Faithful to his memory, we shall tell our sons of the actions of this just man, who has passed from this life to the life immortal." So wrote the members of Concord Lodge in London on sending to President Andrew Johnson their condolences in a communication that they described as "A Message from Descendants of Slaves."

In the story they would relate to their children, Negroes would lay stress on the enduring Lincoln, in whom death was swallowed up in victory. The Lincoln they had in mind was described by an elderly former slave at Chapel Hill, North Carolina, on May 23, 1865:

> He is gone out of glory to glory,
> A smile with the tear may be shed.
> Oh, then let us tell the sweet story—
> Triumphantly, Lincoln is dead.

BECAUSE FREEDOM is a deep river, Negroes would prefer to cross over in a calm time. But cross over they must, being Americans. And the Negroes of the Civil War years and after could find strength for the struggle by reflecting upon the life of a man who, on the threshold of his career, had said that this nation could not endure half slave and half free; a man who, at the midpoint of his presidency, had called upon his generation to highly resolve that America should have a new birth of freedom; and a man who, as the unseen shadows gathered around him, had exhorted his countrymen to strive on to finish the great work they were in.

Bibliography

The chief source used in putting this book together is *The Collected Works of Abraham Lincoln*, Roy P. Basler, editor, with the assistance of Marion D. Pratt and Lloyd A. Dunlap. Published in eight volumes in 1953, this compilation is replete with voluminous notes and sidelights on the myriad men and measures that crop up in Lincoln's speeches and writings. Unless otherwise indicated, this is the source used herein whenever Lincoln himself is quoted.

Other printed works focusing on Lincoln that have proved of marked service to this writer include the standard biography by his secretaries, John G. Nicolay and John Hay, *Abraham Lincoln: A History* (10 vols., 1890), which still stands the wear of time; William H. Herndon and Jesse W. Weik, *Herndon's Lincoln: The True Story of a Great Life* (3 vols., 1889), a source that cannot be ignored, although it outraged Lincoln worshippers when it appeared; J. G. Randall, *Lincoln the President* (4 vols., 1945-55), whose impressive scholarship is often spiced with acid judgments; Allan Nevins, *The Emergence of Lincoln* (2 vols., 1950) and *The War for the Union* (2 vols., 1959-60), lucidly presented and interpretive, capturing the large sweep of events; Carl Sandburg, *Abraham Lincoln: The Prairie Years* (2 vols., 1926) and *Abraham Lincoln: The War Years* (4 vols., 1939), an impressive series in both the beauty of its exposition and the drama of its text; Earl Schenck Miers, editor in chief, *Lincoln Day by Day: A Chronology, 1809-1865* (3 vols., 1960: Vol. I, 1809-1848, edited by William E. Baringer; Vol. II, 1849-1860, edited by Baringer; Vol. III, 1861-1865, edited by C. Percy Powell), a series that furnishes far more data on Lincoln than its title indicates; and Benjamin P. Thomas, *Abraham Lincoln* (1954), understandably the most popular of the hundreds of one-volume biographies.

Aside from the Basler-edited *Collected Works*, the chief printed documentary source used in this study was *The War of the Rebellion: A Compilation of the Union and Confederate Armies* (128 vols., 1880-1901). Occasional use was made of the *Congressional Globe* for the war period, and of the *American Annual Cyclopedia and Register of Important Events* (Appleton's) for the years 1862 to 1865 inclusive.

251

Books by Negroes of that day include those of two former soldiers—Joseph T. Wilson, *The Black Phalanx* (1882), and George Washington Williams, *History of the Negro Troops in the War of the Rebellion, 1861-1865* (1888) —both of which reveal much industry, but are hard to follow, being either haphazard in organization or discursive in tone. The abolitionist lecturer William Wells Brown brought out *The Negro in the American Rebellion* (1867), long on anecdote but short on solid substance. Worth noting for their views on the war as well as for their personal experiences are the writings of two other Negro reformers: *The Journal of Charlotte Forten* (edited by Ray A. Billington, 1947) and *Life and Times of Frederick Douglass* (1884). Elizabeth Keckley's ghost-written *Behind the Scenes* (1868) places all Lincoln scholars in debt for its description of his family life in the White House.

Recent works devoted to the Negro of Lincoln's day include the following: Herbert Aptheker, *The Negro in the Civil War* (1938), four essays wedding scholarship to interpretation; Dudley T. Cornish, *The Sable Arm: Negro Troops in the Union Army, 1861-1865* (1956), a definitive work whose worth is enhanced by an excellent critical bibliography; Benjamin Quarles, *The Negro in the Civil War* (1953), a general account, treating the Negro on the home front and the battlefront, North and South; John E. Washington, *They Knew Lincoln* (1942), an original series of sketches of Negroes who had the run of the White House; and Bell Wiley's revealing, well-organized study, *Southern Negroes, 1861-1865* (1938).

As to periodicals, use has been made of newspaper dailies, picture weeklies, reform weeklies, and Negro publications. Dailies most often quoted from (with dates in parentheses indicating the span of time over which they were consulted) are as follows: *Baltimore Sun* (1861-65), *Chicago Tribune* (1863), *New York Herald* (1864-65), *New York Times* (1864-65), *New York Tribune* (1861), *Philadelphia Press* (1864-65), *Washington Daily Chronicle* (1862-65), and *Washington Star* (1863). The picture publications used were *Harper's Weekly* (1861-65) and *Frank Leslie's Illustrated Weekly* (1861-65). The reform periodicals include the abolitionist bellwethers, the *Anti-Slavery Standard* (New York, 1863) and the *Liberator* (Boston, 1861-64), plus the more moderately toned *Independent* (New York, 1861-62) and the pro-Negro emigrationist sheet *Pine and Palm* (Boston, 1861-62). Negro-edited publications include the *Anglo-African Magazine* (New York, 1859-61), the *Anglo-African Weekly* (New York, 1861-65), *Black Republican* (New Orleans, 1864), *Douglass' Monthly* (Rochester, 1861-63), which was the personal organ of Frederick Douglass, *New Orleans Tribune* (1864-65), and *L'Union* (New Orleans, 1862), a French-English weekly.

The chief manuscript source used in this work is the Robert Todd Lincoln Collection of the Papers of Abraham Lincoln, 1790-1916, comprising 194 volumes and located at the Manuscripts Division of the Library of Congress. Unless otherwise indicated, every time a letter addressed to Lincoln is quoted from or referred to, it comes from this treasure house.

Not all of the manuscript and printed sources that were consulted are listed above. But a number of these unmentioned titles are included in the bibliographies for each chapter, which follow immediately. In these I have attempted to be selective, furnishing sources only for those statements that might not be easily found in the general literature. Page numbers have been omitted, but in many instances these may be found without trouble in the work cited.

1 CHARLOTTE SCOTT'S MITE

Sources used for Charlotte Scott were Joseph T. Wilson, *The Black Phalanx* (1882), and excerpts from the *Marietta Register*, furnished through the courtesy of Mrs. Edith S. Reiter, formerly curator of the Campus Martius Museum, Marietta, Ohio. For William G. Eliot and Archer Alexander, use was made of the former's *The Story of Archer Alexander* (1885). Thomas Ball tells of his role in executing the monument in his *My Threescore Years and Ten* (1891). For the unveiling exercises, these contemporary newspapers were used: *Washington Chronicle*, *Washington National Republican*, and *Baltimore Sun*. Also dealing with these exercises are John Mercer Langston, *From the Virginia Plantation to the National Capitol* (1894), F. Lauriston Bullard, *Lincoln in Marble and Bronze* (1952), and Benjamin Quarles, *Frederick Douglass* (1948). Lorado Taft's opinion is found in his *History of American Sculpture* (1924); the Boston replica gets full coverage in *Bronze Group Commemorating Emancipation: A Gift of the City of Boston from Hon. Moses Kimball* (City Document No. 126, 1879); and the three-cent-stamp reproduction is described in *Lincoln Lore*, August 1958, No. 1446. Freeman H. M. Murray's criticisms are found in his *Emancipation and the Freed in American Sculpture* (1916). Bob Maynard's words are from B.A. Botkin, *Lay My Burden Down* (1945); B.T. Washington's appraisal is from his "An Ex-Slave's Tribute to the Emancipator," *Magazine of History*, 1927, Extra No. 133; Kelly Miller's comments are found in "The Genius of Abraham Lincoln," *Alexander's Magazine* (Boston), March-April 1909; James H. Hubert's lines are in *The Life of Abraham Lincoln: Its Significance to Negroes and Jews* (1939); and the Mordecai Johnson address is in mimeograph form at the Moorland Foundation Library, Howard University, Washington, D. C.

2 LINCOLN: THE SHAPING YEARS

The Raymond letter is in the R.T. Lincoln Papers. Villard's story is found in Harold G. and Oswald G. Villard, eds., *Lincoln on the*

Eve of '61 (1941). Lincoln's Kentucky years are touched on in Louis A. Warren, *The Slavery Atmosphere of Lincoln's Youth* (1933); the Minerva incident is found in R. Gerald McMurty, "The Lincoln Migration from Kentucky to Indiana," *Indiana Magazine of History*, Dec. 1937. Lincoln's sojourn in Indiana is detailed in Louis A. Warren, *Lincoln's Youth—Indiana Years, Seven to Twenty-One, 1816-1830* (1959); the figures on Negroes in Indiana are from the U. S. census reports for 1810 and 1820. Lincoln's first New Orleans trip is described in F. Lauriston Bullard, *Abe Goes Down the River* (1948), and Bess V. Ehrmann, *The Missing Chapter in the Life of Abraham Lincoln* (1938); the second trip is treated in Ida M. Tarbell, *The Early Life of Abraham Lincoln* (1896). The Lincoln-Stone protest is well handled in William E. Baringer's *Lincoln's Vandalia* (1949). Lovejoy's activities are described in Norman D. Harris, *Negro Slavery in Illinois* (1906). For Illinois legislation concerning Negroes, slave and free, I am indebted to Mrs. Marion D. Platt, Archival Assistant, Illinois State Archives, for a thermofax copy of "Negroes, Acts Relating to," which covers the period from 1787 to 1945. There is little about Lincoln as a lawyer that is not well covered in John J. Duff, *A. Lincoln: Prairie Lawyer* (1960). The case of Mack Shelby and his wife is found in "Docket Book C, 1840-1844, Sangamo County," at the Illinois Archives in Springfield. "Lincoln and Herndon's Fee Book of 1847," is at the Illinois Historical Society, also located in Springfield. Lincoln's one term in the House is carefully analyzed in Donald W. Riddle, *Congressman Abraham Lincoln* (1957). Lincoln's visits to Kentucky and his general relationship to that state and its inhabitants are examined in William H. Townshend, *Lincoln and the Bluegrass* (1955).

Paul M. Angle, ed., *Created Equal? The Complete Lincoln-Douglas Debates of 1858* (1958), is more than a reproduction of the text of the debates; it includes an introduction and connecting explanatory notes by the editor, plus contemporary newspaper reports. Harry V. Jaffa, *Crisis of the House Divided* (1959), is a brilliant, argumentative study of Lincoln's political philosophy as revealed in the debates. Harry E. Pratt, *The Great Debates* (1955), is a clearly written thirty-two-page pamphlet, deservedly published in quantity by the State of Illinois and distributed gratis. For a fresh look at one of the most publicized questions in the debates, see D. E. Fehrenbacher, "Lincoln, Douglas, and the 'Freeport Question,'" *The American Historical Review*, April 1961.

3 "AMONG US, YET NOT OF US"

For Lincoln's love of Negro melodies, particularly "The Blue-Tailed Fly," see Dorothy Lamon, ed., *Ward Hill Lamon: Recollections of Abraham Lincoln, 1847-1865* (1895). Downing's remarks appear in the *Liberator*, Mar. 15, 1861; those of Hamilton are in the *Anglo-African Magazine*, Sept. 1859; those of J. McCune Smith are in his pamphlet *The Suffrage Question in Relation to the Colored Voters in the State of New York* (1860). For Negro self-improvement societies, see Dorothy B. Porter, "The Organized Educational Activities of Negro Literary Societies, 1828-1846," *Journal of Negro Education*, Oct. 1936. For slaves fleeing to Canada, see Fred Landon, "Negro Migration to Canada after the Passing of the Fugitive Slave Act," *Journal of Negro History*, Jan. 1920. The attitude of Davis toward Negroes is described in Walter L. Fleming, "Jefferson Davis, the Negroes, and the Negro Problem," *Sewanee Review*, Oct. 1908. The date of the *Bee* is July 17, 1860. The Simpson quote comes from Joshua McCarter Simpson, *The Emancipation Car* (1874). *L'Union's* date is Nov. 1, 1862. The free Negro as pest is from the *Bee*, Oct. 10, 1859. The Lumkin quote is from Bertram W. Doyle, *The Etiquette of Race Relations in the South* (1937). Mrs. Harper's "Appeal" was carried in the *Anti-Slavery Standard*, Feb. 18, 1860. H. F. Douglas's strictures on Lincoln are in Norton Garfinkle, *Lincoln and the Coming of the Civil War* (1959). The quoted stanza comes from *The Campaign Songster* (1860; copy at New-York Historical Society). Rhett's remarks are quoted from Charles Eugene Hamlin, *The Life and Times of Hannibal Hamlin* (1899). H. F. Douglas's statement at Tremont Temple is in the *Chicago Daily Times and Herald*, Nov. 20, 1860, quoting the *Boston Post*. For the satisfaction Lincoln's election gave to Negroes, see the *Anglo-African*, Dec. 22, and Dec. 29, 1860. For violence at antislavery meetings late in 1860, see *Twenty-eighth Annual Report of the American Anti-Slavery Society* (1861); the *New York Tribune*, Jan. 19, 1861, and the *Standard*, Feb. 9, Feb. 16, 1861. For the exodus from Chicago, see the *Liberator*, Apr. 26, 1861. Rapier's statement is in an undated manuscript in the James and John Rapier Collection, at the Moorland Foundation, Howard U. Library; the statement from Wells is in his *The Negro in the American Rebellion* (1867). The action of the Boston Negroes is described in the *Liberator*, Feb. 22, 1861. The "everlasting Negro" quote is from the *Providence Daily Post*, Feb. 2, 1861, in Howard C. Perkins, ed., *Northern Editorials on Secession* (1942). The California scene was described by

Charles M. Wilson, "What Is Our True Condition?" *Anglo-African Magazine*, Jan. 1860.

4 HALF SLAVE, HALF FREE

The criticisms of Lincoln's address are from the *Anglo-African*, Mar. 16, 1861; the squib about balls is from the same weekly, May 4, 1861. For the response of Negroes to the war, see Frederick Phisterer, *New York in the War of the Rebellion, 1861-1865* (5 vols., 1912); the *Anglo-African*, Apr. 20, Apr. 27, 1861; George L. Davis, "Pittsburgh's Negro Troops in the Civil War," *The Western Pennsylvania Historical Magazine*, June 1953; *Cleveland Leader*, Oct. 16, 1861. For the Fort Pickens slaves, see *Official Records*, Ser. 2, Vol. I, p. 750; and L. M. Child to S. B. Shaw, May 5, 1861, in *Letters of Lydia Maria Child* (1883). For episodes concerning officers sympathetic to contrabands, see *Autobiography of Dr. William Henry Johnson* (1900) and Edward L. Pierce, *Address and Papers* (1896). Pierce describes his visit to the White House in "The Freedmen at Port Royal," the *Atlantic Monthly*, Sept. 1863, and in much more detail (and highly critical of Lincoln) in a letter to W. H. Herndon, Sept. 15, 1889, in the Herndon-Weik Papers. On the Colyer-Stanly imbroglio, see Colyer's somewhat partisan account in "Brief Report of the Services Rendered by the Freed People to the United States Army in North Carolina" (1864). For Lamon versus Wadsworth, see D. Lamon, *Recollections of Lincoln*; William E. Doster, *Lincoln and Episodes of the Civil War* (1915); and Henry Greenleaf Pearson, *James S. Wadsworth of Genesee* (1913). Lester himself is the authority for Lincoln's remarks to him, in his *Life and Public Services of Charles Sumner* (1874). Elizabeth Todd Grimsley's reminiscences may be found in her "Six Months in the White House," *Journal of Ill. State Hist. Soc.*, Oct. 1926. Harriet Tubman's words are reported by Lydia Maria Child in a letter to John Greenleaf Whittier, Jan. 21, 1862, in her *Letters*. Conway's statement is in Henry W. Wilbur, *President Lincoln's Attitude Towards Slavery and the Negro* (1914). Mrs. Child's "ten-foot pole" remark appears in the *Anglo-African*, Apr. 6, 1861. Anna E. Carroll's statement is from the Carroll Papers at the Maryland Historical Society in Baltimore. The Nell letter is found in Vol. VI of *The Works of Charles Sumner* (15 vols., 1870-83). The Hicks letter to Lincoln has found its way back to the Hicks Papers at the Maryland Historical Society. Hazewell wrote "The Hour and the Man" for the *Atlantic Monthly*, Nov. 1862.

5 "I MAY ADVANCE SLOWLY"

The Smith letter is from the National Archives microfilms, "Records Relating to the Suppression of the African Slave Trade," a rich and voluminous source (which has one or two Lincoln items that escaped Basler's dragnet). Still useful as a general account is W.E.B. DuBois, *The Suppression of the African Slave-Trade* (1895). The letter from Lyons is in Lord Newton, *Lord Lyons* (2 vols., 1913). The Murray incident is in "Records Relating to . . . Slave Trade." Useful general accounts on establishing diplomatic ties with the two black republics are Rayford W. Logan, *The Diplomatic Relations of the United States with Hayti, 1776-1891* (1941), and Ludwell Lee Montague, *Haiti and the United States, 1714-1938* (1940). The letter from Seys is in "Records Relating to . . . Slave Trade." For Cox and Davis, see Henry Wilson, *History of Anti-Slavery Measures of the Thirty-seventh and Thirty-eighth Congresses, 1861-1864* (1864). Lincoln's "shirt-tearing" is told in *Douglass' Monthly*, Sept. 1862. For Mrs. Kasson's experience, see "An Iowa Woman in Washington, D.C., 1861-1865," *Iowa Journ. of Hist.*, Jan. 1954. Payne's White House visit is recorded in his *Recollections of Seventy Years* (1888). For an account of emancipation in Washington, see Alfred G. Harris, "Lincoln and the Question of Slavery in the District of Columbia," *Lincoln Herald*, Spring 1952. For celebrations by Negroes, see the *Liberator*, May 23, June 27, 1862. The Maynard letter is carried in the *American Annual Cyclopedia* (Appleton's) *for 1862* (1863).

Lincoln's colonization efforts are treated in Frederick Bancroft, "The Colonization of American Negroes, 1801-1865," in Jacob E. Cooke, *Frederic Bancroft, Historian* (1957); Elmo E. Richardson and Alan W. Farley, *John Palmer Usher, Lincoln's Secretary of the Interior* (1960); Paul J. Scheips, "The Chiriqui Colonization Plan," *Journ. of Negro Hist.*, Oct. 1952; Warren A. Beck, "Lincoln and Colonization in Central America," *Abraham Lincoln Quart.*, Sept. 1950. The House committee's report is titled *Report of the Select Committee on Emancipation and Colonization* (1862). Kock's Oct. 1 letter to Lincoln is in "Records Relating to . . . Slave Trade." In the same source may be found Mitchell's reports of April 18 and May 18 to Lincoln. The White letter is in the Carter G. Woodson Papers, Lib. of Cong. The response of the Negroes to Lincoln's proposal may be found in the following: *Baltimore Sun*, Aug. 23, 1865; *An Appeal from the Colored Men of Philadelphia to the President of the United States* (1862; copy in Boston Athenaeum); *Liberator*, Aug. 22, Sept.

12, 1862; *New Orleans Tribune,* Aug. 25, 1862; *Douglass' Monthly,* Sept. 1862. Kerr's satire was republished in the *Liberator,* Aug. 29, 1862. The talk by Watkins was carried in the *Toledo Blade,* Sept. 13, 1861, in *Lake Port* (Lucas County Historical Society of Northwestern Ohio, 1951). For a complete description of the inducements offered to emigrants, see *Pine and Palm,* Apr. 12, 1862. Graddick's departure is recounted in *Douglass' Monthly,* Apr. 1861. The Constitution of the American Civilization Society may be found in "Records Relating to . . . Slave Trade," which also has the two Thomas letters to Lincoln, plus the Van Vleet letter; the last-named enclosed for Lincoln's attention a printed announcement of the "First Annual Exhibition of the Anglo-African Institute for the Encouragement of Industry and Art." Lincoln's message to the emigration-minded Negroes gathered in front of the White House is in the *Philadelphia Press,* Nov. 3, 1862. The Purvis letter is from "Speeches and Correspondence of Robert Purvis" (no date, no place), Howard U. Lib.

6 *"THEN, THENCEFORWARD, AND FOREVER FREE"*

Charles Eberstadt, "Lincoln's Emancipation Proclamation," *The New Colophon,* Vol. III (1950), is an excellent general account and is especially notable for its descriptive analysis of the republications and reproductions of the Emancipation Proclamation. David Homer Bates, *Lincoln in the Telegraph Office* (1907), describes the President as he composed the first drafts of the proclamation. Boutwell's statement about Antietam serving Lincoln's purpose is contained in a letter he sent to J. G. Holland on June 10, 1865, in Josiah G. Holland Papers relating to Abraham Lincoln, New York Pub. Lib. The Garnet letter of 1844 is in "Personal Papers—Miscellaneous, GA—GE," Lib. of Cong. The Welles statement is from Albert Mordell, compiler, *Lincoln's Administration: Selected Essays of Gideon Welles* (1960). Mansfield French's visit to the White House is told in the *Washington Daily Chronicle,* Dec. 15, 1862; Mrs. Child's observation is in her *Letters,* and the Sumner letters are in the Chicago Hist. Soc. Miss Remond's statement is from *An Address before the International Congress of Charities, Correction and Philanthropy* (London, 1862). Jackson's activities are described in *Douglass' Monthly,* Feb. 1863. The McClure observation is found in his *Abraham Lincoln and Men of War-Times* (1892). The statement attributed to Seward is from O.H. Browning, in T.C. Pease and J.G. Randall, eds., *The Diary of Orville Hickman Browning* (2 vols., 1927-33). The Adams-Seward interchanges are from *Diplomatic Correspondence, 1863-1864,* Vol. I (*Executive Documents Printed by Order of the House of Representatives during the First Session of the Thirty-eighth Congress, 1863-1864,* Vol. I [1864]). Cobden's letter is in Belle Becker Sideman and Lillian Friedman, eds., *Europe Looks at the Civil War* (1960). Gapen's letter is in "Civil War Letters," at the Chicago Hist. Soc. Livermore's letter to Sumner was forwarded to Lincoln and is found in "Records Relating . . . to the Slave Trade." The letter from Sumner is at the Chicago Hist. Soc., the Jan. 5 letter of Livermore is in the R.T. Lincoln Papers; and the quote from the *Wilmington Journal* is in Richard Bardolph, "Malice Toward One," *Lincoln Herald,* Winter 1952. Mrs. Child's hosannas are in Sarah Hopper Emerson, *Life of Abby Hopper Gibbons* (2 vols., 1896). The Turner material is from his pamphlet *The Negro in Slavery, War and Peace* (1913). Elisa S. Quincy's letter is in the R.T. Lincoln Papers. The Leesburg celebration is in the *Liberator,* Jan. 16, 1863; that of the Norfolk Negroes is in the *Baltimore Sun,* Jan. 3, 1863, and the *Anglo-African,* Feb. 14, 1863. The attitude of the Ashley slaves is described in Elizabeth B. Johnston, *Christmas in Kentucky, 1862* (1892). The remarks of the *True Advance* are from Charles Eberstadt's essay in *The New Colophon,* noted above. For quotations from Higginson, Haviland, Clarke, and Carpenter, see Thomas W. Higginson, *Army Life in a Black Regiment* (1900); Edward Everett Hale, ed., *James Freeman Clarke: Autobiography, Diary and Correspondence* (1891); Laura S. Haviland, *A Woman's Life-Work* (1889); Francis B. Carpenter, *Six Months in the White House* (1867).

7 LINCOLN AND THE BLACKS IN BLUE

H.F. Douglas's remarks are in *Douglass' Monthly,* Feb. 1863. Buckingham is in *Official Records,* Ser. 3, Vol. II. The three quotations from Sumner are taken, respectively, from Arthur E. Bestor, David C. Mearns, and Jonathan Daniels, *Three Presidents and Their Books* (1955); Sumner Papers at Chicago Hist. Soc.; Sarah Forbes Hughes, *Letters and Recollections of John Murray Forbes* (1899). The whole story of the Negro soldier is excellently told in Dudley Taylor Cornish, *The Sable Arm: Negro Troops in the Union Army, 1861-1865* (1956). All quotations from C.R. Lowell are in Edward W. Emerson, *Life and Letters of Charles Russell Lowell* (1907). For the Frémont Legion, see *L'Union,* May 30, 1863; *Douglass' Monthly,* June and August 1863; *Appleton's Cyclopedia for 1863* (1869); Nicolay and Hay, *Abraham*

Lincoln, Vol. VI. The Delany-Jones offer is in Herbert Aptheker, ed., *A Documentary History of the Negro People in the United States* (1951). Schenck's letter is in *Official Records,* Ser. 1, Vol. XXVII, Part 3. On Birney, see *Appleton's Cyclopedia* for 1864 (1872) and Wilson, *The Black Phalanx.* Stanton's analysis of Bramlette's assertions is found in the Secretary's letter to Lincoln on Feb. 8, 1864, in R.T. Lincoln Papers. Lincoln's promise to the Kentucky visitors and the War Department order of June 13, 1864 are in *Official Records,* Ser. 3, Vol. IV. The poster used by Ayres is reproduced in John Hope Franklin, ed., *The Diary of James T. Ayres* (1947). The Swails case is discussed in Henry G. Pearson, *The Life of John A. Andrew* (2 vols., 1904). The Hay diary quotations are from Tyler Dennett, ed., *Lincoln and the Civil War in the Diaries and Letters of John Hay* (1939). The Gooding letter to Lincoln is in Aptheker, *Doc. Hist. of the Negro People.* The Sturgis-Trotter episode is described in "War Letters of Charles P. Bowditch," Massachusetts Historical Society, *Proceedings,* 1923-1924 (1925). Moore's letter is in the Moorland Foundation Library at Howard University. For the Seddon-Davis conference, see letter from the former to General Beauregard, *Official Records,* Ser. 4, Vol. II. Early's comment is in his *Autobiographical Sketch and Narrative of the War Between the States* (1912). The Lee letter of Feb. 18, 1865, is found in James D. McCabe, *Life and Campaigns of General Robert E. Lee* (1866). The J.B. Moore letter is in the Moorland Foundation Library. The statement by General Thomas on Negro desertions is in Roland C. McConnell, "Concerning the Procurement of Negro Troops in the South During the Civil War," *Jour. of Negro Hist.,* July 1950. In the *New York Times* of 11 January 1864, a reporter tells of the Christmas Day activities of the Corps d'Afrique. Lincoln's return from City Point is described in Benjamin P. Thomas, ed., *Three Years with Grant as Recalled by War Correspondent Sylvanus Cadwaller* (1956).

8 A STAKE IN AMERICA

The Don Carlos letter is from the R.T. Lincoln Papers. Eaton is the authority for these visits, in his *Grant, Lincoln and the Freedman* (1907). Stanton's letter to Butler is in *Official Records,* Ser. 3, Vol. II. The *Philadelphia Press*'s date of issue was Oct. 23. The unsuccessful efforts to get small farms for Sea Islands Negroes is described in George Bentley, *A History of the Freedman's Bureau* (1955). For the proposal transmitted by Gilmore, see his *Personal Recollections of Lincoln and the Civil War* (1898). For the petition from the freedman's organizations to Lincoln, see Levi Coffin, *Reminiscences of Levi Coffin* (1880). The commission's report is in *Official Records*, Ser. 3, Vol. IV. For the explanation by Forbes and Tuckerman of their role in the colonization effort, see their twenty-page printed letter to Lincoln, entitled "Statement of Circumstances Attending the Experiment of Colonizing Free Negroes at the Island of A'Vache, Hayti, West Indies," in "Records Relating to . . . Slave Trade." The Menard letter and the request of the African Civilization Society are found in the same source. Lincoln's relationships with White House Negroes is fully explored in John E. Washington, *They Knew Lincoln* (1942). The "greenback counting" episode was related by William M. Thayer, *The Character and Public Services of Abraham Lincoln* (1864). The fullest and most recent account of the Colonel Utley story is William H. Townshend, *Lincoln and the Bluegrass* (1955). For the use of White House grounds by Catholics, see Albert S. Foley, *God's Men of Color* (1955), and D. I. Murphy, "Lincoln, Foe of Bigotry," *America*, Feb. 11, 1928. Lincoln's visit to the military hospital is described in Anna L. Boyden, *Echoes from the White House: A Record of Mrs. Rebecca R. Pomroy's Experiences in War-Times* (1884). Mrs. Keckley has a ghost-written, but fairly reliable, account of her White House experiences, *Behind the Scenes* (1868); a quite helpful portrayal of her is in J.E. Washington, *They Knew Lincoln;* and for some interesting sidelights, see Smith D. Fry, "Lincoln Liked Her: Story of Elizabeth Keckley, a White House Factotum," in *Minneapolis Register*, July 6, 1901. The letter to Mrs. Shearer is in Charles V. Darrin, "Your Truly Attached Friend, Mary Lincoln," *Jour. of the Ill. State Hist. Soc.*, Spring 1951. For Mrs. Lincoln's donations to the contrabands, see the *Anglo-African*, Jan. 24, 1863, and *First Annual Report of Contraband Relief Associations of the District of Columbia, organized August 12, 1862* (1863). Douglass's statement about his reception by Lincoln is in the *New York Times*, Jan. 14, 1864. Accounts of the Sojourner Truth visit may be found in the *Liberator*, Dec. 23, 1864, and the *Anti-Slavery Reporter*, Mar. 1, 1865. Sojourner's jest is from Bernice Lowe, "Michigan Days of Sojourner Truth," *New York Folklore Quarterly*, Apr. 1956, and Mrs. Stowe's analysis is from her article, "Sojourner Truth, the Libyan Sibyl," *Atlantic Monthly*, Apr. 1863. The Bible from the Baltimore Negroes is in the *Washington Chronicle*, Sept. 8, 1864, and the *Washington Star* and the *Baltimore Sun* of the same date. The Brooks story is in his *Washington in Lincoln's Time* (1896). It is William O. Stoddard who tells of being asked to look like Lincoln, in his *Inside the*

BIBLIOGRAPHY

White House (1890). The Betsey Canedy experience is in F.B. Carpenter, *Six Months in the White House;* Saxton's reference is in *Official Records,* Ser. 3, Vol. IV. The "praise man" incident is related in *Preliminary Report Touching the Condition and Management of Emancipated Refugees, Made by American Freedmen's Inquiry Commission, June 30, 1863* (1863).

9 "GOOD NEWS, CHARIOT'S COMING"

The Fleurville letter is in the R.T. Lincoln Papers. The Langston comment is quoted from the *Toledo Blade,* May 28, 1864, in *Lake Port;* that of Garnet is from the *Washington Chronicle,* Nov. 2, 1864; and that of Ruffin is from the Ruffin Papers, Howard U. For "The Lincoln Catechism," see "Lincolniana Notes," *Jour. of Ill. State Hist. Soc.,* Autumn 1953, and Emma Lou Thornbrough, "The Race Issue in Indiana Politics during the Civil War," *Indiana Mag. of Hist.,* June 1951. The Mills observation is in Basler, *The Collected Works of Abraham Lincoln,* Vol. VII. The Rapier letter is in the Rapier Papers at Howard U., and that of Douglass is in the R.T. Lincoln Papers. The one-sided election returns from Nashville were reported in the *New Orleans Tribune,* Nov. 29, 1864. Seamen's pamphlet was entitled *What Miscegenation Is* (1864). Dismore's missive is in R.B. Harwell, ed., "Edgar Dismore Letters," *Jour. of Negro Hist.,* July 1940; the convention at New Orleans is in the *New Orleans Tribune,* Jan. 15, 1865. The Hay characterization is from his diary of Oct. 23, 1863, in Tyler Dennett, *John Hay.* Taussig's remark is in *Appleton's Cyclopedia for 1863.* The *Herald's* light jest is in its issue of Nov. 23. The late October serenade is from Sandburg, *War Years,* Vol. III. Welles's diary for 5 February 1865 describes the Cabinet's reaction. For Garnet's statement about Negroes being present at the passage of the bill, see the *Anglo-African,* Apr. 15, 1865. For the Negro petitions to Congress, see Aptheker, *Doc. Hist. of Negro People.* The Syracuse convention is described in *Proceedings of the National Convention of Colored Men Held in Syracuse, New York, October 4-7, 1864* (1864). The meeting of the New Orleans Negroes with James McKaye is carried in *L'Union,* Feb. 11, 1864; the petition is reproduced in Aptheker, *Doc. Hist. of Negro People,* although a few paragraphs are omitted (compare with the *Liberator,* Apr. 1, 1864). Carpenter, *Six Months in the White House,* is the source for the Forney quotation. The Boston reception for Roudanez and Bertonneau is mentioned in the *Washington Chronicle,* Apr. 18, 1864. Blaine's observation is in his *Twenty*

262

Years of Congress (2 vols., 1884-86); the career of Banks is portrayed in Fred H. Harrington, *Fighting Politician, Major General N. P. Banks* (1948). The Sumner letter to Chandler, dated Jan. 3, 1865, is in the Sumner Papers at the Chicago Hist. Soc. For Chase's reprisals against those who disliked Negroes, see *Cincinnati Daily Gaz.*, June 23, June 24, 1863. The Bates decision appeared as a pamphlet, *Opinion of Attorney General Bates on Citizenship* (1863). The Xenia meeting is described in *Proceedings of a Convention of the Colored Men of Ohio, January 10, 11, 12, 1865* (1865). The invitation to Lincoln is in the R.T. Lincoln Papers; for the meeting, see the *Baltimore Sun*, Feb. 1, 1865. For Rock's admission, see the *New York Tribune*, Feb. 9, 1865; a pen-and-ink drawing of Rock, plus a brief account of his career, appears in *Harper's Weekly*, Feb. 25, 1865. The New Year's reception of 1865 is described in *Appleton's Cyclopedia for 1865* (1876). For Negroes in the Inaugural Day parade, see *Philadelphia Press*, Mar. 6, 1865, and the *Philadelphia Inquirer* for the same date. Douglass describes his experiences at the inaugural reception in his autobiography, *Life and Times of Frederick Douglass* (1884). For Lincoln at Richmond, see the following: George A. Bruce, *The Capture and Occupation of Richmond* (n.d.); Charles Carleton Coffin, *Four Years of Fighting* (1866); William H. Crook, *Through Five Administrations* (1910); J.J. Hill, *A Sketch of the 29th Regiment of Connecticut Colored Troops*, in Aptheker, *Doc. Hist. of Negro People*; Rembert D. Patrick, *The Fall of Richmond* (1960); David D. Porter, *Incidents and Anecdotes of the Civil War* (1885). The T. Morris Chester dispatch appears in the *Philadelphia Press*, Apr. 11, 1865.

10 A SLEEP AND A REMEMBERING

Sanford's letter, addressed to E.P. Goodrich of Ann Arbor, Mich., is reproduced in *The Civil War*, a booklet describing a special series of lectures and exhibitions sponsored by the 1961 summer session of the University of Michigan. For Swisshelm, see Arthur J. Larsen, *Crusader and Feminist: Letters of Jane Grey Swisshelm, 1858-1865* (1934). Mrs. Keckley tells of her grief in *Behind the Scenes*. For the annual conference of the A.M.E. Church, see the *Baltimore Sun*, Apr. 17, 1865. The unplanned lead role of the Negro regiment is described in the *Sun*, Apr. 20, 1865; for a list of the numerous colored organizations in the line of march, see B.F. Morris, compiler, *Memorial Record of the Nation's Tribute to Abraham Lincoln* (1865); the *Times* issue is that of Apr. 20. The date of both the *Philadelphia Press* and the *National Intelligencer* accounts is Apr. 24. The Springfield groupings arrangement is in the *Illinois State Journal,* Apr. 28; the meeting of the Springfield Negroes, held on April 19, is in the same for May 2. For the Negro soldier contributions to the fund, see Paul M. Angle, "The Building of the Lincoln Monument," in *Lincoln Centennial Association Papers for 1926* (1926). The scene at Beaufort is from the pen of Elizabeth H. Botume, *First Days Among the Contrabands* (1893); the one at Mobile is from the *Black Republican,* Apr. 29, 1865. The meetings of Negro organizations are described in the following: *Proceedings of the Colored Men's Convention of Michigan, Held in Detroit, September 12 and 13, 1865* (1865); *Proceedings of the Annual Meeting of the National Equal Rights League, Cleveland, October 19, 20, 21, 1865* (1865); *Proceedings of the Illinois State Convention of Colored Men Assembled at Galesburg, October 16, 17, 18, 1866* (1867). Douglass's letter of thanks may be found in Howard W. Coles, *The Cradle of Freedom: A History of the Negro in Rochester, Western New York and Canada* (1951); the horse's mane letter is in the Woodson Papers; the Slade lock of Lincoln hair is discussed in Charles W. White, "The Lincoln Cult," *Saturday Evening Post,* Feb. 16, 1957; Mrs. Keckley's mementos are described in *Behind the Scenes;* her letter to Weik is in the Herndon-Weik Papers (Group 5, Vol. XXIX). The message from the London Negroes is in Belle Becker Sideman and Lillian Friedman, eds., *Europe Looks at the Civil War* (1960). The concluding stanza is from a communication from Martha Mitchell Bigelow in the *Lincoln Herald,* Winter 1956.

Index

INDEX

Lynch, Althea, 81
Lyons, Lord, 96, 100

McClellan, George B., 70
  Democratic nominee for President
    (1864), 213
McClure, Alexander K., 137
McDowell, Irvin, 77
McIntosh, Frank, 20
McKaye, James, 226, 228
Mack, Polly, 23
Mammy Sally, 32, 202
Marcia C. Day (ship), 192
Martin, J. Sella, 59, 67, 137
Maryland
  Negro troops enlisted in, 162
  slavery abolished in, 219f.
Massachusetts, Negro troops enlisted
    in, 156
Massachusetts Anti-Slavery Society,
    47f., 59
Matson, Robert, 23ff.
Maynard, Bob, 12
Maynard, Horace, 107
Menard, J. Willis, 122, 193
Miller, Dr. G. P., 67
Miller, Kelly, 13
Missouri Compromise, 17
  repealed, 32f.
Mitchell, Rev. James, 115, 193
Mobile Bay, Battle of, 216
Moore, Jason B., 181
Moore, Western H., 170
Mott, Lucretia, 59
Murray, David D., 17
Murray, Freeman Henry Morris, 12
Murray, Robert, 97
Myers, Stephen, 44, 105

Nance (slave), 21f.
National Intelligencer, 243
National Republican, 122
National Union party, 212
"Negro Bob," *see* Smith, Robert

Negroes
  acceptance for military service,
    controversy over, 153ff.
  attitude toward: in Illinois, 19; in
    Indiana, 17; in South, 52ff.
  colonization of, 108ff. (*see also*
    Chiriqui; Cow Island)
  in Confederate army, 180f.
  discrimination against: in North,
    42f.; as prisoners of war, 173ff.;
    in Union army, 167ff.
  education of, 44, 74, 76f., 190
  in elections: 1860, 55ff.; in 1864,
    211ff.
  emancipated: economic problem of,
    73; education of, 74; Lincoln's
    attitude toward, 187ff.
  emancipation of, *see* Emancipation
  escape of, to Union lines, 68f. (*see
    also* Contrabands)
  flight on repeal of personal-liberty
    laws, 61f.
  free: re-enslavement of, 54f.;
    Southern attitude toward, 52ff.
  grief on death of Lincoln, 240ff.
  and land ownership, 185, 189
  Lincoln "elected" by (1864), 216f.
    at Lincoln's funeral, 241ff.
  permitted to use White House
    grounds for picinic, 198
  of Richmond, Lincoln welcomed
    by, 235
  self-improvement, 43ff.
  as soldiers: discrimination against,
    167ff.; recruitment of, 155ff.;
    rejected, 66ff.
  suffrage for, 224ff., 229, 246
Nell, William C., 48, 88, 105
Nevada admitted to statehood, 222
New England Anti-Slavery Society,
    46
Newman, J. P., 10
New Orleans
  funeral exercises for Lincoln in,
    245f.

271